BEST MATE

TRIPLE GOLD

DEDICATION

I am dedicating this book to my mother, Hester, who inspired me to achieve my ambitions.

ACKNOWLEDGEMENTS

I am greatly indebted to Andrew Longmore for the assistance he has given me during the writing of this book. We planned the chapters together and, over the months, he has painstakingly read and corrected my writings. His expertise and patience combined with a brilliant sense of humour and plenty of enthusiasm have proved invaluable. I could not have managed on my own.

Nor could I have proceeded without Terry. He has been amazingly tolerant and we have conferred on a large number of issues; it was through his constant encouragement that I had the confidence to write. I would also like to thank my loyal owners who have strongly supported me over the past years in my training ventures; in particular, Jim Lewis, the owner of Best Mate, who has been an enormous help with the piecing together of this book.

Further thanks are due to the Costello family, John Fowler, Michael Moore, Philip and Jane Myerscough, Jacques Van't Hart and Declan Weld for their contribution from across the Irish Sea.

Finally, I am grateful to the whole team at West Lockinge Farm, in particular, to Debbie Bollard, Christine Douglas-Home, Andy Fox, Jackie Jenner, Drew Miller and Dave Reddy as well as to everybody who has made it possible for Best Mate to win his races, which includes Jim Culloty, our loyal jockey, Mervyn Richings, our farrier, Roger Betteridge, our veterinary surgeon, and neighbouring trainers Mick Channon and David Gandolfo.

This new edition published in 2004 by Highdown,
an imprint of Raceform Ltd
Compton, Newbury, Berkshire, RG20 6NL

Raceform Ltd is a wholly-owned subsidiary of Trinity Mirror plc

A catalogue record for this book is available from the British Library.

ISBN 1-904317-68-5

Printed by Creative Print & Design

BEST MATE

TRIPLE GOLD

HENRIETTA KNIGHT

CONTENTS

CHAPTER ONE

THAT MAGICAL DAY

The moment Best Mate passed that winning post with his rivals trailing in his wake, I tore out of the tiny press tent behind the weighing room and scuttled across a couple of tarmac pathways to start my now famous run down that lightly gravelled walkway, flanked on either side by safety barriers, which leads straight to the course. If the definition of euphoria is 'a feeling of well-being based on over confidence', then I was certainly experiencing it. It was as if a door had suddenly opened and I had entered another world. Maybe it was like this for Judy Garland in The Wizard of Oz – my favourite film as a child – when she was carried away in her sleep to a dreamland. I wanted to run and jump and laugh. My instinct was to hug everybody who got in my way, but above all I needed to find Terry and bury my head in his chest and squeeze him tightly. I wanted to say to him, 'We've done it!' I did not mind any more what I did or how I did it. The roars of the crowd were ringing in my ears and hundreds of people were shouting congratulations and trying to touch me, but I was free, and all my inhibitions had vanished.

That long, nightmare wait was over. The pressure was finally off, and Matey, our wonderful horse, the people's horse, had made history. He had just won his second Cheltenham Gold Cup back to back, overturning a 32-year-old hoodoo for defending champions that stretched back to L'Escargot in 1971. He had shown himself to be something special, the worthy new champion of steeplechasing.

Amid a sea of people, and running in a semi-daze, I eventually caught sight of Terry in his tattered old hat. I could hardly miss him. He was close to the course and surrounded by cameras. He spotted me and turned up the hill to greet me. In a state of pure ecstasy, I threw up my arms and he ran straight into them for a huge, well-earned embrace. The tears were rolling down his cheeks, and his face was red with emotion. The occasion had moved him deeply. He says that Best Mate's victory that day meant even more to him than winning the Gold Cup himself on Woodland Venture in 1967. We pressed onwards up the horsewalk beside the course and in front of the huge crowds lining the rails at the edge of the lawn. The shouts of 'Well done, Hen!' and 'Well done, Terry!' rang in our ears, but at last we made it to Best Mate – the new king. In his full glory, and glowing with pride, he was walking majestically towards us amid the deafening cheers.

Jim Culloty's face said it all. It was no longer etched with tension as it had been twenty minutes earlier in the paddock; instead, it was a broad-smiling face of happiness. He too felt the relief; it was the end of months of pressure. The partnership had just left their fans with a race to remember for the rest of their lives. Jim had asked Matey for a star show, and his performance had been faultless. How many great days has Cheltenham witnessed down the years? How many great horses have galloped to glory up that fearsome hill? How many have made it all look so blissfully simple? Jim and Matey didn't just win, they put on an incredible show, and etched into people's minds a memory that will survive long beyond the lifespan of those who were privileged to have been there.

To train a horse for that special race needs team effort, and most of Best Mate's team were present to see that glorious victory. Jackie

Jenner, his lass, had one hand on his rein as she proudly walked beside her star, while Drew Miller, Andy Fox and Dave Reddy all flocked to his side as he made his way back to the winners' enclosure. The Fates had been with us that day, and our plans had worked well. Even Chives, Best Mate's stable companion, ran a superb race and deserved a placing.

The crowds at the entrance to the paddock were unbelievable, even greater than the year before. The cheering seemed twice as loud. Two fine hunt horses had followed the procession, their riders smartly attired in red coats, and Terry had even held on to a neckstrap on one of these horses to get an extra pull up the hill and keep up with Matey's fast walk. I had been present at Cheltenham in 1986 when Dawn Run had been victorious, and I believed that there would never be such an amazing reception again. She was so popular, and had been virtually engulfed by her screaming fans. Together with Jonjo O'Neill, she had almost disappeared among the multitude of people, but now, seventeen years later, history was being replayed. Yet this time there was a difference: I had trained the winner myself. The only missing links were my parents. How I wished they could have been there to enjoy those magic moments. They would have been so proud. Indeed, my father, with his sense of humour, would probably have told everybody that he had done the training himself.

The unsaddling enclosure at Cheltenham is unique. The many rows of tiered steps, built as they are in a semi-circle at the end of the paddock, allow the crowds to look down on to the grass below and admire the horses like spectators in a Roman amphitheatre. Thankfully there is never any fighting, just joyous scenes in an arena packed with people gathered to welcome the winning horses. The sensation of being at the centre of that hallowed bowl is indescribable. There is so much excitement, so much emotion, so much noise and movement. Everywhere one turns there are owners, trainers and supporters, together with journalists, cameramen and racecourse officials. It is a hive of activity. It is hard to know where to stand or what to do next, but it is always reassuring to see so many friendly faces and to witness such happiness.

There were huge cheers when Best Mate appeared with his ecstatic owner, Jim Lewis, by his head. The concrete steps were seething with fans, and they gave the horse a true hero's welcome. Many of the racegoers, frightened that they would lose their pitch on these steps, had taken up their positions even before the race had started, and had watched the drama unfold on the big screen beside the paddock. Many of them had followed Best Mate right from the start of his career and they did not want to miss his crowning moment.

The press also gave him a marvellous reception; several of its members had become special friends over the winter months. They had scarcely left us alone in terms of telephone calls or visits, but they had also kept up my morale and convinced me that a second Gold Cup was well within Best Mate's grasp. Interviews and clicking cameras, together with endless kisses and the welcome presence of my sister, made me realise that this win was extra special. The prize-giving ceremony, introduced by my brother-in-law, Sam Vestey, who is chairman of Cheltenham racecourse, will always remain a treasured memory. Her Majesty the Queen presented the trophies and was especially popular with the crowd. She is known to enjoy Flat racing and has bred many famous winners, but by agreeing to attend the 2003 Gold Cup she gave National Hunt racing a much-needed boost. She has a deep understanding of horses and is extremely knowledgeable. Both Terry and I always enjoy talking to her.

It was not easy to leave Cheltenham racecourse that evening. We had been fully occupied after the big race, and having visited the Royal Box, attended a press conference and then given a number of television interviews – the last of which was for Central Television – we attempted to make our way back to the car, but everywhere we turned we were confronted by more and more people. We were swamped by racegoers wanting autographs. I felt like a film star at a première. We were unable to move; we were stopped at every corner. It was a wonderful feeling, but I was longing to get home. We ended up going behind the weighing room and past the saddling-up boxes along the path to the racecourse stables; it was the only way we could escape the crowds. As darkness fell, we reached the car park. We drove home alone, Terry at the wheel, and were able to mull over the day, hour by hour.

It was one of the happiest journeys home I have ever made. I was still on a cloud, but so many thoughts were racing through my mind. How lucky I had been to see a load of straw that morning, as I left the yard. My superstition – 'A load of straw you draw, a load of hay you pay' – had been proved right again. I believe I would have been suicidal had the trailer contained hay! I had worn the same clothes and the same pearls as I had worn in 2002. Terry wore the same lucky hat, and I had forced Charles Egerton to sit with me during the race in the same two chairs we had occupied the previous year.

As we neared the yard with our day nearly over (or so I thought), we noticed that the gates and railings were once again adorned with banners, balloons and impromptu placards: WELCOME HOME!, and WELL DONE, MATEY! We were immediately reminded of the previous year's display. The staff, once more encouraged by Christine Douglas-Home, my irreplaceable secretary, had really gone to town. She had given them money from the petty-cash tin and they had celebrated with champagne at the end of evening stables. After this they had decorated the yard and Best Mate's stable, as well as the front door to my house and also my kitchen. Triumphant, they lined the driveway and cheered us as we drove up to the front door. They were red-faced but happy. Even though they had stayed at home, their contribution had been considerable. Some Channel 4 cameramen were also there. We knew them well: they had been our mascots for the season and had filmed Best Mate right the way through from his previous summer at grass. On this special day they had followed their horse from his stable to the races and back again. They had arrived at seven a.m. and did not leave until after seven p.m. We would miss their monthly visits from now on, but maybe they would return next season.

Then we checked on our hero. I hugged him in his stable beneath the bunches of balloons and the streamers, and thanked him for what he had done for us that day. He had made yet another of my dreams come true. He had won a second Gold Cup. He was a superstar.

So ended the day outside, but indoors there was more to come. There were numerous messages on the table, and the fax machine kept up a constant chatter. The telephones rang and rang. There were more balloons and streamers, with confetti thrown everywhere. Not even at our wedding reception had we received so much attention. A quick call to the Chinese takeaway, the Peking Dynasty in Wantage, followed by a visit from my fellow writer, Andrew Longmore, preceded our first look at a replay of the race. We watched in silence and in wonder. It was even better than I had remembered, and Channel 4 had done us proud, lacing a great and historic occasion with plenty of humour and a fine closing commentary. 'I thought you were running on well there at the end,' said Terry as he watched my gallop from the weighing room. I was not so sure.

It was time to get back to business. I needed to assemble my workbook for the next day and to plan the celebration party for the morning. Time flew by, and it was soon midnight. I was ready for some sleep and more special dreams.

What a horse! In four amazing years he had completely changed our lives. Yet people still asked, 'How did you ever find him?' and 'How were you able to persuade an owner to buy him?' In the pages of this book I have tried to answer these questions. I have attempted to show how, in the course of our lives, Terry and I have gained enough experience to train a racehorse of Best Mate's calibre, and how we were able to point him in the right direction to give him the chance to win two Cheltenham Gold Cups.

CHAPTER TWO

THE FAMILY TREE

Best Mate was born unexpectedly on the morning of 28 January 1995 in a field near Trim in Co. Meath. When he was found by his owner, Jacques Van't Hart, he was lying on a thin carpet of wet snow, a barely moving little black shape contrasting with the white background. His mother, the eight-year-old Katday, was proudly watching over her first-born foal. How would he cope with this unorthodox start, and what were the origins of that little brown mare?

Katday has an interesting background. She comes from a top Flat family and won three races on the level in France as a three-year-old, as well as being placed three times, in the colours of Sheikh Mohammed. She showed plenty of ability, and in 1990 was sent over to Ireland to race over hurdles. She joined John Fowler, and raced in Saeed Manana's name. Unfortunately, however, she did not shine in her new career, and although she jumped well, she ran only three times. She was placed third on one occasion but had developed a few physical problems in training, and these affected her enthusiasm as well as her ability. In 1991 she was retired and went through the Tattersalls December Sales in Newmarket as part of the Darley Stud Management draft. She was sold for 4,000 guineas.

The following spring, Katday was put in foal, but slipped the foal early in 1993. Without much expectation, she was re-entered for another sale, this time the Tattersalls (Ireland) November National Hunt Sales in Fairyhouse, which have a special day for mares. As 'Lot 1587' she attracted the attention of Declan Weld, the owner of Old Meadow Stud at Donadea in Co. Kildare. He is a shrewd man, and a good judge of a horse. He has an excellent eye for pedigrees and had recently acquired a most interesting new stallion from France called Un Desperado. He was on the lookout for extra mares for 1994. He liked Katday's breeding and knew that she had a half sister called Charlie Turquoise who had won ten French jump races including a Listed Steeplechase at Auteuil. This mare could well suit his new stallion. She had the potential to produce a decent National Hunt horse.

Declan did not expect Katday to make much money due to her unimpressive race record in Ireland, but was nevertheless delighted to secure her for as little as 1,400 punts. Within a couple of hours he resold her for a profit of £IR 200 to Austen Lyons, a renowned Co. Meath Gaelic footballer, but she would still visit Un Desperado. It all looked like a good day's work, but the very next morning Declan received a telephone call from Mr Lyons to cancel the deal. He had spoken to John Fowler, who had given the mare an unfavourable report. He had therefore changed his mind and no longer wanted her. Unperturbed by this sudden change of events, Declan re-purchased Katday, and in February 1994 she was duly covered by Un Desperado. She was scanned in foal a few weeks later and was turned out to grass for the rest of the summer.

At the end of August 1994, Jacques Van't Hart, who owns about 30 acres of land near his home in Co. Meath, asked Declan to find him another brood mare. He already had several mares, and it was not long before he added Katday to his collection for £IR 5,500. Mr Van't Hart, who is Dutch by birth, has important business interests in the pharmaceutical world both in Ireland and Holland. In the

1990s he frequently travelled between the two countries, and whenever he went abroad he carefully arranged to have his horses checked by neighbours. Fortunately, he was at home towards the end of January 1995, which was how he discovered Best Mate's birth in one of his paddocks.

According to 1994 covering dates, he was only a few days early, but somehow Jacques had not expected his mare to foal for another couple of weeks and was duly shocked by what he saw in his field. He telephoned Declan Weld immediately, who suggested that mother and son be taken into a stable (there were several stables opening out on to the mares' paddocks). He also advised calling a vet. The foal was barely strong enough to stand up and had not suckled from its mother. Jacques recalls that he partly carried him to the nearest shelter, but he was breathing normally and the veterinary surgeon was not unduly worried. The little fellow was just cold, wet and hungry. Once he had dried out, warmed up and learnt to drink, he would be fine. He soon recovered – he was always tough – and within a few days the stable door was once again left open so that Katday could take her son back into the fields for exercise. The foal had found his feet, and was happy to accompany his mother on those first canters on Irish soil, but there were further hardships to endure.

February 1995 turned out to be one of the wettest in history. Ireland was hit by incessant and unprecedented heavy rainfall. Many race meetings and point-to-points were abandoned through waterlogging. Yet this was a very important month for Best Mate, who needed to develop and put on weight. It was essential that he keep dry and warm as exposure to the elements could easily prove damaging. The fields were well protected by hedges and trees, and the mares had access to stables, but unfortunately, since this first foal was a novelty to Katday, she preferred the open spaces rather than the confines of a shelter. It appears that, for most of the time, she kept her son outside in the sodden fields, in the pouring rain.

In early March, Jacques Van't Hart needed to return to Holland on business, so he asked Declan Weld to look after Katday and the five-week-old Best Mate. On 9 March the mare and foal travelled to Old Meadow Stud, but by this time, as a result of the endless rain and lying on wet ground, the little foal had lost most of his hair. Declan recalls that he was a most unusual sight, 'completely naked bar a few hairs under his tummy and whiskers under his chin'. Apparently, he looked 'more like a tiny gazelle than a foal, and his skin, which was black, resembled that of a seal'. He weighed only 60lb but was healthy and inquisitive. Katday's milk supply had virtually dried up, which is not unusual for a mare rearing her first foal under conditions where there is little goodness in the grass. It was therefore necessary to give the foal extra milk, and the lads in the yard soon nicknamed him 'Gonzo'. At first, they wondered whether he would live, but he was quick to respond to his new diet. To start with, he was introduced to goat's milk from a basin, but gradually this basin was replaced by a bucket and the goat's milk changed to powdered milk, specially manufactured for foals. It is mixed with water and is extremely palatable. Gonzo eagerly awaited the buckets, and Declan recalls that he was clever and greedy right from the start.

Gradually, his hair began to grow again, and his confidence increased. Katday also gained in weight and improved her condition. The foaling and the days that had followed had obviously taken a lot out of her, but at Old Meadow she received extra concentrates and these helped to bring back some of her own milk. March was another wet month which necessitated stabling the mare and foal at nights, but they exercised in one of the stud paddocks each day. Katday never liked being caught, but her son would come up to the gate at the sight of a bucket, thus forcing her to follow him.

As Best Mate continued to improve, he began to look more like a normal foal, even though he was undersized. Declan states that he was never robust nor tall, but quite leggy. However, he was extremely healthy and never needed any extra injections, bar those for flu and tetanus. His early weeks had obviously turned him into a tough cookie, and he had built up an excellent natural immunity to cope with his environment.

Later in April, Katday revisited Un Desperado. She was again successfully covered and scanned in foal.

During the month of May, Best Mate returned, with his mother, to Jacques Van't Hart's land, where they were joined by several other mares and foals. He enjoyed those summer days playing with his friends in the quiet sheltered fields. It was very peaceful. There was a good carpet of grass beneath the horses' feet, and instead of the saturated turf and squelchy mud that had characterised the winter months, the ground was warm and dry – perfect for a foal. Yet, inevitably, this tranquillity would not last for long; further upheavals lay ahead. As autumn approached, Mr Van't Hart decided to sell his foal at the November Sales in Fairyhouse, so Best Mate's lifestyle would be changed again. He would shortly be taken away from his mother's side to fend for himself. Another chapter was about to be written.

Best Mate was not officially weaned from Katday until just before those November Sales. He virtually went from the fields, near Trim, to the sales ring, but he had become extremely independent and had almost weaned himself. He no longer needed his mother. Even so, it must have been quite a shock to his system when he was boxed up and delivered to Fairyhouse. After two days on his own at the Tattersalls complex, shut in a strange stable and away from his friends, he began to pine for company and lost some condition. He was stabled in box 216 in Barn F and was catalogued as 'Lot 1016', to be sold on Tuesday, 14 November.

The surroundings at Fairyhouse were totally different to the open fields and it took Best Mate a while to adjust to the hundreds of faces and the unaccustomed noises, in particular to the loudspeakers. He no doubt resented being pushed and pulled along the concrete walkways on a little headcollar, and, according to one observer, he looked small and light for his age. There is always a lot of neighing at the annual foal sales and plenty of distraught weanlings, but surprisingly they quickly learn to accept their new way of life.

Declan Weld had grown fond of Katday's unusual foal and, with his heart ruling his head, almost ended up buying him. For sentimental reasons he would have been happy to take back his little 'Gonzo'. However, he had to compete with another shrewd horse coper, Tom Costello. He too had been attracted by the young colt's breeding, and he liked his loose easy walk. If he had not spotted the foal, Declan considers that he might have pinched him for £IR 300, but instead the bidding was lively between the two men and Best Mate was eventually knocked down to Tom for £IR 2,500. He would now move down to Co. Clare and be reared in one of the finest nurseries in the country. He had been sold to an expert and had been given a great chance to go the right way. The next three years would be of vital importance and would lay the foundation stones for his future National Hunt career.

Best Mate was just two years old when Terry and I went to see his sire, Un Desperado, at Old Meadow Stud in the spring of 1997. I will never forget Un Desperado; he had so much presence and was full of quality. I remember him standing up in Declan Weld's yard – he was such a proud horse, and stood there as if he owned the place. He was a big, powerful bay with striking dapples, and his conformation was hard to fault. We loved his strong, almost 'over at the knee' forelegs. He had a wonderful shoulder and a huge front. It was then that we both agreed that we would love to have a horse by this stallion in our yard, but little did we imagine that two years later we would be training one of his finest sons.

Declan Weld had chosen Un Desperado carefully. He has strong views on National Hunt stallions. He believes they should have speed and be Group winners. 'To produce good jumpers, a stallion must have gears,' he says. Un Desperado won over a mile at Longchamp as a two-year-old, and then won a ten-furlong Group race on the same course at three. He beat Sharrood by two lengths and, just for good measure, broke the track record. This was good enough form for Declan. Following his years in training, Un Desperado was retired to stud in France in 1987, but he was not well managed and attracted very few mares. By 1991 he had sired only a small number of foals, despite being by the good stayer Top Ville, who has since proved to be an influential sire of National Hunt stallions. It so happens that Shardari, Pistolet Bleu, Toulon, Norwich and Beneficial are all by Top Ville, and not only were they all decent racehorses on the flat, they have now produced good jumping winners too.

When it was apparent that Un Desperado's owner was in financial difficulties and that the horse would have to be sold, Pierre Charles Le Metayer, the much-respected French agent, stepped in. He told Declan Weld about the horse and organised for him to go and see him in Normandy. It now seems a strange coincidence that Pierre Charles was involved in this deal because he was also a good friend of Jim Lewis, having been responsible for selling him such good horses as Nakir (Arkle Chase, Cheltenham) and Edredon Bleu (Queen Mother Champion Chase, Cheltenham). Nobody could have foreseen the future, or dreamt that Jim would later end up owning Best Mate. Happily, Pierre Charles knew all about Best Mate before he sadly died in 2000, and was proud to have been responsible for his sire.

When Declan travelled to France to see his future stallion, he recalls that he was shocked by what he saw. He was poor and thin, but in particular Declan loved his head and 'the eyes that looked straight through you'. He agreed to buy him and never once regretted his decision, though it was some while before the horse was strong enough to travel to Ireland. During his eight seasons at Old Meadow Stud, Un Desperado – or Dessie for short – became a great favourite. It appears that he showed a lot of the characteristics we have now learnt to associate with Best Mate. He was a highly intelligent horse, and an impatient one too. He liked being the centre of attention and would make so much noise banging his stable door when anybody entered the stable yard that he ended up being as good as any guard dog. There were three stallions at Old Meadow Stud in the 1990s, and all three had their own bridles. The moment anybody picked up Un Desperado's bridle in the tack room he would recognise the jingling of the bit and know it was the signal for him to be led out to cover a mare. If either of the other two bridles was taken out, he ignored them and barely stirred in his stable.

It was a tragedy for the Weld family and for National Hunt racing when, in 2001, Un Desperado suffered a fatal brain haemorrhage in his paddock. He was only eighteen years old and was still extremely active. He was at last getting the recognition he deserved when disaster struck. Fortunately, there are still a number of his offspring left to continue flying the flag, and he had already sired a number of high-class horses, notably the brilliant miler Riton, who was champion older horse in Argentina in 1995 and won six Group races including three Group 1s; Ranger, who won the Prix de Guiche Group 3 in France and the Bay Meadows Derby Group 3; and Ventana Canyon, victorious in the Arkle Trophy at Cheltenham in 1996.

One man who remains a particular fan of Un Desperado is Philip Myerscough. He is an astute breeder of racehorses and has successfully bred a number of good winners on the flat. He stood Fairy King at his former stud, Ballysheehan in Co. Tipperary, before the stallion's transfer to Coolmore. He is married to Vincent O'Brien's daughter, Jane, and fortunately they both love jump racing as well. It was Philip who owned and bred Ventana Canyon. The horse also raced in his colours, even though he shared him with his good friend Peter Curling, the well-known artist. Since breeding this Arkle Chase winner, the former managing director of Goffs was always on the lookout for another mare with similar bloodlines to those of Ventana Canyon's dam. He would then be able to send her to Un Desperado. By chance, he spotted Katday when she was catalogued for a sale at Goffs in February 1996. Jacques Van't Hart had suddenly decided to sell his broodmares, and this one, in particular, greatly appealed to Philip. There was an added attraction: she was already in foal to his favourite National Hunt stallion.

Ventana Canyon's dam, Adariysa, was by Shirley Heights, a son of Mill Reef; Katday is by Miller's Mate, another Mill Reef stallion. Philip subsequently bought Katday at these sales for £IR 5,500, the same price as Jacques Van't Hart had paid when he bought her from Declan Weld. On 19 March she had another colt foal whom he later named Inca Trail. It was Miller's Mate who gave the Costellos a clue to the naming of Best Mate when they were searching for a really good name for their young star at the beginning of the 1999 point-to-point season. Indeed, this stallion was an interesting racehorse himself, since in 1985 he won the Wood Ditton Stakes at Newmarket, beating Supreme Leader, but was then injured – he fractured a cannon bone – when finishing second to Law Society in the Chester Vase. By all accounts Miller's Mate was as talented as he was good looking. Trained by Sir Michael Stoute, his dam, by Vaguely Noble, was a daughter of the famous Pistol Packer who won the Prix de Diane and the Prix Vermeille, as well as finishing second in the Prix de l'Arc de Triomphe.

Katday's ancestry on her dam's side is also interesting. Not only did her mother, Kenara, breed Charlie Turquoise, which appealed so much to Declan Weld, but her third dam, Pretty Lady, produced several top-class racehorses. Her most notable son was Dynamiter, who won the Champion Stakes in 1951 and 1952, and another son, Abdos, winner of the 1962 Grand Criterium, is the broodmare sire of Acamas, Akarad, Darshaan and Epervier Bleu.

In June 2000, Terry and I made a special journey from Dublin to see Katday and look at her three-year-old son, also by Un Desperado and now called Cornish Rebel. She is kept at Philip Myerscough's Baroda Stud in Co. Kildare and is proving a real gold mine for her owner. She is a brown mare, barely sixteen hands, and fairly compact. She has a lovely head, a deep girth and a sloping shoulder together with an active walk. We liked her a lot, particularly since we knew that she was Best Mate's mother! Apparently, when she is turned out in the paddocks, she is still somewhat aloof and tends to graze on her own, away from the other horses. She obviously likes her independence, as was demonstrated at the time of Matey's birth in 1995. When we saw her for the first time she had no foal at foot, but we saw her yearling filly, by Un Desperado, who is a full sister to Best Mate; she is now called Flying Iris. We have seen her several times since and she has striking similarities to her eldest brother. She is the same colour and is full of quality. She is a real gem, not only because of her relationship to the champion but because she is from her sire's last crop. Whether she will be risked on a racecourse or just kept for breeding remains to be seen, but the Myerscoughs are extremely proud of her. The filly born in 1999 by Oscar is called Sidalcea. She is not in the Best Mate mould and is shorter in front. She is neater and more like her sire, but she is nevertheless a most attractive individual, and is currently in training with Edward O'Grady. Sadly, the 2002 Pistolet Bleu colt foal died when he was a yearling and there was no offspring in 2003, but Katday is now back in foal, this time to Bob Back, so all fingers are crossed for 2004.

Of Katday's sons who have raced, other than Best Mate, Inca Trail impressively won his bumper at Naas in January 2002 from the O'Grady yard before being transferred to England to join his elder brother at West Lockinge Farm. He is stabled in the next-door box to Matey and they talk through a hole in the wall. He is a fine-looking, almost black horse, and in temperament he is a lot like Best Mate. He is always impatient to get on with his daily exercise and very greedy. He likes to have his own way. So far he has won only a small hurdle race on English soil, but has run well in competitive races. He will go chasing in the coming season and he looks every inch a chaser. The 1998 Roselier gelding Inexorable, who Philip sold as a yearling for £IR 32,550 at the Tattersalls November National Hunt Sales in 1999 and who was then resold at Doncaster May Sales in 2002 for £185,000, has to date won his only point-to-point from David Wachman's yard. This was at Nenagh in Co. Tipperary in January 2003. He looks destined for a good career on the track. Cornish Rebel, whom we saw at Baroda as a three-year-old, and who was sold for £IR 110,000 at the Derby Sales in 2002, won a competitive bumper at Newbury in the spring of 2003 and is now trained by Paul Nicholls. He is highly regarded.

It can thus be seen that Best Mate has a strong supporting pedigree and some interesting ancestors. It was the French connection that was later to appeal so much to Jim Lewis owing to the success of his own French-bred chasers. It was pure good fortune that Declan Weld pinhooked Katday at those Tattersalls sales and then had a stallion to match her pedigree. The hardships

Matey endured during those wet early months of his life have highlighted the strengths of his character. He was a fighter right from the start and was somehow different to the other foals of his generation. He continues to attract attention wherever he goes. Not just one in a million, he is one in ten million. He is irreplaceable.

CHAPTER THREE

BEST MATE GROWS UP

When Tom Costello bought Best Mate as a foal at Fairyhouse in November 1995, he was accompanied to the sales by several of his sons. It was Tom Junior who took a particular shine to the future star, and he later took over the ownership of the horse. 'He was a such a small, light foal that you could almost bring him away under your arm,' he remembers. 'But he had such a lovely swing to his stride as well as good front legs and a nice head on him.' Young Tom was confident from the start that he would be something special, and he also liked his breeding since Un Desperado was just beginning to sire some notable winners. All the little foal needed to do was to develop and grow.

Around twenty foals returned to Co. Clare that year after the sales. They were over-wintered in two groups at two different places on the Costello farms. The weanlings are always regularly dosed and vaccinated, but they are not mollycoddled. They spend the winter months in big open sheds with the run of the adjoining fields, are fed twice daily with special concentrates, and have as much hay as they want. The extra feeding – mostly oats – continues well into the spring and summer and is considered to be of vital importance to the future well-being of these young horses. They soon acquire strong necks and powerful hindquarters, as well as good hard bone. The minerals in the soil and the well-managed pastures also aid this development.

Best Mate gradually showed some improvement in his condition, but he remained small and light. He developed a little more during the summer of 1996 when the yearlings were divided into smaller groups and joined up with the store cattle to graze the bigger fields. They could gallop and roam over many acres. During the second winter, a number of the young horses were stabled by night, which meant they had more handling in preparation for the following spring when, as two-year-olds, they would start their education in earnest and get ridden for the first time.

Tom Jr began Best Mate's early training in April 1997. He broke him in himself, but continued to give him plenty of food as he was still only medium-sized. He remembers him as a sharp, intelligent horse who was easy to handle and took his lessons well. The weeks of long reining were accompanied by plenty of loose jumping, without a rider, which he found particularly easy. He was a natural jumper right from the start. When ridden, he was extremely sensitive and quick to react to the rider's movements. He was not averse to getting his head down for a good buck, and over the next eighteen months there were several occasions when he deposited his jockeys on the ground by producing powerful bucks when they were least expected. He was about fifteen hands three inches when broken in, and several good judges looked at him and turned him down for being too small. He measures a whole hand higher now, and to stand up to him he is a tall horse.

After the initial riding in the summer of his two-year-old year, Best Mate was turned away for further development, and the next step in his education did not start until the end of July 1998, when he was three. He was easy to re-break and had remembered all his previous lessons. He would now be aimed at the four-year-old point-to-points the following spring. He was stabled in the same box as The Thinker had occupied in the early 1980s. Tom Jr wonders whether this was a special omen as that chaser won the Cheltenham Gold Cup in 1987.

All went well with Best Mate until early October 1988 when he began taking lame steps with his riders. Until then he had always moved impeccably. The lameness mystified his connections, but they soon discovered that he was only unlevel when he wore a bridle and had a bit in his mouth; when walked and trotted in the yard on a headcollar he was perfectly sound. Eventually it was discovered that he had two blind wolf teeth that were causing great discomfort, the nerves around them presumably catching on the metal bit when he was ridden. He could not bear any pressure in this part of his mouth, in the region of the first molars. He was incredibly sensitive to touch and would throw his head up into the air. It was therefore decided to give him an anaesthetic and surgically remove these offending little teeth, each of which was about the size of a large almond. The incisions into his gums would then need time to heal, so he was given a six-week rest before restarting work. To everyone's relief, the operation was a success and he was once again completely sound. The 'bridle lameness' disappeared, although even to this day there are times when he obviously remembers the pain and the habit he developed to evade the bit. He still throws his head around when he is walking home from the Downs, and sometimes takes a while to accept the bit during his lessons on the flat.

As a result of Best Mate's enforced lay-off during the last months of his life as a three-year-old, he dropped behind the others in terms of education. In particular, he missed several valuable schooling sessions away from home. It has always been the pattern in the Costello training camp to travel the young horses to different places and accustom them to jumping in company, either on a racecourse or on a point-to-point course, prior to their first public appearance. But it was not until February 1999 that Best Mate had his first away day, and on this occasion it meant a visit to Clonmel racecourse.

He travelled to Co. Tipperary in the horsebox with several other point-to-pointers, and Tony Costello partnered him in this first schooling session. The plan was to follow the lead horse round the whole track and jump all the racecourse fences. Be My Manager, with Dermot Costello, was chosen as the leader. He was the same age as Best Mate but had already been given plenty of practice. The two horses set off at a steady pace, but Matey's eyes were on stalks. He had never been asked to do anything like this before and he was clearly unsure of himself. The ground was very soft and the fences looked big and black. Tony had a nightmare ride. He could not get his horse to pick up the bridle and carry him into the fences; instead, Best Mate almost froze on his approaches and went into each fence like an eel. Unless he met the take-off point spot on he would climb into the air and cat-jump the obstacle, often landing on all four legs at once. Be My Manager, jumping smoothly and accurately, soon went out of sight and gave him no further help. 'I did not know whether I was on a racehorse or a donkey,' recalls Tony. The morning went so badly that it was imperative that they returned the following day in an attempt to improve upon their performance. Luckily, Matey had obviously learnt something. Keeping closer to his lead horse, he suddenly got the hang of the game, and although far from foot perfect he seemed much happier and more confident.

With only a week to go before the first four-year-old race of the season at Lismore, Best Mate still needed more practice. He was green and inexperienced. The penny had not yet completely dropped and he was still not ready for his racecourse debut. Tony and Tom Jr decided on another journey away from Fenloe – Tom Costello's house, about eight miles from Shannon airport to the east of the small but busy town of Newmarket-on-Fergus – and this time the chosen venue was Killaloe point-to-point course, which is situated between Nenagh and Limerick. The East Clare Point-to-Point had been held here on Sunday, 21 February on heavy ground. The Costello lorry drew up for schooling the next day, but imagine the riders' horror when they found that all the wings on the fences had already been taken away. The ground had been literally 'ploughed up' by the point-to-point runners. It was a cold, windy Monday, and Killaloe, a rollercoaster course, is not ideal for schooling at the best of times. Undaunted, the boys set off to educate their horses, but once again Best Mate was all at sea. He spooked and shied at these strange-looking island fences, and Tony had a very uncomfortable time in the saddle as his partner jumped from left to right or right to left at these horrible obstacles; he was almost never straight. However they completed the circuit with no damage, a tribute to the courage of both. There were now only six days to go. Would Best Mate ever be ready to race on Sunday? The Costello family were emphatic that the answer was 'yes', and, loaded up with several other runners, the box set off on 28 February to Co.Waterford.

When Terry and I saw Best Mate walking round that paddock at Lismore, the horse looked knowing and confident. He showed no signs of greenness when he cantered to the start and had obviously put his past schooling experiences well behind him. Tony, who had not been looking forward to the ride, could not believe the horse's change in attitude. He felt different from the moment he sat on his back, and he jumped round the course one and a half times in that four-year-old Maiden race like an old pro. He was foot perfect and galloped as straight as a die; indeed, Tony found it hard to pull him up at the bottom of the hill, but he knew his horse was short of a gallop and that a hard race on that heavy ground might damage him for life. Connections were delighted with their embryo chaser. For once, everything had gone according to plan. His run had been full of promise.

The two-horse race at the point-to-point at Tuam in Co. Clare one week later might have looked a farce on paper, but Best Mate put up an excellent performance to beat his sole opponent. Michael Hourigan's mare Well Then Now Then, was well fancied, yet he beat her by eight lengths showing a good turn of foot. *Formcard*, Ireland's point-to-point formbook which is published each autumn and lists the top horses of each preceding season, described Best Mate as having found an extra gear, and in the end-of-season summary stated that he was likely to find further successes between the flags, and possibly more – a description that hardly fitted a future Gold Cup winner. It was probably fortunate that the book had not been published when we took Jim Lewis to see his future champion. Yet, a spotter for Marten Julian had noted the run, and in his *National Hunt Guide* for the

1999/2000 season Best Mate was highlighted and given a half-page write-up. 'Best Mate,' the guide stated, 'who had enjoyed a quiet school round in a race run in a hailstorm a week earlier at Lismore, comes from Tom Costello's academy of young talent. A son of Un Desperado out of a mare by Miller's Mate who won three races on the Flat in France, Best Mate is a lovely looking horse who stood head and shoulders above his rivals when observed in the paddock before his debut. It is therefore no surprise that he caught the eye of Henrietta Knight as few trainers buy a better-looking horse. Furthermore, as the horses she buys from Ireland tend to come to hand more quickly than those bought by other trainers, expect to see this interesting individual in the winners' enclosure sooner rather than later.' It was an accurate assessment.

The Costellos knew they had a good horse but were in no particular hurry to sell him after Tuam, where his run had gone virtually unnoticed by the point-to-point experts. It suited them well as they had decided to train him for the four-year-old bumper race at Punchestown at the end of April. He apparently grew more in the months of February and March 1999 than at any other time in his life, and was fast developing into a fine-looking chaser. No wonder Terry had been so impressed by his appearance at Lismore, and how lucky it was that we saw him on that day and were able to buy him before the Punchestown festival came round.

CHAPTER FOUR

FIRST SIGHTINGS

Terry and I left home, West Lockinge Farm, at eight o'clock on that Sunday morning in late February 1999 for Heathrow airport. Our flight to Cork was on time, and we arrived in Ireland around 11.30 a.m. There was nothing unusual about this journey as at the beginning of every year we make several similar visits to Irish point-to-points. It suits us well as the meetings are usually on Sundays and there is seldom any racing in England on those days during the winter. A large number of top chasers have started their careers at these events, and in order to put in a bid for a nice horse it is easier to be on the scene, in person, than to talk business over the telephone at a later date. On this particular occasion our journey to the West Waterford Point-to-Point at Lismore was to mark the beginning of a fairy story.

During the flight across the Irish Sea, I well remember glancing through the entries for the first race. Michael Moore, a close friend who lives and farms in Co. Cork and is our chief spotter at the point-to-points, always faxes us a list of entries in advance. He also collects up as many pedigrees as he can find and sends these to us as well. I had not had time during the previous week to look at the list of horses for Lismore, so sitting by the window on the Aer Lingus flight gave me my first opportunity to study the entries. Even at this stage I was attracted by the name Best Mate, by the then little-known sire Un Desperado. By chance, both Terry and I had seen this stallion three years previously at Old Meadow Stud in Co. Kildare and we had been most impressed by the horse, who was a fine upstanding individual with a big front, excellent limbs and a good bold head. Un Desperado was by Top Ville, and in the early 1990s we had trained Edimbourg by Top Ville to win nine races. Was this a coincidence? There were plenty of entries and several had interesting breeding on paper. It would be fascinating to see them.

Our enthusiasm for the point-to-point diminished somewhat as we drove from Cork airport in driving rain past sodden fields and flooded rivers towards Co. Waterford. It was a typical Irish winter's day – wet, grey and dreary. We had seen many similar days before, but on this occasion we had arranged to meet a party of enthusiastic owners headed by Martin Broughton, who had flown to Ireland the previous afternoon. Martin had already enjoyed successes with Easthorpe from our yard and was now searching for a new horse for his syndicate of close friends. Together with his wife Jocelyn, he was much looking forward to sampling the atmosphere of an Irish point-to-point for the first time. What a day to choose! We spoke to Michael on his mobile telephone as we drove along, and he reassured us that no cancellation was expected. He also gave us the good news that he had loaded up the Land Rover with our waterproof jackets (which we always leave at his house for the winter) and a big picnic that had been specially prepared by his wonderful mother, 'Mrs E'. She is well known for her smoked salmon sandwiches and chocolate eclairs!

After about an hour's drive we reached Lismore. The point-to-point is staged in a most attractive part of Ireland in the grounds of Lismore Castle on the banks of the Blackwater river, which is famous for salmon fishing in the spring and summer. On arrival, it was immediately obvious that the car park was virtually unusable. Hundreds of cars were parked down side roads and avenues to avoid the mud. Terry found an ideal spot for our hired car, which we then abandoned before trudging across two fields to see the action. We found Michael and the Broughtons, marked off the runners for the first race on a soggy racecard, and waited for some horses to appear in the paddock.

It was this opening race which was all important. It was for maiden four-year-olds, none of the horses had run before, and there were sixteen of them, despite the atrocious conditions. The unsuspecting youngsters, already saddled, were led across a muddy grass field from the horsebox park to a roped-off area close to the secretary's tent. This was the parade ring, where brave spectators gathered round in the pouring rain to look at the horses. We stood at the entrance to this pen and watched every horse go by, trying to assess what we were looking at, but it wasn't easy under those dreadful conditions.

The horses walked round and round, and one of them stood out. This was Best Mate. He seemed unperturbed by the underfoot conditions and walked proudly through the mud with his head held high. He took in everything around him and occasionally broke into a jog to readjust his footing as his leader slipped and slithered beside him on the wet ground. Terry spotted him at once. He loved his alert manner and the athletic way he moved. I liked him too, but I was also carefully watching a fine big chestnut horse called Bruthuinne. He looked impressive, and was the favourite. He was a lean, fit-looking individual trained by David Wachman, and was due to be ridden by Noel Fehily, who in those days divided his time between England and Ireland as a successful amateur rider (he is now a leading professional jockey based with Charlie Mann in Lambourn). The Broughtons also seemed to like Bruthuinne, who was a half brother to the good chaser Aghawadda Gold trained by Thomas Tate in England. Best Mate came from Tom Costello's yard. We had heard a lot about these 'Costello horses' over the past years but had never been to Tom's establishment in Co. Clare. We knew, however, that many good young horses had passed through his hands. He was already responsible for five Cheltenham Gold Cup winners (The Thinker, Cool Dawn, Cool Ground, Imperial Call and Midnight

Court), while Florida Pearl, another graduate of the Costello school, had made a winning debut in the four-year-old Maiden race at Lismore in 1996. This point-to-point track had produced good horses, and so had Tom Costello.

The horses made their way to the start, and we watched them canter down across the heavy ground to a line of trees beside the estate wall. Here they walked around prior to being lined up for the off. A number of the horses looked green and unsure of themselves, but several were barely four years old and still had a lot to learn. Many National Hunt-bred horses are foaled later in the year than their Flat-race counterparts, and this is especially noticeable in Ireland where the breeders often prefer to wait for warmer weather and better grass.

Best Mate, under Tony Costello, sensibly made his way to the start. He looked well balanced and held himself correctly, with his neck arched and his head low to the ground. Terry watched him carefully from the time he left the paddock until the moment he was pulled up, three fences from home. He liked everything he saw, and he always reads a race exceptionally well.

There were fifteen fences to be jumped at Lismore and all races were run over three miles. The four-year-olds carried 11st 7lb. The course is left-handed and undulating with two tight bends at the top end; indeed, the last bend, just before the finish, is almost set at 90 degrees and a lot of horses hang right here towards the horsebox park. It is not ideal for a young horse. The fences are portable and made of brush. They are shared throughout the season by other point-to-points in the same area, and unsurprisingly they suffer a lot of wear and tear as the months progress. They are built differently to our fences in England and do not slope gradually from the widest point at the base to the highest point. The Irish fences are constructed more in the shape of a garden seat, with a horizontal base and an upright back. We have noticed that horses tend to run into these fences, and even step on the take-off rails. They are not particularly stiff, and frequently encourage some indifferent jumping. Some horses learn bad habits and get away with mistakes, but both Best Mate and Bruthuinne jumped well. The former was up with the leaders for three parts of the race and was given plenty of light. He still looked full of running when he was pulled up; Bruthuinne also raced close to the front and kept on well in the testing ground. He looked the certain winner when he jumped the last, but after a schemozzle on the final bend he was collared by the smaller and nippier Bob Back mare Prometteuse. He was beaten by two lengths but was later awarded the race when the winning horse tested positive for caffeine and was disqualified.

It was a strange day. Best Mate had looked the class horse in the opening race but had failed to finish. We talked to Tom Costello, and even introduced him to Martin Broughton, but he was not interested in selling until his horse had managed a win. By the end of the day, everybody was drenched but it had been an enjoyable and constructive afternoon. The picnic had been the saviour for the Broughton party, and its members had experienced yet another aspect of National Hunt racing. The next morning we visited David Wachman's yard and, fired with enthusiasm, they bought Bruthuinne. As events turned out, he was an unlucky horse for them and he took four seasons to win two small races. Terry and I wrote Best Mate's name down in our notebook. He had enormously impressed us. Perhaps we should look at him again when he'd won his first race?

CHAPTER FIVE

THE SECRET DEAL

Three weeks after our excursion to Lismore, we were once again back in Ireland for the Cloyne Point-to-Point near Midleton in Co. Cork. We had another enjoyable day, educational and worthwhile, but we saw no horse of special appeal. We left the course at around 3.30 p.m. and drove a few miles further down the road towards Ballycotton Bay to spend the night at Ballymaloe House, which is one of our favourite places to stay and is renowned for its superb food. It is closely linked to the world-famous cookery school of the same name.

As soon as we arrived the telephone rang; it was a call to say that an impressive four-year-old of Tom Costello's called Be My Manager had just won the Maiden Race at the Galway Blazers' Point-to-Point in Athenry. Our spotters had done their work and we were notified immediately. On the strength of this news, and with a strong desire to take another look at Best Mate, we decided that now was the time to drive to Co. Clare and see Tom Costello's establishment. It was not difficult to change our tickets home on the Monday, so we cancelled our early flight from Cork and booked the midday one from Shannon. We rang Tom to ask if we could be with him at 8.30 a.m. and he seemed happy to see us at that hour. Michael Moore agreed to accompany us on that memorable journey, and we left Ballymaloe at dawn.

During our drive to the west of Ireland we also learnt that Best Mate had won a race since we last saw him – that two-horse affair, the four-year-old maiden race at Tuam, also in Co. Galway, where he had beaten Michael Hourigan's mare Well Then Now Then, who was making her first appearance in public. The meeting had taken place on 7 March, but the race had obviously not impressed many of the experts. Best Mate was now for sale, but he had not been snapped up in the week following the win. Many promising Irish point-to-point winners tend to get sold immediately after their races, so it was lucky that this two-horse contest had not set the point-to-point world alight because we still had a chance to buy him.

The narrow and winding approach road to Tom Costello's house, Fenloe, runs beside the shores of a strikingly beautiful lake and nature reserve. There are all sorts of species of wildlife to be seen. The entrance to Fenloe faces the lake, and as we drove through the gateway and up the short drive we were immediately impressed by the extreme tidiness of it all. The tarmac roadway was edged by well-kept grass verges. The fields, surrounded by stone walls or post and rails, were immaculate. Several groups of fine Charolais-cross beef cattle grazed contentedly as we passed by. There were superb views across these fields to the woods and hills beyond. Magnificent old trees added to this picturesque scenery. It was certainly a most peaceful setting, and we were soon to learn that attention to detail rates high on Tom's list of priorities.

The man himself was waiting on the steps as we drove up to the front door. He was watching our arrival intently (he never misses a trick). Terry parked the car facing towards the way we had come in. He always does this wherever we go since he says that at least we can then make a quick exit if we don't like the horses we see. That was not to be the case on this Monday morning; he could have parked the car anywhere as it turned out.

We were quickly taken into the house to the sitting room on the left of the front door, with its blazing log fire. The walls were hung with numerous photographs showing many of the good horses that had been sold by the Costello family. Jo, Tom's wife, brought us some coffee – she is a charming lady, and always makes us welcome; she is also an excellent cook. We then sat down to watch the previous day's race featuring Be My Manager in Galway. We viewed the race intently; the horse looked good and won well. Unfortunately, there had been no video of Best Mate's race two weeks earlier, but we were later shown a good photograph of him jumping the last fence.

After a short discussion in the house, we wandered up a narrow path to the imposing stable yard with a high stone wall around it. It is over two hundred years old, and the main part is in the shape of a square with horses' heads looking out over their half doors towards the centre. Once again, everything was neat and tidy. It was quiet and peaceful too, and it was here that we met Tom Junior for the first time. He was in charge of the yard. He had been a top showjumping rider as a child and then a good amateur jockey, having won races in England as well as Ireland. He was responsible for the breaking in and training of all the horses at Fenloe and he has a quiet, knowledgeable way with the animals he handles. He had, of course, known Best Mate and Be My Manager ever since they'd been bought as foals by his father. He had watched them develop and had ridden them many times. He believed that they were two exceptional young horses.

First, we were shown Be My Manager. Although he had run fewer than 24 hours earlier, he had taken his race well. He was a tall horse, about sixteen hands three inches, and still looked immature, but stood up impressively in the yard. Despite being a little 'on the leg', he moved well, well balanced and light on his feet. He had a good head, a large front and plenty of bone. We liked him a lot; he looked a real chaser.

When we had seen enough of this horse, Tom Junior went back to fetch Best Mate. As he walked him out of his stable, which was tucked away in the corner of the yard, he looked every bit as good as we had remembered. He covered so much ground with every step and patiently stood there against one of the bare stone walls while we stepped back and marvelled at him. At that time he was about sixteen hands two inches, and he, too, still looked unfurnished, but we were struck by his lovely sloping shoulder and deep girth. As Terry put it, 'all the heart room in the world'. He had a special head, too, a wide forehead, a bold eye and big ears. He looked an intelligent horse, and his limbs were almost faultless. My camera was busy that day. I photographed both horses and was able to get some good pictures. We still look at those photographs back at home. It must have been fate that we ever made that journey to Co. Clare. It was a memorable morning. We saw two impressive four-year-olds and we wanted to train them both, but how could we buy them?

As we left Fenloe for the airport, I asked Tom if he could give us 24 hours to mull over what we had just seen. He said that he would only sell us one of the horses as other people had been ringing him to buy them and he could not sell both to the same trainer. We sensed that he favoured us buying Be My Manager. Certainly he was the best horse 'on paper', and he was by the much-sought-after stallion Be My Native. Indeed, the 1999 version of Ireland's point-to-point form book *Formcard*, had Be My Manager top of the list of the four-year-olds. Best Mate was not even mentioned in the top ten, but we knew nothing of this when we saw them. Yes, Be My Manager looked a fine prospect and we had one good order to fill, but surely we could not leave behind such a perfect specimen as Best Mate?

By the end of the day we had talked to one of our most loyal and straightforward of owners, Lord Cadogan, and although the price was high he agreed to buy Be My Manager. We were delighted with this news and rang Tom Costello to clinch the deal. It was then that I asked him to wait another 48 hours while I tried to persuade a second owner to take a look at Best Mate. Tom gave us this chance, but we knew that we would have to act fast since good horses do not stay long with him once he has made up his mind to sell and the horses have shown their form in public.

It was now that fate once more came to the rescue. We decided to tell Jim Lewis about Best Mate. Jim is another of our long-established and most valued owners. I trained his first winner for him, Pearl Prospect (Wincanton, 1989). Afterwards Jim had several French-bred horses with Simon Christian, who had a short spell of training next door to the Lewises in Fred Rimell's old yard at Kinnersley in Worcestershire. When Simon stopped training, Jim and Valerie Lewis sent us a new horse from France, Edredon Bleu. But how could we possibly persuade Jim to buy an Irish horse when his best horses, Nakir and Camitrov, had been bought in France through his agent and friend Pierre Charles Le Metayer?

There was one possible link: Best Mate's pedigree was French. Not only is he by Un Desperado, but his dam, Katday, won her races in France too. I seldom telephone Jim unless there is a drama with one of his horses; almost all our communication is by fax, so I dispatched one. It was well worth a try. 'Dearest Jim & Valerie,' I wrote, 'Terry and I have just seen the horse of our dreams. He is the perfect racehorse and we would train him for nothing. He is in Ireland but he is French-bred.' Amazingly, Jim agreed to fly to Ireland and see this special horse.

On 29 March 1999 we met him at Heathrow for the 11.15 EI 735 Aer Lingus flight for Shannon. Tom Costello met us at the airport and within half an hour we were once more walking up to the front door at Fenloe. This time we did not spend long in the house. Neither Terry nor I dared to breathe as we again followed Tom up that garden path to the yard. Jim and Valerie were shepherded through the gates and must have wondered exactly what they were going to see. Would Best Mate be as special as the picture we had painted? Straight to the corner box they went, and there, for the first time, they caught a glimpse of their future star. Tom Junior led him out, across the cobbles and on to the smooth tarmac. We were not let down. Yet again he looked superb, and once more he stood up against the wall for a thorough examination.

Tom then led him onwards and through the doors of the huge indoor school behind the stables. We followed behind and were told to stand in the middle of this huge covered area. Down the long sides of this rectangular-shaped building were two jumps. One of these comprised various timber poles balanced on large barrels, and on the other side there was a plastic steeplechase fence. The poles were about three feet off the ground and the chase fence was over four feet high. It looked solid and imposing. The two 'Toms' picked up a couple of lunge whips and stood at either end. Best Mate was let loose. Off he went, with a buck and a kick. He cantered round and round the outside of the school on the deep sandy surface, jumping the two obstacles every time he reached them. He always met them correctly and 'in his stride', demonstrating his athleticism. They stopped him with a shout of 'woa' and he obediently stood still, head held proudly, nostrils barely moving despite the sudden, somewhat violent exercise. He returned to the yard, and Jim Lewis took another look at him in the stable. Best Mate was so inquisitive and friendly. He was really interested in all the attention. He put his head on Valerie's shoulder. I had taken some more photographs, and they came out well.

After all the excitement in the yard, we returned to the house and Jim Lewis disappeared with 'the boss'. He returned with a smile some twenty minutes later. He had just bought a new horse! Jim describes the dealings in his own words. 'Hen and Terry left it to us. I asked Tom, "How much do you want for this horse?" knowing that whatever he said I'd say, "You must be joking!" When he told me the figure, I said, "I told you, Tom, you're going to break my heart." But then we discussed how I might pay. Now, if I want to buy something, I buy it. There's no messing around. So I told him he could have the money in ten minutes. I'd adjusted the price, and I put my hand out to shake on the deal. I maybe rushed him a little bit, but we shook on it, and he said, "The only reason I've sold you this horse is because I know Henrietta will train the horse better than anyone else. But I want you to do me a favour. I want you to promise that you'll never tell anyone how much you paid for him." "Deal," I said. We shook hands again, and I've never told anyone, not even Hen or Terry. And I know he hasn't either.'

Terry and I could not hide our joy. We were delighted. It was the best news we had heard for years, but the story had only just begun. On the way home I remember saying to Terry, 'Let's pray that our judgement is right. Best Mate has got a lot to prove. Our heads are on the block if things go wrong.' But from that March day onwards Best Mate was to change the whole pattern of our lives. We had taken a huge gamble, but how true is that famous Shakespearean quotation: 'There is a tide in the affairs of men which, taken at the flood, leads on to fortune…'

The well-respected veterinary surgeon from Co. Waterford, Walter Connors, examined Best Mate three days later, and he passed with flying colours. On 31 March Michael Hinchliffe collected the two horses from Tom Costello's yard, and after a night on the ferry and a short journey by road, Best Mate took his first steps from the horsebox across our gravel drive to his new stable at West Lockinge Farm.

It was 1 April 1999, and a new era had just begun.

CHAPTER SIX

IDEALS AND INSPIRATIONS

When I look back over the years I find it hard to trace the source of my lifelong passion for horses. I have certainly inherited some strong genes to push me in that direction, but they do not fully explain why, for over half a century, horses have dominated my thoughts. They are like a drug; I am hooked on these animals. From the early hours each morning, when Terry and I get up to feed all the inmates of our yard, to last thing at night, when I finish my workbook for the following day, they are always on my mind. My love of horses has always been the driving force behind my ambition. I have always wanted to improve and learn more, but it is not easy to climb up the ladder and gain respect in such a hard, competitive world. Jim Lewis calls me 'the weaver of dreams'; perhaps he is right, as I have constantly aimed at the top, and when I began training I used to dream of one day winning the Cheltenham Gold Cup.

I have wonderful memories of my childhood years, such happy days. I have spent most of my life at Lockinge, close to the stables from which our horses are now trained. We were always a close-knit family, but sadly neither of my parents is now alive. My sister Celia (Ce), although two and a half years younger, has always been a close companion and my greatest friend. She is married and has her own family but we still speak to each other most days. When she had a stroke in 1995 and was unconscious for three weeks, those days were easily the worst of my life. Now that she has recovered so well, she is once again my greatest supporter. She loves the racing.

As children we had ponies from our earliest days, and everything that I did, Ce followed suit a few years afterwards. We were certainly spoilt, but we enjoyed our lives to the full. Apart from ponies and horses we were surrounded by animals, from dogs, bantams, rabbits and guinea pigs to the cattle on the farm and the mynah bird in the house which wolf-whistled to anybody who came in through the front door. I never had dolls, but plenty of toy horses and a few teddy bears. I remember playing for hours in my bedroom organising my collection of 'Julip' horses and sending them out on rides around the house. I had toy stables and a model farmyard, but no dolls' house. Each horse had its own stall and would be carefully put to bed at night. For a while, we had a proper old-fashioned nanny, but at times she must have despaired of her charge. All I ever wanted to do was make the poor dogs jump over cushions in the house or over fences, made out of sticks, on the lawn. Then I would disappear with Ce to ride the hobby horses.

My mother, Hester, was a special person. She had an extraordinary way with people and with animals, and was also a fine horsewoman. She was universally popular and did so much to help others less fortunate than herself. She was so gifted with animals that she could catch even the wildest horses or ponies in the fields. It seemed that she almost talked to them. Her own upbringing also took place in Lockinge, so she knew every inch of the place and completely understood the countryside. When we were still fairly young she began to breed Shetland ponies, and she quickly built up a highly regarded stud. Within the space of ten years there were over 60 ponies on the farm, comprising broodmares and their offspring as well as three stallions, one of whom was regularly taken to the major shows and won many championships, including at the Royal Show. On several occasions Mum organised the Shetland Pony Breed Show on Newbury racecourse, and it was great fun for us to see the workings of a racecourse at first hand. The breeders and their helpers all camped down in the stable lads' dormitory and the ponies occupied the official stables, even though they could barely see over the tops of the doors.

We learnt a lot when helping with these animals. They were character-building years, and we had plenty of fun, but there were always heartaches as well. On the good days, when everything seemed to go right, it taught us to appreciate how lucky we were, yet when disasters occurred we were rapidly brought back down to earth and there were often plenty of tears.

My father, who had spent a large part of his life in the army, finished his career as a major in the Coldstream Guards with a Military Cross from the Second World War. He began farming in 1947. He liked horses, but was more interested in agriculture and cricket as well as organising his social diary. Yet he successfully rode in a number of point-to-points and was, for a long time, secretary to the Old Berkshire Hunt. He was a strict father and was not always pleased when his daughters and wife spent whole days away from home at horse shows. He often tried to discourage my obsession for ponies and my life in the stable yard, although later on, when any successes came along, he was the first person to say 'well done' and was secretly proud of what I achieved. He had a wonderfully dry sense of humour and we all adored him, but I'm sure he wished I'd been a son and had taken up shooting since he was a wonderful shot himself. Sadly for him, the only interest I ever showed was when I accompanied him pigeon shooting in the woods or killing rabbits on the farm, yet he gave me a sixteen-bore gun for my seventeenth birthday and I still keep my shotgun licence up to date. Luckily, he did teach me how to use this gun properly, and over the years I have managed to put a number of rabbits suffering from myxomatosis out of their misery.

We rode regularly as children, starting on a special Shetland pony called Florian, who was almost human. He frequently came into the house and travelled in the back of the Land Rover; he even appeared in the film *Follow That Horse* starring David Tomlinson and Dora Bryan. In 1960 he was chosen for the Personalities Parade at the Horse of the Year Show at Wembley. Ce and I took a week off school and led him in the twice-daily performances. Later on, we had an assortment of bigger ponies, several of which came directly from Ireland. We used to meet them off the train at the now defunct Wantage Road station. It was always a great treat to be driven to the station, watch the ramp go down on the platform and then ride the new ponies back to the farm. They had probably been travelling for two or three days and were fairly tired so they seldom caused us any trouble on the way home. Nowadays, the racehorses come over from Ireland in a horsebox on the ferry and the journey lasts about fifteen hours from door to door.

My love for horses and the fascination for training developed further during my childhood years when Reg Hobbs came to live in our village. He had been a most successful trainer, and Battleship, ridden by his son Bruce, had won the 1938 Grand National under his expert eye. Reg was a fine horseman and had a tremendous understanding of horses. He was quiet and patient but very firm. I remember being struck by the way he used his voice and sung to his charges. I used to watch him for hours, spellbound, as he lunged, long-reined and backed the many youngsters. On his retirement from racing Reg advised my uncle, Christopher 'Larch' Loyd, who at that time had a number of homebred horses to be educated from Lockinge Stud. He even persuaded Larch to convert a disused double tennis court into a loose jumping school. It was well sited in the former gardens of Lockinge House, which had been demolished after the war, and it was expertly designed along the lines of a similar training aid Reg had used in America. We still use it today for the racehorses, and there is no finer place to teach a horse to jump. Reg would stand in the middle and quietly encourage the horses to show off their paces and develop their jumping techniques. Sometimes he wanted the horses to be ridden, and it was on these occasions that I was able to gain valuable experience. He would leg me up on to the three- and four-year-olds and I would canter round over the poles dreaming of the future and loving every moment of the present. Reg filled his pupils with confidence and was a wonderful teacher. He later helped my mother to train her point-to-point horses and was always on call to offer his advice. I often rode along the Downs with him, on my pony, and he reminisced about his training days, but it always surprised me when he happily cantered the four-year-olds up the middle of a tarmac road. He maintained that it was safer to canter on a smooth, firm surface than on a softer rough one. Admittedly he never seemed to do any damage to the horses he rode.

While most summers were taken up with horse shows, Pony Club camps, rallies and Pony Club Interbranch team competitions, during the winter months we usually spent the weekends and holidays hunting our ponies or travelling to point-to-points. I was particularly fond of those racing days and followed the form closely. I even made my own point-to-point form book, taking the results each week from the *Horse & Hound* magazine.

I was fortunate in that most of my education was spent at day schools. My parents decided to allow me to attend Didcot Girls' Grammar School rather than the private boarding school St Mary's in Wantage. This was one of the best moves they ever made, at least in my eyes. I had never liked the idea of leaving home and deserting the animals during term time. As it was, I was still able to ride in the evenings, after school, before settling down to piles of homework. At school, I was highly competitive, always striving to keep my place close to the top of the class, and as my home life was so idyllic I did not want to let my parents down. While I was at Didcot, my idol was Ann Packer, who became the golden girl of British athletics when she won a gold medal in the 800m at the 1964 Olympics in Tokyo. She was my house captain, and I marvelled at her popularity and the press coverage she generated. Sadly, my ability in athletics was limited: I was confined to the sack race on sports day.

It was during our rides after school one spring in the late 1950s that Ce and I decided to train our own donkey for the Donkey Derby due to take place that summer in the neighbouring village of East Hendred. Sheba was a huge black donkey and very stubborn; she was also extremely unpredictable, but we sweetened her up and in her training we used Florian as the lead horse. We would canter them bareback across the fields and up through the cleared pathways in the nearby woods. I usually carried a long stick broken off from an elder bush, and I left the leaves on the end of it. If I were to hit Sheba she would stop completely, but I could coax her to go forward by shaking the leaves. It was so much fun, especially when she won the race and we received a huge silver cup. I felt as though I had made it as a trainer, even in those days.

During the winter months, when the days were short and darkness fell soon after four o'clock, it was less easy to ride after school, yet my pony, Peewit, who was stabled full time, needed her daily exercise, and since she was a thoroughbred she had to be carefully managed. I looked after her myself, mucking out and feeding her each morning before school. I treated her like a little racehorse and she became extremely fit. I saved up my pocket money to buy a special stirrup light which I had seen advertised in a horse magazine. It was most effective (until the battery gave out), and I went for many miles in semi-darkness with this light close to my foot. Nowadays, nobody would dream of allowing a twelve-year-old child to ride out alone, with dusk falling, on deserted downland tracks. There were no mobile phones in the 1950s.

By a strange coincidence, my mother had bought Peewit on the advice of Ginger Dennistoun, who trained locally at Letcombe Regis. He became a great family friend, and it was from Ginger's yard that I first rode out on a racehorse, when I was fourteen years old. He was a great character and a very astute trainer. He would accompany his string up to the Downs riding an old hack, smoking a pipe and dragging a reluctant Springer spaniel behind him on a piece of baler twine. Yet I learnt a number of good tips from Ginger, and his horses always looked a picture of health. He never liked them to walk home too quickly as walking fast was too easy for them; they needed to be held together and kept on the bridle in order to work all their muscles correctly. He always liked them to be relaxed, though, and allowed them to pick leaves and twigs from the hedges beside the roads. My interest in racing grew when Ginger trained a horse for my mother. Several times we accompanied him to the racecourses to watch it run. It was a huge thrill when it managed to win a race.

By that time, of course, I was bitten by the racing bug. Each year during Cheltenham week, Ce and I would rush back from school as fast as we could to watch the last televised races. In 1961, Ravenscroft, owned by my uncle Larch and ridden by Fred Winter, won the National Hunt Handicap Chase. He was trained by Fulke Walwyn, and we watched it live on the television. I can remember the excitement even now. It was through Fulke that my father had acquired some of his good point-to-point horses. Silver Measure had won a number of races from his yard in Lambourn, and then gave our family a lot of fun in point-to-points. In the early 1960s my mother was given another good old chaser named Rowland Ward. He had been retired from racing proper and needed a good home. Luckily for me, she didn't particularly enjoy riding him as he frequently whipped round and, from time to time, dropped her on the floor, so she allowed me to exercise him in the winter months. I adored the horse, and even got him fit enough to win the Old Berkshire Hunt Members' Race at Lockinge in 1964. This was my first training success – apart from the Donkey Derby – and I still proudly show off the engraved winner's tankard. That victory gave me another taste of things to come.

After successfully passing my O and A level exams by 1964, I bought my first proper event horse, Borderline, a big bay thoroughbred, from a 'for sale' advertisement in the *Horse & Hound*. He belonged to Van de Vater, who later became a good friend during my eventing days. Van has a brilliant sense of humour and gave me plenty of help with this horse. Borderline cost me £500 and drained my Post Office savings, but I was immensely proud of him. He was only five years old, but we learnt together and we did quite well, winning several BHS events. He quickly upgraded to Intermediate level. He was a very fast horse, so one spring I entered him for a couple of point-to-points. He was placed several times, and later went into training with Tim Forster.

It was during those early eventing years that I met up with Lars Sederholm, who was beginning to build up his well-regarded training centre at Waterstock near Oxford. He had already educated a number of top riders, including Caroline Bradley. He helped me enormously and gave me a lot of valuable advice. They were wonderful days, and my lessons at Waterstock will never be forgotten. New horses were bought, made and sold under Lars' guidance. He is an exceptional teacher with a special eye for a horse. He likes his horses to be athletic, naturally well balanced and, if they are on the wrong stride, with an inborn ability to put themselves right and adjust their feet quickly in front of a fence. (Interestingly, Best Mate possesses all these qualities.) I spent some fascinating days with Lars, and I learnt so much. Even now, when I look at a racehorse, I wonder what Lars would say about it. To my mind, racehorses are no different to showjumpers or eventers. They all need to be quick-thinking athletes.

It was through Lars Sederholm that I came to be given Blitzkrieg in 1972. He was a well-made thoroughbred gelding by Reverse Charge. He had already been round the Badminton Three-Day Event in 1970 with John Birtwhistle, Monica Dickinson's brother; he had also won a couple of point-to-points. Lars had found the horse for an American rider, Mason Phelps, but the horse went lame and needed a long rest. Mason soon gave up his three-day eventing interests and returned to America, but his eventer needed a home. We agreed to have him at Lockinge. He eventually came sound again, and in 1973 my number one ambition in life was fulfilled as I was able to ride Blitzkrieg at Badminton. We finished twelfth. I could not believe my good fortune; he was a wonderful horse and a very safe conveyance. Even my dear father enjoyed the week, and was quite emotional during the prize giving.

Although allowing me to pursue my eventing career in the 1960s, my parents also tried to encourage me to broaden my horizons and get away from my everyday life at Lockinge. They wanted me to have a wider circle of friends. In those days it was generally considered good, for country girls, to spend some time in London in order to meet eligible young men. Certain mothers, who could afford to take the time away, accompanied their daughters to the capital and familiarised them with many different aspects of life. Thus, in 1965, somewhat reluctantly, I was introduced to the world of debutantes, but it was not altogether my scene. There were tea parties and cocktail parties followed by numerous dances. Many of the parties were held in beautiful places, and even though I didn't enjoy them all, it was most educational. And I loved the food!

The opening event of the 1965 season was Queen Charlotte's Birthday Ball at Grosvenor House in early May, with several hundred debs in attendance. We were all well prepared and had duly learnt to curtsy properly before being introduced to the guest of honour. I will never forget the ordeal and all the fuss, not least because I loathed having to wear long white gloves. Frankly, the best part of the evening was when the national anthem was played at two a.m. and we were all allowed to go home. I went along with it during those summer months in order not to offend my parents, but in retrospect it was fairly pointless and a ridiculously costly experience. Some of the dances were amazing spectacles, but I never did meet my Prince Charming – Terry came later – and most of my evenings were spent on the sidelines with a bunch of other wallflowers, watching the dancing. Yet there were a few benefits: I learnt how to talk to guests on either side of me at dinner parties, for instance, and I also met several people who are still good friends today. Most significantly, during those months, when I yearned to be back in the country with my horses, I had plenty of time for thought and I began to plan my career.

In 1967, I embarked on a three-year course of teacher training. I enrolled in the autumn at Westminster College of Education near Oxford and I obtained my Certificate of Education in 1969. I then did an extra year to study for the Bachelor of Education (Oxford) degree, which I passed in the summer of 1970. Those years at college were brilliant, a striking contrast to the summer I had spent in London. As I travelled daily to the college, I was able to live full time at Lockinge and once more stay close to my horses. I learnt a great deal more about life during my spell of teacher training than I ever learnt in my debutante days, and the weeks of teaching practice in particular provided a whole new experience. I had opted to teach at secondary education level, and a number of the schools in which we were placed were in fairly rough areas on the outskirts of Oxford. Good manners in the classroom were rare, and students were prime targets for unruly teenagers. Indeed, I well remember being locked in a book cupboard by the pupils during one history lesson. It was a claustrophobic experience, and I remained in that dark hole for nearly an hour until the next teacher entered the classroom and heard animal-like noises emanating from behind the door. On another occasion the boys in my biology class took great exception to a lesson on photosynthesis and set up a series of booby traps along the bench at the front of the laboratory. Totally oblivious to their pranks, I received a number of painful electric shocks when setting down my books. But there was no point in getting angry, and I remember laughing, which both surprised and annoyed the pupils. In the end they laughed too, and I never had any more trouble.

After my four years at Westminster College I was on the lookout for a job. As luck would have it, there was a vacancy for a teaching post at St Mary's School, Wantage, and I was accepted. I taught my two best subjects, history and biology, and remained at the school for the next four years. I enjoyed the teaching, but horses were still the first priority in my life, and it was only a matter of time before they completely took over. I had originally refused to attend St Mary's as a pupil because it would have meant living away from Lockinge, but as a teacher I could still live in the village and carry on with my riding interests in my spare time and during the long holidays. It was during my last summer at St Mary's that Tim Forster asked me to break in a couple of his racehorses.

At times, in the 1980s and 1990s when life was not running quite so smoothly, I blamed Tim for giving me a taste for this new and dangerous way of life, but now I thank him for having started me on the road to success. With just two horses, I began my own livery yard and was drawn inexorably into the world of racing.

CHAPTER SEVEN

GETTING MY EYE IN

When I first began to run my horse livery business in the autumn of 1974, I realised that its success would be largely dependent on the goodwill of my relations and friends. My parents were tremendously helpful and allowed me to use two sets of stables: four at Lockinge Manor, where at that time we all lived, and another twelve at West Lockinge Farm, though the facilities at the latter were extremely basic. Most of the stables were conversions from existing farm buildings; they included calf pens, calving boxes and carthorse stalls as well as the covered part of an old cattle yard. Yet, strangely enough, the horses always seemed relaxed and happy in these boxes. Even today, the racehorses still enjoy the farmyard atmosphere with the many bantams, chickens, ducks and geese around their feet.

The outdoor facilities were simple, but they served us well. We had a small enclosed arena in the farmhouse garden and there were plenty of quiet roads and tracks, together with woodlands and grassy fields for hacking. The horses could also be exercised along the Berkshire Downs, and the hills were invaluable for getting them fit. There was a lot of variety and it was never boring. Lockinge was the perfect place to educate young horses, largely as a result of the peace and the space; for this reason several trainers entrusted us with their charges. I was also allowed, by my uncle, to use the loose jumping school at the top of the village – the very same one that Reg Hobbs had built in the 1950s. Unsurprisingly it needed resurfacing, and a number of the broken wooden structures required mending, but for a livery yard like mine it was invaluable. Indeed, many horses came to Lockinge for jumping education alone, and they gained so much confidence in the loose school without any riders.

To begin with we accepted every type of horse from hunters and eventers to racehorses and children's ponies; the majority came to us unbroken, but a few needed rehabilitation or retraining. I was fortunate to find some loyal and dedicated helpers, and we all learnt together. The days were extremely busy and the hours were long, but it was rewarding and satisfying. We handled some top-quality thoroughbred horses, and I became more and more fascinated by the breeding of these racehorses which passed through our yard. I felt the need to learn more and to branch out further. It was important for me to train my eye if these horses were to continue to dominate my life.

Many of the unbroken National Hunt horses came our way through Tim Forster, and they were similar in mould. He liked a particular stamp of chaser, the big old-fashioned type of horse which needed plenty of time. He trained some of the best in the country, but he would not allow them to be hurried and everybody needed endless patience. I learnt so much from him which was to prove valuable when I began to train. Nowadays, with everything costing more, owners seem to expect quicker results, and there are many fewer of the Tim Forster-type chasers around. The climate and the ground conditions have changed too, and there are more races run on sounder surfaces, especially with the inclusion of summer jump racing in the programme book. There is a greater emphasis on speed, and there are fewer true three-mile chasers.

Most of Tim's horses were bought in Ireland, but since he hated travelling and was a nervous wreck when boarding an aeroplane – I know, because I often accompanied him – he went less and less to that country. Luckily he had several excellent contacts across the Irish Sea who found him horses, and as he began to trust my judgement he gradually allowed me to go over to Ireland and look at the potential purchases. It usually meant meeting up with Tom Cooper or Arthur Moore, and I would travel with them to see the horses. I used to take photographs and report back. The experience I gained from these trips was enormous, and I had the utmost respect for his 'agents'. Tom Cooper would stress the importance of a good front leg and was fanatical about knees. He loved a horse who walked well, but strangely never wanted to see it trot. He was one of the finest judges in the bloodstock world and he put me right on so many different aspects of conformation. Arthur was, and still is, very clever with pedigrees, and could find horses in the most obscure places. We went on some interesting drives looking for these horses and had a lot of laughs, but he is also an excellent judge of a correct horse.

It was during those days in the 1970s that my love for Ireland grew. It was well known that the best steeplechasers were born and bred there, and I needed to find out the reason. I gradually learnt a little more about the geography of the country and I gained a large number of friends, many of whom were to prove enormously helpful when I began to train. One of my favourite counties in Ireland at the time was Co. Cork, and this is where Terry and I now go to so many of the Irish point-to-points.

I was also introduced to a very special man called Paddy Flynn. He was in his sixties and was extremely knowledgeable about horses. He successfully trained a few from the little yard behind his bungalow close to Fermoy and had sold a number of winners to England. I would sit for hours with Paddy and his wife in their small kitchen, sipping home-made soup from a mug while picking Paddy's brains on stallions and pedigrees. He would drive me around in his rickety old car up roads and pathways some of which were virtually impassable to motorised vehicles. He drove everywhere in fourth gear, and I remember there were several big holes in the floor of his car; I could often see the ground beneath me as we tottered over the rough terrain. Many a time I thought the bottom would fall out and we'd be stranded on the top of a mountain.

Paddy seemed to know every farmer and breeder in his area, though occasionally I found it hard to believe that any horse could be reared in some of the places we visited. Many of the buildings were falling down, and the fencing was either non-existent or full of wire. A number of the horses were wild and nervous, yet Paddy still ordered their owners to catch these creatures and stand them up so that we could see them at closer quarters. I was told that in his younger days, when he hunted with the Avondu hounds, Paddy never wore a hard hat, preferring instead a cloth cap which he took off and kept in his hand on the approach to a bank or a thorny hedge. He would then fearlessly put his head down, 'drive on', and hope for the best. Paddy was a legend, and when he died I was asked to write a few paragraphs about him in the *Irish Field*. I will never forget him.

My own days hunting in Co. Limerick were also a lot of fun. Pat Hogan, who often lent me his horses, another fine judge of horse flesh and also gave me valuable advice. He had been a champion amateur rider in his heyday and was famous in the hunting field, where he continually took his own line across country to keep up with the hounds. Few people were able to follow him for he was a gifted horseman and knew the capabilities of his hunters. In the late 1960s and into the 1970s, P. P. Hogan was king of the point-to-points. He bought and raced high-class horses; top jockeys such as John Fowler, Ted Walsh and Enda Bolger successfully rode his charges and helped him increase his tally of winners. My sister and I visited several of the Irish point-to-points during Pat's golden years and they gave me an appetite for more.

Thirty years ago, many of the top National Hunt horses were bought privately in Ireland, although a number came from the annual sales, and these sales became the highlights of my summers. I seldom missed them; they were a continuation of the learning curve. The

Doncaster National Hunt Sales in May and the Tattersalls (Ireland) Sales in June were a 'must'. I would sit for hours watching horses being sold and seeing the buyers select their purchases before they entered the ring. Tim Forster always went to Doncaster because he could reach the sales by road, and he usually forced himself to travel to Ireland in June as well, even though it meant boarding an aeroplane. He would tell me to look at every horse and report back to him on the ones I liked. He frequently purchased several of the highest-priced lots, and afterwards they would be sent to West Lockinge to begin their education.

My eye gradually improved the more we handled such good horses, and as the livery yard gathered momentum we began to take in horses from other trainers including Fred Winter, Peter Bailey, David Gandolfo and, later on, Michael Dickinson. Fred liked a different stamp of horse to Tim Forster; his horses were lighter-boned with more quality. They were proper athletes, and lovely to ride. They came to hand much quicker than the old-fashioned chasers. Somewhere along the line a mixture of these two types was going to be perfect, and this is what I think we saw when we spotted Best Mate.

As my urge to train steadily increased, much of my time was spent watching established experts training their own horses. On many occasions I would accompany Tim Forster to the Downs in his Land Rover and watch his horses gallop and school. It was on one of these days, in the early 1980s, that I asked for permission to school a couple of point-to-point horses which had found their way into my yard. One of these belonged to Charles Egerton (Edgy), and much to our surprise he had expressed a desire to ride it himself in a local point-to-point. It had been placed the previous season in Ireland but was not very big. During this horse's short time at Lockinge it had jumped adequately around the loose school, but Edgy was anxious for further practice. Imagine my horror when, up on the Downs, and faced with a line of fences, it veered violently right at the first obstacle and smashed the captain's wooden wings to pieces. The air was full of unrepeatable swear words, and the trainer almost exploded – never before had any horse dared to damage these indestructible walls of timber.

The point-to-pointer was unscathed, but the jockey, Edgy, had been knocked out. He lay there like a crumpled rag doll on the downland turf until he made enough noises to be bundled into the back of the Land Rover, and there he remained, on the bare metal floor, for another half an hour until Tim Forster had seen the rest of his horses working on the gallops. It was one of those Land Rovers which had a transparent partition between the driver's seat and the open back. I sat in the passenger seat hardly daring to open my mouth, but occasionally peeping through the glass at the body in the back. When we eventually returned to the yard the captain got out, slammed the door, shouted at Edgy to stay where he was and disappeared into the house for breakfast. I remember anxiously ringing his mother, Ann, from the office and was relieved when half an hour later she arrived to rescue him from the freezing cold floor in the back of the jeep. Fortunately, Edgy had broken no bones, but his pride had taken a serious knock. That afternoon, he dispatched his father's gardener to the gallops, where he was spotted, with his friend, repairing the schooling fence wing. I never again asked to school a horse at Letcombe Bassett.

During the summers I would also often visit the highly respected and successful flat trainers Jeremy Tree and Dick Hern to watch them training the two- and three-year-olds on their famous gallops. It provided more valuable experience, and I particularly enjoyed my visits to their evening stables when every horse was individually looked over. They gave me plenty of useful advice which I try to remember, even now.

Despite my main interest being racing, eventing is another equestrian sport that still remains close to my heart. By 1975 I had stopped competing myself, but I had continued to act as a List 2 Dressage judge. This appointment took me to many of the major horse trials, and I was on the Ground Jury at Burghley in 1987. I knew a lot of the top riders and closely followed their fortunes in the three-day events. In 1980, Chris Collins became chairman of the Olympic selectors and asked me to serve on his committee. Chris, and his sister Anna, had always been good friends of mine and we had often competed against each other in horse trials. Chris has always had an excellent brain and is extremely philosophical about life with a wonderful sense of humour. He also loves National Hunt racing. Chris won the Amateur Riders' Championship twice in the 1960s and the Pardubice Chase in Czechoslovakia on Stephen's Society, a horse he'd bought from Tom Costello. He also used to ride some of the best hunter chasers in the country. They were trained by Arthur Stephenson, and many had originated from Co. Clare. We had many interests in common, and it was a privilege to work with him.

His time of office as chairman lasted four years, and when he stepped down in 1984 he nominated me as his successor. Those next four years were most rewarding, and a lot of fun. There was a lot of travelling involved, for the championship competitions were held in Australia, Poland, West Germany and Korea, the latter country hosting the 1988 Olympic Games in Seoul. I visited all these countries and enjoyed seeing other parts of the world. The planning of the team training and the monitoring of the riders and horses were great experiences. Again, I learnt a great deal, and much of it was to be useful later on in the training of the racehorses. In particular, the team veterinary surgeon, Peter Scott Dunn, was superb. He taught me so much, and I still treasure the days I spent with him. So much can go wrong with fit horses, especially when they are also required to undergo long journeys and compete under adverse conditions. The way in which Peter dealt with the horses, the riders and the owners was most skilful. He was both professional and diplomatic. He was the official team vet for 32 years and nobody has been able to equal him since his retirement.

Fortunately, the selection committee work took place mostly in the late spring and summer months, so it did not unduly upset the running of my livery yard, which was at its busiest in the autumn, winter and early spring, and in the early 1980s I also became deeply involved in the training of point-to-point horses from West Lockinge. In 1983, good fortune once more came my way and I acquired another gift horse.

During my travels to Ireland in the 1970s I had tracked down several of the breeders of the racehorses which we had in our yard, and I had grown particularly fond of the White family from Bannow in Co. Wexford. They owned and bred that good horse Bannow Rambler, who was trained by their neighbour, Padge Berry. John White had sold several horses to Tim Forster. In 1982, his son, also called John (now famous for winning 'the Grand National that never was' in 1993 on Esha Ness), came to England as an amateur rider to work and ride for Nicky Henderson. He brought with him a horse called Matt Murphy. This chunky chestnut, by Deep Run, had won a bumper and a hurdle race in Ireland but had remained unsold due to a heart murmur. When in Lambourn, there were further veterinary complications, and the Whites were advised to take him out of training. He was boxed over to West Lockinge Farm where John and his wife, Clare, were lodging in one of our farm cottages. He never left the place thereafter, and ran in my name in numerous point-to-points.

In his first season, Matt Murphy won five races, including an Open Race at Tweseldown, ridden by Richard Dunwoody. Luckily, John White was available to ride him later in the season and won a Hunter Chase at Towcester. This horse won two such races, and twelve point-to-points. He was a marvellous servant to our yard, but his legs were always hot in the mornings until he'd been exercised as he constantly weaved over his stable door. Best Mate now lives in Matt Murphy's stable, and he too is a weaver, but then, according to Fred Winter, so were several of his best horses, including Pendil and Bula. We are never put off buying horses who weave, unless they do so in a crazy way. Fred told me that it shows they are intelligent.

Many of the owners who had point-to-point horses with us during the 1980s later helped to start me off on my training career by giving me other horses to train for them. My brother-in-law, Sam Vestey, kept several ex-chasers in our yard, and they all won point-to-points. Jo

Fenloe House, Newmarket on Fergus, Co. Clare, home of Tom Costello

Tom Costello's fields: where Best Mate and five other Gold Cup winners were raised

Crossing the threshold: Tom Costello invites the Lewises to see Best Mate

*Terry with Tom Costello and Val and Jim Lewis in the Stable yard,
Fenloe House where we first saw Best Mate*

Tom Costello Jnr and Best Mate, March 1999

'You're going to break my heart, Tom'. Val and Jim return to Fenloe House to do a deal. Terry and I left them to it

Smiling faces, deal done. Above: *HK, Valerie Lewis, Tom Costello, Jo Costello, Jim Lewis.* Below: *Terry, Valerie, Tom and Jim*

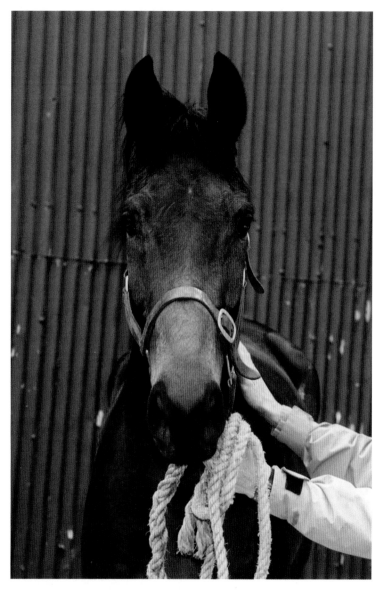

Best Mate on the day he was bought, March 1999

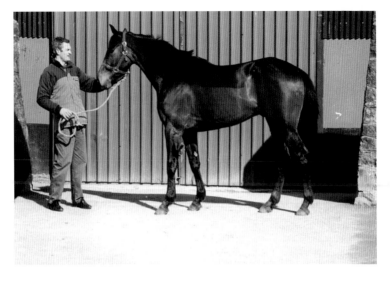

Best Mate at Fenloe, March 1999 (above) and again at Lockinge, April 2002 (below), after his first Gold Cup. Note the development of his neck and general physique © Dinah Nicholson

Farm. We had plenty of goodwill from
...rs and were often able to use their gallops. David
...ster, Barry Hills and even Michael Dickinson,
...ell at Manton, allowed us to pay visits with our
... time, and it entailed a lot of hard work, but those
...varding. They provided me with valuable further
... me a strong base from which to take the next step
...orld of professional racing.

...s in office with the Horse Trials Selection
... an end in 1988, after the Seoul Olympics, and it
...ecided to take the plunge and apply for my
... I had the promise of about eighteen horses to
...ssion from point-to-points to the National Hunt
...med a logical step, since point-to-points were
...e of our horses were capable of winning under
...th full support from my point-to-point owners
...her friends, I travelled to London in the summer
...erview at Portman Square. I nervously sat down
...ng Committee, which at that time was chaired by
...nd after plenty of questions, together with the
...y forms, my licence was granted.

...somewhat anxious as to how events would turn out,
...I could always return to schoolteaching if training
...about the extra capital that was required, and about
...new boxes on his farm, but he agreed to several
...llowed me to put stables in his haybarn. Despite his
...theless followed my runners closely. My mother was
...tic and gave me tremendous moral support. She had
...ind me in my horse ventures, and this was exciting
...ved racing, had a number of friends in the racing
...d forward to helping me with my new career.
...had taken out my licence, it remained to be seen
...could be successful. I knew it would not be easy, yet
...ready for this new challenge. Nobody had trained
...n West Lockinge Farm before, but my training

*'He is my Ming vase, my Kohinoor diamond.' Jim Lewis gets to
know his horse for the first time. Two weeks later, on April
Fool's Day, 1999, Best Mate arrived at West Lockinge*

Best Mate's paternal grandfather Top Ville

Best Mate's maternal grandfather Miller's Mate, who helped with his 'name'

Un Desperado, Best Mate's father

Katday, Best Mate's mother at Baroda Stud 2003 © Caroline Norris

Best Mate's full sister, Flying Iris aged two at Baroda Stud, 2003

Sidalcea, Best Mate's half sister at Baroda Stud aged four, 2003

Newton Taylor s
Niece who provi
the United Hunts
marked the begin
had a taste of this
there, with my ho
today, the thrill of
the water jump, bu
race and win there.

The best poin
Hogan's yard in
Leyland. He wa
championship, and
bought top horses a
He was extremely
points and always l
hard to follow. Yet
excellent owner. He
the most loyal suppo

I had some wond
trained them for five
hundred winners, an
During those years, I
head girl. She was de
hunting the point-to-p
youngsters. When I e
proper, she branched
more point-to-point w
young National Hunt h

As well as having so
point days, I also manag
ride for me. Mike Feltc
occasions, partnered a
successful. In addition, R
Daresbury), Tim Thomso

for West Locking
neighbouring traine
Gandolfo, Tim For
during his short sp
horses. It was a bus
years were most re
experience and gav
forward into the w

My four year
Committee came t
was then that I
trainer's licence.
train, and progres
world proper see
seasonal and som
Rules as well. Wi
and from many o
of 1989 for an int
before the Licensi
Mrs Embiricos,
presentation of m

My father was
but I assured him
failed. He worrie
my plans to buil
conversions and
worries, he never
a lot less pessimis
always been beh
and new. She lo
world, and looke

Now that I
whether or not
I believed I was
racehorses fron

methods had worked with the point-to-pointers. I would apply the same principles now that I had a licence. I had been with horses all my life and had gained plenty of outside support. With my competitive nature and my determination to succeed, I would tackle the new task with enthusiasm. It didn't bother me that I was a 'girl in a man's world'. After all, it could prove to be an advantage; it might attract more owners. I certainly hoped so.

CHAPTER EIGHT

TERRY BIDDLECOMBE'S RETURN

My first winner under Rules came on 18 August 1989 at Bangor, where the Grey Gunner, owned by Jo Newton Taylor and ridden by Bruce Dowling, won a three-mile Novice Chase. He was an ex-point-to-point horse with a poor jumping record, but he was honest and stayed well. He happened to be my first ever runner. A spell in the loose school must have sharpened him up because he barely made any jumping errors that day. It was a memorable win, and I have always had a soft spot for the course ever since. I enjoy going back there.

Since I had never been an assistant trainer, my training methods were developed largely from my own experiences and observations. I reasoned that it would be best to continue to train the racehorses along the same lines as the point-to-point horses. I have always trained the horses in my own, somewhat unorthodox, way at Lockinge; I have never liked the idea of sending them out of the yard in a long string, like regimented soldiers, one behind the other. It strickes me as soul-destroying for a horse to go along, day in day out, with its head up the backside of the horse in front. At Lockinge, the horses are encouraged to absorb the landscape and take an interest in where they are going. It keeps them happy and also helps to keep the riders awake. Most of our racehorses are exercised either in pairs or in small groups. Fortunately, I know the geography of the surrounding countryside like the back of my hand so I am able to state exactly where I want each one of them to go. The girls and the lads have daily instructions, and the work plan is written down in a book for all to see. This system has now worked well for nearly fifteen years of training, and there is no reason why it shouldn't continue to do so for the foreseeable future.

Those early training years went well, which was a big relief for all concerned. I might have been a girl in a man's world, but I was enjoying the challenge. We had plenty of winners and attracted more owners and more horses. During the first season, Ronnie Beggan rode a number of the horses and was most helpful with the schooling. Soon, however, we were to have a second claim on Jamie Osborne, who was then Oliver Sherwood's stable jockey. He rode many winners for the yard and is a talented rider. He always kept his horses well balanced. Jamie has a natural eye for a stride and he never interfered with the horses' mouths. All the horses jumped well for him. As a child, Jamie had successfully ridden working hunter ponies at the top shows, and I am sure this helped him when it came to riding racehorses.

As we took in more horses we built more boxes, and the yard expanded from around 25 horses in 1989 to 40 in 1994. I had the most wonderful assistant for the first eighteen months, Johnny Wrathall, but he was tragically killed in August 1990 while completing a summer job as a long-distance lorry driver in France. Ironically, he wasn't even driving his vehicle at the time of the accident. Johnny was a huge loss, and we were shattered by his death. He got along so well with everybody in the yard, and with my owners. He was a special horseman and a most enthusiastic and understanding person. He knew exactly how I wanted the young horses to be educated and had successfully done a lot of showjumping and race riding himself, although mostly at point-to-point level. I still think of him now, at certain moments, and I know how delighted and proud he would have been with our successes. He would have adored Best Mate. Yes, John's death hit us very hard, but we picked ourselves up and I carried on without an assistant for the next two years.

A tally of fifteen winners in the first year rose to 24 in the 1990/91 season, but by the end of the summer of 1993 the pressure was mounting and I needed more help. There were times, especially in the evenings, when I longed to sit down in the house and discuss the training in greater depth with someone who understood the problems and could give constructive advice. As it was, I lived on my own at West Lockinge Farmhouse and took on everything alone.

A chance meeting with Julian Pritchard in June 1993 marked the start of a big change to my life. Julian had turned up on the farm to do some contract work for a couple of Welsh farmers who were collecting straw bales from our fields. We began to discuss racing, and I sensed that he was anxious to become more involved in the National Hunt world. He had already ridden plenty of point-to-point winners and was well known in the Herefordshire area. He offered to come and help me, and to lend a hand on the farm too. Julian moved into Johnny Wrathall's cottage in August. His approach was different to that of his predecessor, and my father was not too sure about his driving, especially with the tractors on the farm. He was already famous for having wrecked a number of his own cars, and many of the farm vehicles looked destined for a similar fate. Nevertheless, Julian was a good strong rider with an excellent sense of humour, and we got on well. He later gained a number of successes for the yard on Toureen Prince, but I never got used to his driving and would sit nervously on the edge of my seat as we swung round bends on the way to the races.

On 3 September 1993, I again plucked up courage and asked him to chauffeur me to the Bloodstock Sales at Malvern, where I'd been invited by Russell Baldwin & Bright to judge the young horses at the show prior to the auction, along with Toby Balding and Jack Doyle. As we drove through the showground and stopped to park by the side of the ring, Julian suddenly exclaimed, 'Oh, there's Uncle Terry!' My reply was, 'Uncle who?' He told me that his uncle was none other than the legendary Terry Biddlecombe – and there, sure enough, was the blond bomber of bygone days, three-times champion jockey, standing nonchalantly at the edge of the railings. I remembered Terry well from when he had been at the peak of his career in the 1960s and early 1970s. I had greatly admired him. Indeed, I had often gone down to the last fence at Cheltenham to watch him ride over it. He was a superb horseman and a strong, highly competitive rider with plenty of dash. After my childhood crush on Ann Packer, I changed, in my early twenties, to idolising Terry Biddlecombe. Alas, in 1985 I had tried unsuccessfully to impress him when, as part of a Central Television team, he turned up at West Lockinge Farm to film my livery yard and report on my work with the young racehorses. Instead of wearing my normal day clothes I'd appeared at the front door in a flimsy blue dress and high-heeled shoes – totally unsuitable for the position I then held at my stables. Terry now admits that when he left the farm, having seen several unusual displays of the breaking-in of horses – one horse had accidentally bucked its way right out of its saddle – he had thought I was half mad! I had tried far too hard and the results had been disastrous.

I remember that September day at Malvern as if it was yesterday. I was surprised to see Terry, and I questioned him as to where he had been for the past eight years, as I'd neither seen nor heard anything about him for ages. I soon learnt that he had spent much of that time in Australia and had suffered a number of domestic problems, not to mention having to fight a major battle with alcohol. He had returned to England in 1992 to reorganise his life and was now ready to start afresh. Terry Court, one of his greatest and dearest friends and the director of Russell Baldwin & Bright, had given him the chance to rebuild his life and had made him an agent with the firm. He protected the former champion and treated him like a son, but it was Terry's own determination, charm and sense of humour that once again won the day.

For the bloodstock sales, he had been nominated by his new boss to look after the judges, and I subsequently spent several amusing hours in his company. I obviously created a better impression than I'd done in 1985 as we got on extremely well. When I left the sales, I remember thinking to myself, 'I hope I'll see Terry again before too long.' Fortunately, our meeting at Malvern was to mark the beginning of some of the happiest days of my life. Fate had intervened once more, and would soon alter the whole pattern and course of my training career; in less than a year, Terry would become an integral part of my life. If I had not re-met Terry at Malvern, would I have noticed Best Mate in the point-to-point at Lismore a few years later? Most probably, I wouldn't even have been there.

The training of the horses at Lockinge was not immediately changed by the rediscovery of 'Strong Tel' – a nickname later given to Terry by one of my owners – but I met him again three weeks later outside the weighing room at Cheltenham racecourse, and I distinctly remember the shivers that ran down my spine. We seemed to have similar interests, and to have many friends in common. I had some runners that day, but they didn't win; more importantly, Terry met my father for the first and only time. It was one of his rare visits to a racecourse and he had lunched in my brother-in-law's box. During the afternoon's racing, I took Terry up the stairs to the box, and the two men got on well. A couple of weeks later my father died of a sudden heart attack. Terry was one of the first people to ring me up, but because of the havoc that the tragedy had caused in our family it was not until after Christmas that I first invited him over to the yard to see the racehorses. The visits increased from that day on, and in the spring of 1994, after the Cheltenham Festival, he moved into the Farmhouse for good.

It is strange how certain events tend to happen at the right time in one's life. It was almost as if the timing of Terry's arrival at Lockinge had been pre-arranged. There had been some bad days and weeks during the 1993/94 National Hunt season. Not only had I missed my father enormously and been extremely upset by his death, but a virus had hit the yard and the horses were running badly. Morale was at a low ebb, and I managed to train only fourteen winners that year. Terry's arrival at West Lockinge raised my spirits, and he proved a huge help to all of us. His advice was invaluable. At last I had somebody to talk to who understood racing. Most importantly, he got along extremely well with my mother, and this meant a lot to me as she had always played a vital and prominent role in my life. As her eldest daughter, and living as I did in the same village, I had remained amazingly close to her. I was always guided by her sound advice. Thanks to Terry, I soon gained fresh enthusiasm, and was once again hungry for further successes.

Terry had spent nine years with Fred Rimell during his hugely successful riding days and had learnt a great deal from that brilliant trainer. He had been brought up with horses in a similar way to me, and his father, Walter Biddlecombe, was highly respected in the horse world. On account of his reputation as a brilliant and fearless jockey, Terry immediately got on well with the staff in the yard. He proved a great help with the jockeys, who admired and respected him, and he gave valuable advice in the schooling fields. His swear words were, and still are, fairly extensive, but there is so much humour behind their frequent use that they are never taken seriously by those who know him. Indeed, were he not shouting abuse at somebody we would think there was something wrong with him. I have been told by his friends that he had an identical vocabulary 40 years ago. I welcomed the presence of a man so famous and popular in the racing world. He is a natural extrovert, and our characters complement each other well. At last I was able to share the training responsibilities with somebody I trusted and loved. My owners accepted him quickly too, which was a big relief, and they also gradually learnt to understand his wicked sense of humour.

Terry had lived through some tough years since his retirement from race riding, but the new teetotal Biddlecombe was an example to many. When he first came to West Lockinge Farm, I was accustomed to a good few glasses of champagne and white wine each day to counteract my tiredness and constant worries, but it wasn't long before Terry gave me an ultimatum. I had a choice: I could have Terry or the bottle. Unsurprisingly, I gave him the nod. Indeed, I stopped my drinking habits almost immediately through fear of losing him. I have never wanted a sip of alcohol since. My mind has become sharper as a result, and I find that I have far greater energy. Terry certainly did me a good turn. He also saved me some money.

Many people call Terry and I the odd couple, most probably due to our different backgrounds and outward appearances, but in reality we are similar in many ways. Over the past decade we have gradually developed a mutual understanding on numerous topics. We share everything, and we talk about everything. Indeed, due to our common interests, we are seldom far apart from each other for any length of time. We are both motivated by horses and by racing, so it's fortunate that we both instinctively like the same type of horse. Terry has an unflappable temperament, but his laid-back, almost casual approach to life sometimes drives me mad. I have always tended to worry, chew my nails and lean on my superstitions, but his cool, calm outlook counterbalances my moments of panic. He accepts me for what I am and goes along with my idiosyncrasies, though he does not always agree with my pessimistic views. I rely upon him so much, and enjoy having him by my side. Four eyes are better than two, and I could certainly never go back to training on my own.

Right from the start, Terry and I shared the same ambition. From day one we were looking out for a horse that might be talented enough one day to win a Cheltenham Gold Cup.

CHAPTER NINE

THE PERFECT START

Best Mate first set foot on English soil on April Fool's Day 1999, but there were no practical jokes on this occasion. He travelled over with Be My Manager, his close companion from Co. Clare, with whom he had spent three months in an Irish field during the summer of 1998. Since the two horses were good friends they were put into adjoining boxes so that they could continue to communicate through a window in the wall. They had each won their respective four-year-old point-to-points in Ireland in March and were now ready for a gradual let-down. They needed time to acclimatise and get used to their new surroundings, but they settled in quickly and were straightforward to deal with. They ate extremely well too, which is a bonus for any trainer. Indeed, Best Mate has always been a greedy horse and never says 'no' to food.

In those early weeks in April, the weather was still unsettled and the nights were cold. The spring grass had not yet started to grow in the fields. The two new horses were quietly exercised in the mornings and then gradually introduced to the paddocks on the farm where they could start to unwind. Equipped with New Zealand rugs, they enjoyed rolling in the wet mud and exploring their new environment. Their nanny at turnout time was the 22-year-old Sir Wattie, who had won the Badminton Three-Day Event in 1986 and 1988 and the individual silver medal at the Seoul Olympics when ridden by Ian Stark. Wattie had been retired to West Lockinge Farm when I began training and was a brilliant influence on the young thoroughbreds. He kept them sharply in their place and refused to join them on their crazy gallops. We christened him the yard mascot.

There was no special treatment for Best Mate during his early days at Lockinge. Those who saw him agreed with us that he looked a good prospect for the future, but it was obviously going to be some months before he started racing, and to the members of staff in the yard he was 'just another young horse Terry and Hen have found in Ireland'. He had no set minder – Jackie Jenner, his current lass, didn't even work for me then – but Paddy Young, a talented horseman who spent a lot of his time teaching and riding the green horses, partnered Matey on a number of occasions on the hacks around the Downs. He was particularly impressed by the future champion; he was, he said, a lovely horse to ride and gave him an excellent feel, especially in canter. He nominated him as his first choice for future honours.

By the middle of May it was time for Best Mate and Edredon Bleu to move to Jim Lewis's home, Crabbe Farm near Evesham, for the summer months. We made sure that the two horses had been introduced to each other before they left, and they were quick to settle down in Jim's paddocks. Until Jim and Valerie moved house in 2000, they always had their horses at home from May until August. Understandably, they enjoyed seeing them on a daily basis, and in 1999 they were much looking forward to getting to know their new acquisition. During those summer months they were fortunate to secure the services of John Taylor, who carefully monitored the horses and brought them into stables each night for extra food and attention.

Overall, the weeks were peaceful and the horses thrived, but there was one notable hiccup. Jim had two fields which he used for his racehorses. These nice, sheltered paddocks had plenty of grass and were separated by post and rail fencing, but there was a rusty metal gate in the middle of the fence line. A new wooden gate had already been ordered but the old one was unexpectedly reshaped before the replacement arrived. John recalls that as he returned to the yard one afternoon to catch the horses and bring them in for their night's rest, they were no longer in the same field as the one he'd left them in that morning. It was then that he saw the badly buckled gate and the horses grazing in the other paddock. He feared the worst. Best Mate or Edredon Bleu could have suffered serious injuries, yet miraculously there was no permanent damage to either horse.

Edredon Bleu had painful-looking cuts on his hind legs where he had skinned them on the top rail, and he looked decidedly sorry for himself, but the grazes were only superficial. In France he had been taught to brush through the tops of the steeplechase fences and had presumably hurdled the obstacle, which is characteristic of his style of jumping. Best Mate, in contrast, did not have a scratch anywhere to be seen and had obviously made a perfect jump. He had been educated differently, schooled over upright poles at Tom Costello's from the age of two. He had remembered his early lessons.

It later transpired that both horses had taken fright on hearing the sudden and deafening noise of a huge pile of stones being unloaded from a lorry in the nearby builders' yard. They had set off at full gallop across the field and been unable to stop at the gate. The incident gave Jim a huge fright, but at least he could say that his new horse was a clean and talented jumper. Later that summer, John Taylor began riding the two horses at Crabbe Farm. He spent six weeks walking and trotting them before they returned to West Lockinge and was struck by Best Mate's athleticism. He told Jim that he could barely feel the horse's feet touching the ground and that he thought he was real 'class'.

When Best Mate came back into full training, during the month of August, he was placed in the care of Jane Hedley who was beginning to work in our yard for the first time. She had won point-to-points in the Borders and was a good rider. She was well suited to her new charge and much enjoyed the time she spent with him. He was much stronger by the autumn of 1999, and there were days when he was so bursting with energy that Jane would come back from exercise looking exhilarated, saying, 'Matey was awesome today!' I well remember helping her with him in the loose jumping school. He was so powerful, and his style of jumping was immaculate. He was a joy to watch. Jane often rode him during his work on the gallops, but gradually Jim Culloty was allowed to sit on his back, thus beginning to forge a formidable partnership for the future. 'I gave him a canter up the Eurotrack gallop and I rode him over a fence,' Jim remembers. 'He was every inch a chaser in the making, although he was only four. I thought he would win his bumper, but I didn't know he'd be as good a hurdler as he was. I knew he would be a good chaser, and there were plenty of rumours going around that he was a good horse.'

Best Mate certainly enjoyed life to the full. He seemed a playful horse with a sense of humour, and during those early days he would put in some huge bucks, especially when pheasants flew out of the hedges. Jane sat tight on every occasion and did an excellent job with her favourite horse. Those months were so important to his future career. We were learning about his character every day and beginning to work out how to train him for future stardom. At the owners' open day on 19 September he made a big impression on all who saw him in the parade. He walked proudly around the paddock, and I remember remarking, on the loudspeaker, that he was my idea of the perfect racehorse and that we hoped he would be something special.

It was soon time to find a race for Best Mate's first public appearance. He was working well on the gallops and the ground had improved after some days of rain. Happily, he seemed easy to get fit and always recovered quickly from any exertions. Unlike many former point-to-point horses he did not take long to understand our training methods and was soon at home on David Gandolfo's woodchip track, which we were using that autumn for the more serious workouts. Since we seldom run horses in National Hunt flat races (bumpers) if they have already had experience in point-to-points, we looked for a suitable hurdle race. As a general rule, we tend to use bumpers as stepping stones towards hurdling and chasing careers. They are useful for giving a horse its first look at a racecourse and for getting it used to crowds or galloping under race conditions with a number of others. We do not train our horses specifically to win these Flat races since we do not like them too revved up for their first outing. We like to think that there will be plenty more to work on afterwards and that a horse will progress further after its first run, but it is obviously a bonus when a horse finishes in the placings.

Unfortunately, I could not find a suitable National Hunt Novice Hurdle for Best Mate's debut. I entered him for an EBF Hurdle at Newbury in early November, but was told by Weatherbys that he was ineligible: his sire, Un Desperado, had not been registered with the EBF scheme during the year of Best Mate's birth. As there were no other suitable hurdle races for over three weeks, and knowing that Jim Lewis loved Cheltenham, the original plan was shelved and Best Mate was entered for the £10,000 added bumper on the Sunday of the Murphy's November meeting. I explained the predicament to Jim and we decided that at least we could see how he coped with the Cheltenham hill. It would be a competitive race, but there was no alternative. Best Mate needed a run.

I remember the day well; his race was the last on the card. I was on my own as Terry had gone to Towcester with two other runners. If he did not run up to expectations it would be my head on the block, but I could always tell Jim Lewis that he was a three-mile chaser and not a Flat-race horse, so I had my excuse prepared! The light was starting to go as the horses began to parade in the paddock, yet Best Mate looked authoritative and stood out. Did he sense that this was his place? Jane Hedley found it hard to keep up with his amazing stride. He certainly looked the part; I just prayed, in my usual pessimistic way, that he would not let me down. After all, the

Costellos had considered entering him for the prestigious four-year-old bumper at Punchestown in April so he ought to be up to the task, even though he would undoubtedly be better with obstacles to jump.

My immediate instinct was to hide once Jim Culloty and Best Mate had left the paddock, but I knew that I would have to watch every inch of the race as Terry would want a blow-by-blow report. I crept into the Tote Credit building and hoped that nobody would see me, but I was soon aware of a large figure by my side. It was my good friend Charles Egerton (Edgy). He watched the race with me and gave me moral support. Little did he know what a precedent he was setting. He has since kept me calm through two Cheltenham Gold Cups. I have enormous respect for Edgy's judgement and he has a rare gift in that he can read a race correctly – something I have never been able to do.

Jim Culloty gave Best Mate a perfect ride and Edgy kept telling me that he was going to win. Jim produced him at exactly the right moment, and the horse accelerated up the hill to get his head in front just before the line. The winning distance was three quarters of a length. It was a most exciting race, and the best possible result. I could breathe again. The telephone line between Terry and I was red hot. The following day, when I wrote my comments on to Best Mate's card, I put 'Excellent performance. A very good horse and a good race. Has class.'

In the end, it was fitting that Best Mate's first ever race was at Cheltenham; it didn't matter that it was a bumper race. He familiarised himself with the course and proved that its gradients and final hill suited him well. Jane proudly led him into the winners' enclosure. The daylight had almost gone but I could still see the big smile on Jim Culloty's face. I remember telling the press that we believed him to be a very good horse and that we hoped he would go a long way. Jim and Valerie Lewis were overjoyed, and they accompanied me to the Royal Box after the race; Sam Vestey, my brother-in-law, who is chairman of the racecourse, invited them up there. We sat round a big table and drank cups of tea with hot buttered toast and crumpets while we watched the replay on the television screen. It remains a vivid memory. At last I could relax and enjoy the end of the day. I could dream of the future and what it might bring. Could this horse go right to the top? There were plenty of unanswered questions, but I kept on dreaming. And I knew that sometimes a dream can come true.

CHAPTER TEN

A SEASON OVER HURDLES

A fter winning the bumper race at Cheltenham in November 1999, Best Mate was extremely perky and recovered quickly. The race had taken very little out of him, yet he had come through it with flying colours. It would not be long before he would be ready for his first run over hurdles, but with the EBF non-registration problem it would be less easy to find a suitable race. A good look through the Racing Calendar helped me to unearth an ordinary National Hunt Novice Hurdle at Sandown on 3 December. We thought the course would suit him, as it has a similar uphill finish to Cheltenham, and the day out appealed to his owners, even though it was the last race on a Friday, which can be a nightmare for racegoers when they have to battle with the London weekend traffic.

Fortunately, it proved a most enjoyable day for everybody. There was an attractive card and some good horses on view; indeed, both What's Up Boys, the Hennessy Gold Cup winner in 2001, and Looks Like Trouble, the 2000 Gold Cup victor, reached the winners' enclosure in the early part of the afternoon. As there was so much time to fill and Best Mate was our only runner, Terry and I joined Jim and Valerie Lewis for an excellent lunch in the Members' Restaurant, which has a wonderful view across the course. We were both rather nervous about Matey's first run over hurdles, but the race looked ideal and only eight horses had been declared. It is always such a bonus for a young horse to run in a small field where it can get a good view of the obstacles.

Once again, Best Mate walked around the paddock with his head held high, demanding attention. He was clearly delighted to be having another outing and another chance to show off. He behaved well in the preliminaries and cantered sensibly to the start on ground officially described as good. During the race, Jim Culloty tucked him away in mid-division and he jumped beautifully. Two hurdles from home he cruised into the lead, and won impressively by ten lengths. He was described in *Superform* as 'a well regarded, potentially top class gelding who must be followed'. Accurate words indeed. We were all delighted by Matey's performance, and Jim Lewis looked a happy man as he patted his new star in the winners' enclosure. Terry and I were also delighted with the run, and relieved that everything had gone according to plan and Best Mate's future looked exciting. Plenty more wins could lie in store for a horse of such talent.

That first hurdle run at Sandown had been so encouraging that we entered him for the Tolworth Hurdle on 8 January 2000, on the same track but a considerable step up in class from his debut. The Tolworth is a Grade 1 event over two miles which invariably attracts a strong field. It meant that Matey would have just over four weeks to recover. We would give him a short break with a few easy days in his paddock and then train him for this prestigious race. We knew he would face a much stiffer task, but at least we would learn more about him and the level of his ability.

By that first week in January there had been a lot of rain and the ground was described as soft. We have since realised that this is not Best Mate's ideal racing surface, even though he has the talent to cope with it. The favourite for the race was Mark Pitman's unbeaten six-year-old Monsignor, who had won the previous season's Festival

Bumper as well as two good novice hurdles. He was obviously a high-class horse and had also come from Tom Costello's yard. On the day, Best Mate was unable to accelerate past Monsignor on the soft ground up the hill, but he only went down by two and a half lengths. Both horses stayed on well and finished a long way clear of their opponents. Mark's horse was a year older than ours and obviously stronger. He had also benefited from two previous hurdle runs as opposed to Best Mate's single outing. In defeat, though, we had found out a lot more. Matey had run well and was clearly in the top league. Monsignor went on to win the Royal & SunAlliance Hurdle at Cheltenham two months later, and one can only sympathise with his trainer that after that race injury prevented him from pursuing an exciting career over fences. The two horses did not meet again after Sandown.

The Cheltenham Festival was high on the list of Jim Lewis's priorities in 2000 following the encouraging run in the Tolworth Hurdle. He always likes to have runners at this meeting in March, as every owner does, and after some discussion we entered Best Mate for the two novice hurdles, the Capel Cure Sharp Supreme Novices Hurdle and the Royal & SunAlliance Novices Hurdle. The former would be run over two miles, the latter over two miles five furlongs. We were sure that Matey would stay a lot further than two miles – after all, he had won a three-mile point-to-point as a four-year-old – but nearer the time we would have to decide which race looked most suitable. We did not particularly like the idea of trying a new distance for the first time at the festival, and his two previous hurdle races had both been over two miles, but we would nevertheless carefully weigh up the pros and cons when we knew the entries and the likely going.

As the days drew closer to Cheltenham, the fax machine became red hot. Jim and I put all the known cards on the table and placed our final votes. I always like to discuss running plans with my owners, especially for the high-profile races, but it sometimes takes hours and hours to assess the form and reach conclusions. We knew Monsignor would go for the longer race, and we were not keen to take him on again so soon. Our best chance, therefore, could be in the two-miler.

At least we would get the best ground as it was the first race on the three-day card. The official going was good, but the forecast was for a dry week and there were fears that the ground might change to good to firm. We certainly did not want to risk Best Mate on a firm surface, so this was another case for choosing the Supreme Novices Hurdle. Indeed, the ground did ride faster than good, even on day one, and there were four course records broken during the three-day meeting. The ground on Wednesday and Thursday was described as good to firm on both courses.

In retrospect, we chose the right race for Best Mate at Cheltenham in 2000, but it was to prove a nightmare to watch, and it pitched Jim Culloty into an unwanted spotlight. By losing the race to Sausalito Bay, Jim had to contend with the wrath of thousands of punters. The media were also critical of his riding and race tactics, and he must have experienced some agonising moments as he came down that Cheltenham hill. The plan had been to track the favourite, Youlneverwalkalone, and the race went smoothly for the first three quarters of a mile. Terry is always responsible for the big-race orders and he was happy with Matey's position until he reached the far side of the course, close to the water jump on the chase track. It was here that the trouble started. Best Mate began to get shut in. It had not been a particularly strong gallop, which was surprising for this race, and a pocket was forming which, according to Terry, can easily happen around Cheltenham. Jim needed to extricate his horse before the crucial part of the race. At the top of the hill a gap appeared and Jim found a clearer run down the inside, but unfortunately Best Mate made a slight mistake at the third-last hurdle and encountered further traffic problems. He lost his position again. Jim was forced to pull out and go round the other horses to find room. This gave Best Mate a lot of extra work to do, but by the last hurdle he was ready to make his move up the rails beneath the stands. Once he could see the daylight, he flew up the hill and only failed to peg back Noel Meade's ex-Flat-race horse Sausalito Bay by three quarters of a length. Youlneverwalkalone was one and three quarter lengths back in third.

Now, a few years later, Jim Culloty recalls the race: 'Youlneverwalkalone was the favourite and our plan was to track him. Conor O'Dwyer, who rode him, said he was going to be handy, but he didn't have a great start so he was mid-division. I also expected them to go very quickly and they didn't. They crawled for a mile and a half, so it became a sprint finish, and I got tapped for toe. Everybody was bunched so I couldn't get a run. I should have been handier. Also, when I was able to make a move I had nowhere to go, and when the race did quicken up I was caught flat-footed. He was just a bit slow over the third last, at the very moment the rest of the field were quickening, and the leaders got first run on me. Down the hill, he was always going to be hammered, but as soon as they hit the rising ground, he got going and they began to tire.'

Jim thought it was a good run to finish a fast-closing second, but he was heavily criticised for the ride – in my opinion, unfairly, though it might not have seemed like it at the time. It cannot be easy for a jockey when the pressure is on and there are a lot of runners in an important race. Terry has a brilliant record at Cheltenham, but he admits that it is a tricky course to ride, and one which takes a lot of knowing. It is easy to be critical watching in the grandstand or on television, but when there are races featuring top-class horses, everybody wanting a winner, the longed-for gaps so often close up, and inexperienced horses find it hard to work their way through a close-knit bunch of runners. One sees it happen so often, especially in flat races, when jockeys and horses do not get an opening and lose their races as a result.

For my part, I was both thrilled and disappointed by the result. Best Mate had run a wonderful race and I felt proud that he had shown such a staggering turn of foot from the last hurdle. Yet on looking back at the race there was no doubt in my mind that he was the best horse and should have won, though I have never blamed Jim for the defeat. Racing is all about ups and downs; if everything was plain sailing there would be no excitement. It could even become a boring sport, with every race a foregone conclusion. Noel Meade's horse, under an excellent ride from Paul Carberry, deserved to win that day, and to give his trainer his first ever success at the Cheltenham Festival. It was a popular win for the Irish.

Although Best Mate had only finished second in the Supreme Novices Hurdle, his lass, Jackie Jenner, was to be compensated the next day when her other charge, Edredon Bleu, won the Queen Mother Champion Chase. Jackie, who joined our team in January 2000, had replaced Jane Hedley as Best Mate's minder. Jane had returned home to Northumberland for the spring point-to-point season, and Jackie had come to West Lockinge from Dai Willam's yard. She had also spent several seasons with Gardie Grissell and had handled a number of different horses. Her link with our stables is now widely known and she has become quite a celebrity in her own right, sometimes getting as much publicity as her horses. Jackie fits into our system extremely well and is a most trustworthy and likeable member of our staff. She is unflappable on all occasions, and she turns out her horses to a high standard; she can always be depended upon and gives her 'boys' confidence, which is so important before the big races.

That Champion Chase was magical. There was an epic battle up the Cheltenham hill between Direct Route (Norman Williamson) and Edredon Bleu (Tony McCoy) which had the crowds on the edges of their seats right to the line. It was a race that will go down in history as one of the most exciting ever seen, and even to this day I find it hard to believe that Bleu prevailed by a nostril. I had always dreamt of winning the Cheltenham Gold Cup, but had secretly longed to win the Champion Chase as well. The Queen Mother had for many years been a close friend of several members of my family. My grandfather had known her since his childhood, and both my mother and father had spent many hours in her company. She had given me some treasured memories too, especially when I was privileged enough to stay with her on several occasions in the 1970s and 1980s at the Royal Lodge in Windsor Great Park for that great race at Ascot in July, the King George VI and Queen Elizabeth Diamond Stakes. She knew that even then I adored racing, but I doubt that she ever imagined she would one day be presenting me with the trainer's trophy following a victory in her own race at Cheltenham.

She used to follow the fortunes of Edredon Bleu and Best Mate, and I often discussed the two horses with her. In the spring of 2001, when the Queen Mother was lunching with my mother at Lockinge Manor, I well remember Jackie Jenner bringing Edredon Bleu into the garden to meet Her Majesty, who admired him and stroked him on the lawn. I photographed them together and sent Jim Lewis a copy. It was a wonderfully happy occasion and a beautiful day. Terry was also present at that family gathering, and the Queen Mother always enjoyed his company. He had ridden numerous winners for her and had spent time with her at Sandringham during the making of the film *The Queen Mother's Horses* towards the end of the last century. Together they had witnessed some memorable triumphs, and she always appreciated his smile, coupled with his sense of humour, though it was noticeable that he modified his language in her company, which relieved me enormously. Goodness knows what she would have thought had she heard him shouting abuse in the stable yard!

It was back to the drawing board after the Cheltenham Festival, but we knew that Best Mate was top class. Should he be put away until next season, or should he be allowed to have one more run at Aintree? One of the people who was pressing for another race was Declan Weld. He knew that the two-mile four-furlong Martell Mersey Novice Hurdle at Liverpool in April had Grade 2 status, and he felt sure that Best Mate could win it. This would give a further boost to his stallion, Un Desperado.

In the end, however, Jim Lewis would make the decision in consultation with Terry and I, and as the days approached Best Mate seemed so well and fresh that we decided to let him run.

He appreciated the longer trip, even though he had probably gone a little over the top after his Cheltenham exertions and was still immature. Jackie reported that he kept whickering to the many police horses that were used for crowd control. Every time she led him past one of these horses he would turn and look at it. He was fascinated by them. Fortunately, despite these distractions, he won easily enough, beating Copeland, who has since proved himself to be a top-class hurdler, by two and a half lengths. The result of the race was a big relief to us all, not least to Jim Culloty, who was able to ride his favourite horse into that hallowed winners' enclosure at Aintree. It had put the smile back on to Jim Lewis's face too, and both Terry and I felt we could breathe again. It is always a risk to run a horse at Aintree after Cheltenham, especially with less than a month in between. It can so often lose its form in those few weeks, yet the effects of a hard race do not show until it is too late.

Thus ended a highly satisfactory season for Best Mate. He was only a five-year-old and had done nothing wrong. He had caught the eye of many racegoers, and the start of his chasing career in the early autumn would be eagerly awaited. It seemed a long time since we had first seen him, at that point-to-point in Co. Waterford, but in reality it was only thirteen months earlier. He'd promised so much that day, and now the stage was properly set for the unveiling of his true talent. We would guard him carefully and rest him well during the summer months. By now, Jim Lewis had sold his land in Worcestershire, so Matey and Bleu would stay with us at West Lockinge Farm that summer, where we could turn them out in the paddock by day and bring them into their stables by night. They were already changing our lives, and I started to dread going away from home and leaving them behind. These were special horses, and Best Mate was to prove the horse of my lifetime.

CHAPTER ELEVEN

GOING CHASING

In the second week of July 2000, after spending ten weeks on holiday, Best Mate was ready to resume gentle exercise. Since his last racecourse appearance at Aintree on 7 April, the pressure had been off and he had been slowly let down. His lass, Jackie Jenner, had ridden him out on most mornings that spring right up until the beginning of May, but he had also been spending two or three hours a day in the field. For the rest of May and the whole of June he had been out all day. His companions were either Sir Wattie or Edredon Bleu, and he was never turned out with more than one horse.

We have always been careful to choose the right grazing companion for Matey because he is very bossy and boisterous in the field. If we were to put a horse with him of similar character there could well be a clash of personalities. The risk of injury is too great. Wattie was perfect as he was such a laid-back horse; he never moved far and never got involved in a brawl, but sadly he was getting older and a lot more arthritic and in June 2002 he had to be put down on humane grounds. There were many wet eyes that day. Edredon Bleu, who tends to be slightly timid, is also an ideal companion. He is polite, and knows his place. He never takes Matey on and accepts the pecking order. If anybody visits these two horses in the paddock, Best Mate is always the first to come forward, and he pushes his nose into everything. Bleu stays a few paces behind until he sees that the way forward is safe. He is wary of the schoolboy show-off, especially when his ears go back and he threatens to give him a sharp nip. At catching time, Matey is always easy and willingly allows the girls to attach the lead rein to his headcollar. Bleu sometimes takes advantage of his own shyness and enjoys a game. He dodges the handlers and refuses to be caught at all – until the polo mints are produced. On occasion, he has kept a member of staff in the field for over half an hour and then cantered off to the furthest point. One has to be extremely patient.

Best Mate tends to do himself extremely well during the months of May and June. If he were a human being, I am sure he would revel in taking a luxurious summer holiday abroad. He would spend his days lazing in the sun and eating his head off. At Lockinge, he always comes into his stable in the evenings for an extra feed, even when the weather is good, since Jim Lewis likes all his horses to be stabled by night throughout the year. He is scared of thunderstorms and the possibility of his chasers being struck by lightning in the fields after dark. His fears are quite understandable, and in many ways it suits us well to give his horses extra attention during the summer, and we also bring in a number of other inmates for supplementary feeding. Fulke Walwyn always liked his charges to come in at nights. Eating oats throughout the summer does them so much good and keeps them hard. Too much grass is not good for them at this stage of their careers. Hard food helps to eliminate unsightly grass tummies and ensures that the horses do not fall apart during their weeks of rest.

Restarting Matey's fitness programme is not a difficult task. He never takes any notice of the saddle when it is put back on, nor does he mind the feel of the girth. He enjoys hacking out around the villages and along the quiet country lanes. He happily climbs the hills and barely realises that he is back in work. There is so much to see during those warm summer months, and the scenery is constantly changing, especially when the harvest begins. His only dislike is the flies, and he tends to revert to his old habit of throwing his head up and down at the walk when there are a lot of insects around. For this reason we take him out first lot each day, before they get bad. Best Mate gets about one-and-a-half-hour's slow exercise in July and August but is still allowed to go back into the field on most afternoons, until the weather deteriorates and his races draw closer. He starts steady cantering on our all-weather track after a month of walking and trotting. This is combined with regular schooling on the flat, in our outdoor arena beside the garden. We employ an experienced event rider for this work, and the gentle but positive trotting in circles helps to further build up the muscles that will be needed for galloping and jumping during the National Hunt season. I like to see all the racehorses carry themselves in balance and go forward with a rounded outline. It encourages them to jump in the right shape and to use their necks and backs correctly. If they are confident and well-schooled, they must be better rides for the jockeys during a race, but it is not as easy as it sounds since the horses vary enormously and temperament is all important.

While Matey was steadily regaining his former fitness, Jim Lewis, Terry and I were planning his programme for the coming season. It was decided that a two-mile one-and-a-half-furlong novice chase at Exeter would give him a good introduction to steeplechasing. It is a course that is not used during the summer months, and as a result it usually produces good even ground in October and November, provided that there has been enough rain to remove any jar. It is a well-managed course and the grass is regularly mown to a set height in order to establish a decent bottom. The fences are well presented too, and beautifully built. With the exception of the first open ditch, which is sighted after the bend beyond the stands, they are inviting for a novice. The ditch in question is a little out of character with the rest of the fences, and its brightly painted take-off board tends to cause inexperienced runners to back off more than usual. There are often some awkward jumps at this obstacle, but it was unlikely to trouble Best Mate since he had already seen plenty of coloured poles in the showjumping paddock at West Lockinge Farm. He is not a spooky horse. A circle was put round 17 October in our diaries, and we organised his training programme around that day.

Every season, we insist that each chaser has a school over our home fences before taking part in a race. An older horse usually only needs to be refreshed and to sharpen its eye, but a younger one may be jumping these obstacles for the first time. We like to give all our novice chasers three good schooling sessions before they run, and we often jump them the day before a race so that fences are fresh in their minds. In the case of Best Mate, chase fences were not new to him. He had already experienced plenty of schooling in Ireland and he had run in two point-to-points. When we asked him to jump our line of fences we expected him to jump like an old handicapper, but we obviously trusted him too much. Jim Culloty was over confident. Believing implicitly in his horse, he set sail for three small schooling fences which had been freshly built and positioned in a field where the grass produces a good cushion for that time of year. Unfortunately, horse and jockey were not on the same wavelength, and, possibly remembering his adverse schooling sessions at Clonmel racecourse and on the Irish point-to-point course at Killaloe, Best Mate suddenly jinked violently to the left, threw Jim off balance and soared effortlessly over the four-foot-six-inch wing beside the second fence. Terry and I were standing close by and were shocked by what we saw. Jim Culloty would not get off lightly. He subsequently received reprimands from us both, and the language was strong. Yet an important lesson had been learnt, and never again did he take Best Mate for granted. At the next time of asking the horse was brilliant, and he jumped faultlessly. We gave him two more schools before Exeter, and each time he was spot on.

As that Exeter day drew closer, there was some rain and the ground on the course improved; on the day of the race it was given as good. Best Mate set off from Lockinge at 8.30 a.m., even though the novice chase was not until 4.10 p.m. It so happened that we had two other runners in earlier races, so all three horses travelled together.

He would have a long wait in the racecourse stables, but he doesn't mind travelling and tends to enjoy an away day. On these occasions the only thing he misses is his food. All our horses are fed at six a.m., and if they're racing they don't receive any further food until after their exertions. Five hours without food is the shortest time we allow before a race, and on many occasions the time span is longer. No athletes run on full stomachs, and the same should apply to horses. It is the muscles that need the best blood supply since they are greatly needed for galloping and jumping; digestion in the gut should therefore be slowed down to a minimum.

Matey had not been to Exeter before, so running on that course would give him a new experience. Until then, he had raced only on Grade 1 tracks, but it was about time he went back to his grass roots and mingled with the true country enthusiasts, deep in the heart of Devon. There is such a lovely atmosphere in that part of the country and it is a most picturesque track, with plenty of room for the horses in each race. There are a number of gradients and a steady uphill climb from the back of the course to the home straight. It is always a true test. Hopefully, Matey would think he was back in a point-to-point.

There was a big turnout of spectators to witness Best Mate's first run over fences, and he didn't disappoint his supporters. Despite a couple of decent opponents – in particular Bindaree, who was to win the 2002 Grand National, and Shooting Light, who subsequently won the Thomas Pink Gold Cup at Cheltenham in 2001 – he won the race in impressive style. He travelled and jumped superbly throughout. He cruised into the lead approaching the last and won hard held by two and a half lengths. It was the perfect start for the future champion. 'I can remember at the last ditch, which is the last fence on the far side at Exeter, I gave him a squeeze and he put down on me,' recalls Jim Culloty. 'The picture in the *Racing Post* the following day was of Best Mate leading over that ditch, and you wouldn't even know he had made a mistake. He's so neat and balanced... He's intelligent, and he has the physique to go with it. With some horses you have to balance them, help them over an obstacle. With Best Mate, you're better just sitting tight and not interfering with him. He needs rhythm because he does everything gradually. Being pushed and pulled, being fired into fences, he doesn't like that. But we are learning about him all the time.'

Everybody was ecstatic in the winners' enclosure and his run earned him plenty of praise from the racing journalists. It was a thoroughly satisfactory day out, and he had now got his foot on the bottom rung of the steeplechasing ladder. There would be plenty more climbing to do, but this first chase had gone like clockwork.

One of the beauties about Best Mate is the way in which he comes out of his races. The day after Exeter was no exception, and having eaten all his supper he was fresh and well the next morning when the time came for the customary post-race 'trot-up'. All our horses are trotted up the day after their races; this is usually done after first lot and takes place on the level, but worn, part of the gravel drive. First of all, the clay which is applied to the forelegs after a race is washed off, and then each horse is led up to the front door for me or Terry to see. We feel their tendons, joints and shins carefully before the lads or lasses walk away and trot back towards us up the drive. It reminds me of the trot-ups that happen at three-day events on the morning after the cross-country phase. One is always relieved when one feels cold legs and the horses move off with level steps. Matey tends to trot up Jackie rather than the other way round. He always pulls her along and shows off like a dressage horse. Later in the day she takes him for a couple of walks on his headcollar and a chain, and lets him pick grass along the verges. On most occasions we don't let the horses out into a field for a couple of days after a race until we are completely sure that we have not missed any hidden problems. With Matey, we are always over cautious and extra careful. We sometimes wait for longer than a week until he returns to normal exercise since he is so over exuberant in the field. Yet he does so much enjoy having a good roll, and the freedom benefits him mentally.

The most obvious follow-up race to Exeter was the two-mile Grade 2 Independent Novice Chase at Cheltenham on Sunday, 12 November. Once again it was during the big three-day meeting this time sponsored by Thomas Pink, and it was on the same day that

Matey had won the bumper in 1999. It would be no walkover, and Nicky Henderson's horse Dusk Duel was a warm fancy, but we already knew that Best Mate acted up the Cheltenham hill, and he was in tremendous form. There was a big crowd, and as always he looked magnificent in the paddock. Jackie was beginning to look like a marathon runner as she struggled to keep up with his steps, and he was not going to wait for her if she lagged behind. Six horses had been declared and Matey was the favourite, but I worried lest his supreme overconfidence would cause his downfall. He needed to pay attention to those Cheltenham fences and could not afford any lax moments. He would have to listen to Jim Culloty's orders.

As it happened, he jumped perfectly for most of the race but had a momentary lack of concentration at the fourth fence from home, the last ditch. Jim says that he came into the fence on a bad stride and needed to shorten a little, but instead he didn't pay attention and rushed at the obstacle. As a result he did not get very high and left his hind legs on the birch – 'he brushed through it and gave himself a bit of a fright', as Jim put it. That ditch is renowned for such mistakes, especially with novices. He lost a few lengths, but the difference of opinion had only caused a minor blunder. In all probability the mistake had done him good, and in future he would concentrate harder. Indeed, it is the only mistake of that kind that he has made to date.

Both horses were going well at the second last, but Dusk Duel slipped badly on landing and thereafter put himself right out of contention. In the end, Best Mate merely strolled up the hill to the winning line. He had once again had another 'good feel' of the Cheltenham course. There was also an added bonus: he had not had a hard race.

He was proud that day when he walked back to the winners' circle. He pricked his ears and gazed into the distance as he stood on that hallowed turf. It prompted me to say that I believed he thought he was Arkle. That great horse always had a look of eagles, and I consider that Best Mate has a similar look. Like his predecessor, he is a confident horse who loves his public and thrives on a big reception.

Unfortunately, my remark was misinterpreted by the media. In the press it was written that I believed Best Mate to be the second Arkle, yet I have never said this, and anyway, it is almost impossible to compare two horses who raced in different generations. I used to idolise Arkle myself. Arkle won three Cheltenham Gold Cups as well as numerous other big races. His was a household name in Ireland and England. It is already an honour to train a horse with a few of Arkle's characteristics.

Best Mate still has a long way to go to achieve Arkle's status, but after that novice chase at Cheltenham he did look a worthy candidate for the 2001 Arkle Chase at the festival meeting the following March. Once again Jim and Valerie Lewis were thrilled with their young star, and it meant another trip up those stairs to the Royal Box together with more drinks and sandwiches at the round table. Best Mate had come a long way in the last twelve months; only a year earlier we had all been there for a Flat-race win, but we always knew chasing would be his real game.

It was a good feeling to have won two novice chases with Best Mate before Christmas, and with the two-mile Novice Championship Chase the Arkle as the season's main objective there would be time to give Matey a short holiday before looking for one more race in the run-up to Cheltenham. He did not have a lot of chase experience, which is why we looked for a third outing. If the weather held, the Scilly Isles Novices' Chase at Sandown in early February 2001 over two and a half miles could serve us well.

Then, on 23 November, disaster almost struck. Jackie had just returned with Best Mate from a routine exercise on the Downs. She had ridden him back down the lane, which is also a bridlepath, at the back of the farm, hosed off his legs in the yard and took him back to his stable. All seemed normal, until she picked out his feet to clear them of mud and stones. It was then that she shouted out in horror on finding a rusty nail embedded, close to the frog, in his off hind foot. At the time he did not seem to be feeling any discomfort, but she called to Andy, our head lad, to take a look. He tried to pull the nail out by hand, but it was firmly embedded and he had to resort to a pair of pliers. It was not easy to keep Matey still and he kicked out repeatedly as he began to feel some pain, yet Andy was fortunately able to remove the whole nail. It was about two inches long but was bent over. Matey lurched forward and was suddenly in quite a state. He was not accustomed to being hurt and was finding it difficult to put weight on his hind foot.

Both the farrier, Mervyn Richings, and the veterinary surgeon, Roger Betteridge, were summoned. Terry and I were quickly on the scene as well. After a short consultation, it was decided to move Best Mate to Lambourn, to the veterinary hospital at Valley Equine. It would be important to take X-rays and scan the soft tissues in order to make sure there was no serious damage. Jim Lewis was immediately informed, and we all waited anxiously for news. The relief was enormous when Roger telephoned to say that we had been extremely lucky: the point of the nail had missed penetrating the navicular bursa by a fraction of a centimetre. There had obviously been considerable haemorrhaging under the sole of the foot which was causing a lot of pain, but Matey, with his hoof well bandaged and poulticed, was able to walk back into the horsebox and return home. It must have been throbbing like the bleeding under a nail when a finger is shut in a door. He was given some painkillers and strong antibiotics for five days but was already covered for tetanus. We were told to watch carefully for any swelling at the back of the pastern, as this might indicate infection running up the tendon sheath from the foot. We were also ordered to leave him in his stable for ten days, but he enjoyed all the extra attention and an increased supply of apples and carrots. He was a model patient. Roger visited him daily and Jim Lewis was given frequent bulletins.

How lucky we had been. Rusty nails can be so dangerous, but they are never seen until it is too late. It must be odds against one lodging in a horse's foot, but in the countryside they are plentiful, especially on farm land, and also in villages close to places where builders have been at work. If Matey had to have a setback, however, it could not have come at a better time as he was due for a rest anyway. When the ten days were up and Jim Lewis could breathe again, Matey resumed gentle exercise and was once more on course for those races at Sandown and Cheltenham.

In 2001, the month of January was extremely wet. Many of the racecourses had heavy ground, especially during the last two weeks. Towards the end of the month Jim and Valerie Lewis went abroad for their annual holiday, but we were left with instructions to run Best Mate at Sandown, even though they would still be away. Yet they stipulated that we were only to run if we were satisfied that the conditions were right. It would not be easy to find an alternative race, and with Cheltenham looming the timing was crucial. The horse was extremely well. He had returned to action in fine form after his enforced lay-off and he seemed stronger than ever. Faxes were flying to and from the Western Cape in South Africa, and as that weekend approached in early February the general opinion was to let Matey take his chance. The ground would be soft – it was in fact heavy on the day – but good horses are supposed to be able to race on any ground. Surely the underfoot conditions could not be as bad as those we had witnessed in the Lismore point-to-point? Jim Culloty schooled his favourite horse once more at home and gave him a nice piece of work on the gallops. He looked magnificent, and his blood test was perfect. We desperately wanted to run, but Terry would walk the course on the morning of the race and we would talk to Jim Lewis from Sandown. Matey got the green light to start after Terry's assessment of the ground, but we scratched Edredon Bleu from the Elmbridge Chase. The ground was wet but safe, yet it was not Bleu's ground; he would definitely get bogged down.

There were eight runners in the Grade 1 Scilly Isles Novices Chase, and it was sponsored by Weatherbys. It was always going to be a lovely race to win, and Best Mate was superb. He put up a sparkling display and jumped impeccably. As he met the rising ground turning into the straight, his stride lengthened and he forged clear over the last two fences. It was unreal to see a novice chaser accelerate so impressively on the rain-softened ground. He won on the bit by thirteen lengths from Crocadee. We immediately spoke to Jim Lewis on the telephone and there was jubilation all round. He apparently spent £82 on his mobile phone that day, speaking to Terry and I as well as to Marvin, his son, who represented him. He also telephoned two other close friends, Nick Craven from Weatherbys and Len Jakeman, a knowledgeable racegoer and part owner of Foly Pleasant. They too had witnessed the victory first hand. Marvin texted the commentary to South Africa, and the last message read: 'Won in a canter. Bloody hell.'

It had been an exhilarating day, and on the way home Terry and I received a call from our great friend, the late Dave Dick. He was a great supporter of our yard and had taken to Best Mate in a big way. As a former top showjumping rider and famous steeplechase jockey in the 1950s and 1960s, his opinions were greatly valued. Dave had ridden some brilliant horses, including many for Dorothy Paget. He had won top races on the likes of Mont Tremblant, E.S.B. and Dunkirk. The former was victorious in the Cheltenham Gold Cup with Dave in 1952, and in 1956 he won the Grand National on ESB. Dave knew a good horse when he saw one, and that afternoon, at the beginning of February, he told us that Best Mate could easily win two or three Gold Cups. I remember saying that I thought 2002 would be too soon for him as he would only be six years old, but Dave insisted that he had not seen a horse of this calibre for years and that he would definitely be ready by then. Mont Tremblant had been the same age when he had been victorious. Tragically, Dave died before Matey's first Cheltenham triumph, but I have always remembered his words. He always spoke his mind and so often gave me advice on my horses. Terry and I adored him. His sense of humour was second to none, but on this occasion he was serious.

After Sandown, the *Superform* write-up said 'impressive, fast time. A high class novice who looks a real star in the making and will prove very hard to beat in the Arkle.' By now, Best Mate was the red-hot favourite for that Cheltenham race in March, and plenty would be written about him in the newspapers over the next weeks. He was fast gaining the recognition he deserved and becoming an extremely popular horse with the public. Yet little did any of us realise that the foot and mouth epidemic was only just round the corner, and that in due course Matey would not get his chance to run in that prestigious race, named after the legend of the 1960s.

By mid-February, foot and mouth had been officially confirmed in Britain. This vile disease spread rapidly across large areas of the country during the last weeks of the month and on into March. Things looked grim for the Cheltenham Festival, yet for a long time we were led to believe that it would go ahead. The horses continued to be trained for their scheduled races, but there was so much uncertainty and such despair. With every news programme on the television the situation worsened, and there were some shocking scenes. It was extremely depressing. Not only did we all feel for the farmers, but many country pursuits were curtailed and it was difficult to foresee what would happen next. It was a case of using Terry's favourite motto: 'one day at a time'. We could not plan anything with certainty. From 3 March, when Doncaster was abandoned, until 9 April, when the Hexham meeting was lost, over 30 jump meetings were obliterated from the programme book as a result of the disease. After a few weeks of hope, the efforts to save Cheltenham were of no avail. There would be no festival in 2001.

It was hard to see what else we could do with Best Mate that spring. He was so well and was ready for a race. He had been cruelly denied a winning chance in the Arkle, and the novice chases at Aintree did not appeal. The distances were wrong. We ruled out the two-mile novice chase on that course because of the sharp nature of the Mildmay track. We did not wish to put him back in distance for a fast-run two-mile race when the Scilly Isles Chase had been run over two miles four furlongs on a stiff course. The three-mile novices chase at Aintree would come too soon, since we did not want to step him up in distance until the next season.

In the end, we went for a hurdle race option, and Matey took his chance in the two-mile four-furlong Grade 1 Martell Aintree Hurdle. He had not run over hurdles since winning on that course as a novice in 2000 on good to firm ground. The ground was atrocious for the big hurdle in April 2001, and was officially described as heavy. It was way different to the going at Sandown, and Matey hated it. He didn't jump a single hurdle with any fluency and got no help from the ground. He bravely kept going, but lost by fourteen lengths to Barton. Mr Cool, Bounce Back and Teaatral followed him up the straight, but Landing Light pulled up, quite unable to cope with these testing conditions. Best Mate had come to no harm, but it was obviously time to stop with him and prepare him for his summer holidays. He had probably gone over the top. He had been super fit and spot on in early March when we thought Cheltenham would take place, but it is difficult to let a horse down and bring it back to peak fitness with no race in between.

His chasing reputation remained high, however, and he looked an exciting prospect for the autumn. At the Racehorse Owners' Association annual awards dinner in London in December he was voted the leading novice chaser of the 2000/01 season. We were set to campaign him over longer distances, and there was further talk of the King George at Kempton on Boxing Day and the 2002 Cheltenham Gold Cup. There would be plenty of decisions to be made in the coming months, but now it was time for a break. On 1 June, Terry and I set off from Heathrow to Naples for a short holiday on the Amalfi coast. We could not be away for long for we needed to keep a regular check on our rising star, and there was plenty more dreaming to be done.

CHAPTER TWELVE

ON THE GOLD TRAIL

After the rigours of Aintree in April 2001 and Best Mate's struggle to act on ground which was almost unraceable, he recovered quickly; his customary let-down weeks went smoothly, just as they had done the previous year. He seems to know when he is not in full training and soon switches off. He most probably senses that there is less tension in the yard, and he enjoys the longer hours in his paddock. There's more time to crunch his polo mints, and the spring grass gets tastier by the day. The month of May soon passed, and Terry and I enjoyed our carefully planned break. We made sure that Andy Fox, our head lad, did not start his own break until after our return.

Over the years we have become increasingly more dependent upon Andy. He always holds the fort at West Lockinge Farm when we are away, and the measure of his reliability is impossible to gauge. He neither leaves any stone unturned nor takes short-cuts. He has now been with me for twelve years – and, by coincidence, he spent his childhood in Lockinge as well. He learnt to ride, with the help of Alan Honeybone, a former steeplechase jockey, on one of my mother's

Shetland ponies, and since then he has steadily learnt more and more about horses. From 1980 to 1988 Andy worked for Tim Forster in Letcombe Bassett. It was during that time that he happened to look after my sister's horse, Drumadowney, who won the Reynoldstown Chase at Ascot in February 1985 and was then fourth in the Cheltenham Gold Cup as a six-year-old the following spring. Andy also spent two years caring for Last Suspect, but gave up this horse two months before it won the Grand National. After spending those eight years in a top National Hunt yard, he turned his attentions to stud work. During the 1980s, two stallions, Decoy Boy and King of Spain, were standing at Kitford Stud in Lockinge; Andy was put in charge of the latter. The time he spent with this stallion, together with the handling of the mares, foals and youngstock, provided him with further valuable experience, and as a result we find him especially good with the numerous young horses who come into training. He handles them quietly but firmly and has endless patience. The horses respond accordingly. Indeed, he can catch even the most difficult ones, with ease, in the paddocks. They all learn to trust him since they know him so well.

During the racing season Andy Fox feels the horses' legs twice daily, and after his evening rounds he gives us a full report on any ailments. He makes clear notes, and we record all his findings in a special book, which can prove extremely helpful if we need to look back. Andy was here when Best Mate arrived in England in the spring of 1999 and he has supervised him, in our stables, ever since. He knows every inch of the horse's body as well as his day-to-day habits, and meticulously prepares his evening feed every night. Indeed, Andy mixes the feeds for all the horses, and we compare notes; I make out lists with him and we determine the special needs of each horse. The daily requirements are written up on a board in the feed shed.

When Terry and I go away each summer, Andy checks all the field horses twice daily, as well as carefully monitoring the ones who come in by night. Even when we are on holiday I talk to him every morning on my mobile phone; I always worry about my charges, especially when I'm not at hand to see them. I feel extremely responsible for their well-being, even during the off season. People say that I should learn to switch off and forget my life at Lockinge, but I'm unable to do this. Yet I do relax abroad once I have rung home and satisfied myself that all is well on the farm. Training racehorses is a 365-days-of-the-year job. The racing may be seasonal, but the day-to-day care certainly is not. Terry is far better at winding down than I am. His more carefree nature allows him to slip into a new routine with ease, but he accepts that I will never change. How can I with so many animals in my life? I even hate saying goodbye to the dogs and the ducks on the pond, yet we have the perfect holiday arrangements with Andy. We are extremely lucky to have such a brilliant head lad whom we trust implicitly.

During the busy months of the winter, Andy shares our worries and we discuss the training programmes of the horses in great depth. It helps him to understand any changes in their eating habits. Andy seldom goes racing and has little time for riding out when the season starts in earnest, but he never misses Cheltenham. His wife, Vicky, who used to work for us, led up our first Cheltenham Festival winner in 1997. She looked after and rode out Karshi when he won the Bonusprint Stayers Hurdle that year. We like to think that Andy brings us luck – we would certainly never leave him behind. He lives for his three days at Cheltenham in March, and is very much looking forward to the four-day festival in 2005.

Andy works longer hours than anyone else in the yard, yet he never complains. He takes pride in what he does and he loves his horses. He has a lot of talent and has become extremely knowledgeable. He could easily train horses in his own right and would undoubtedly be successful, but at the moment he seems content to help us – which is good because we could not manage without him. He is an assistant trainer and a head lad rolled into one, which makes him the backbone of the home team.

The summer of 2001 passed by and the autumn months were soon well under way. Best Mate continued to look good, and he came back into work a stronger horse. We do not weigh our horses at West Lockinge Farm, but I'm sure he had gained many kilos. He had strengthened noticeably behind the saddle and over his quarters. The horse was beginning to mature, and, by putting on weight, was possibly taking after Terry, who always relishes Italian food and does himself so well on holiday. The first objective was the two-and-a-quarter-mile Grade 2 Haldon Gold Cup at Exeter on 6 November. Both Jackie Jenner and Jim Culloty were delighted with the feel Matey was giving them in the run-up to this race. He also looked good while doing his basic dressage work in the arena. We were all full of enthusiasm, but it would be a telling season and there would be some tense moments.

We had no qualms about taking Best Mate back to Exeter for that important early-season race. He had shown his appreciation for the course the previous year and had won his novice chase there convincingly. We hoped that he had remembered the place and his good experience. We thought the race would suit him, and a huge crowd gathered to support him. He strutted around the paddock, proving to his fans that he felt good. He still had his summer coat and he looked a beautiful horse. All eyes were upon him.

It was a strange race. Matey had only three opponents, all of whom were trained by Paul Nicholls. The ground was officially good to firm and good in places, but we were happy with the underfoot conditions when we walked the course. Surely there must be a plot in the Nicholls' camp to overthrow our unbeaten favourite, but what could it be? Cenkos, under Timmy Murphy, set off at a blistering pace but had burnt himself out by the eighth fence. He was wearing blinkers for the first time and did not look particularly happy with them on. Fadalko, under Mick Fitzgerald, ran below par, so it was left to the least experienced horse, Desert Mountain ridden by Jo Tizzard, to follow Matey home. Jim Culloty had been in no hurry in the early part of the race, but after the last ditch Best Mate changed gear and the result was a foregone concluson bar a fall. He sprinted away from his opponents and won by twenty lengths. He got a great reception as he walked back through the paddock to the unsaddling enclosure. It was an emotional moment, and we were delighted with his performance. It was exactly what we all needed, and everybody was smiling in the Best Mate camp. His fans were in raptures. This was some horse; whatever would he do next?

As the month of November neared its end, there remained one more big day in the diary. It so happened that the First National Gold Cup Chase at Ascot – a two-mile three-furlong handicap chase for second-season novices – and the Grade 2 Peterborough Chase at Huntingdon were scheduled on the same date. Jim Lewis would have a runner in each race, but which horse would Jim Culloty ride? Matey was due to race at Ascot and Edredon Bleu was set to defend his crown at Huntingdon in the race he had claimed as his own since 1998. He had won the last three Peterborough Chases and Jim had ridden him on each occasion. This time Jim chose Best Mate, and after much deliberation it was decided to offer the ride on Edredon Bleu to Norman Williamson. It would be a tough weekend, and the adrenalin would certainly be flowing at a strong pace, but we could never have foreseen the added emotions that would also have to be endured.

At the start of the week, the *Racing Post* carried pictures of both my horses on the front page, and they were both given write-ups relating to their Saturday races. My mother, who followed the careers of the horses closely and read the *Racing Post* each day, telephoned my sister and said that she did not know how I would ever get through the week. She always worried about me, and was especially concerned when big days approached. She always wanted the horses to run well. Yet by a strange twist of fate, I survived that week and she did not.

On the Wednesday morning, when Norman Williamson came over to school Edredon Bleu, I spoke to my mother before first lot and she was in great form. However, during breakfast we received a telephone call summoning Terry and me to Lockinge Manor where it was reported that she had taken a fall. Alas, she had suffered a massive brain haemorrhage, and we found her lying at the foot of the stairs. She never regained consciousness and died in hospital later that morning. I was by her side. It was a devastating experience. At the time of the accident, my three runners had left for the day's racing at Kempton Park. They were owned by Jim Lewis, my sister and me. I knew that my mother would have wanted them to run, so we didn't withdraw them, even though the thought obviously crossed my mind. All three horses went on to win their races that day; it was as though Mum had willed them to do well. Stars Out Tonight, Maximize and Red Blazer all rose to the occasion, but it was hard for Terry to supervise them and he could not enjoy the victories. He kept taking himself away from the crowds and sitting down on his own. He regularly called me on his mobile telephone. We were all shattered by the events of the day. I returned from the Oxford hospital with my sister, but remained in a total daze. For the first time in many months neither Best Mate nor Edredon Bleu figured in my thoughts.

It was a tough week, and I found it hard to concentrate on training the racehorses. Everybody felt sad. My mother left a huge hole in my life and her sudden death came as an unbelievable shock. She had been my guiding light for so many years; I wondered how I would ever manage without her. I would miss her dreadfully, but I knew that she would want me to carry on with my daily duties. Everything would have to be right for Saturday. It was an important day. Ironically, Mum was to have accompanied me to Huntingdon and was much looking forward to the outing. I would miss her company on the two-hour drive, but I would cope without her. Jim and Valerie Lewis were wonderfully understanding. They, of course, were in shock too; they'd spent many happy days in my mother's company over the past years. By Friday I had pulled myself together, and Best Mate and Edredon Bleu were ready for action the following day. The stage was set and our lives would continue as normal.

On the day of the race, Jackie Jenner did not accompany Best Mate to Ascot; instead she chose to go with Edredon Bleu to Huntingdon as he was still her favourite and she did not want to let him down on the racecourse he loved so much. She nominated Dave Reddy to lead up her younger star, and Drew Miller, our travelling head lad, assisted him. Dave is a star man and an experienced member of our team. He has worked for me for the best part of eight years and has been in racing all his life. He joined Fulke Johnson Houghton's yard as a sixteen-year-old and, together with his father and brother, worked there for seventeen years. Later on, he had a short spell with Andy Turnell, where he did much of the travelling. He is a popular lad and knows Best Mate well. He has ridden him at home and has a lovely quiet way with horses. He habitually helps Jackie with her wonder horse at the races. He has become a familiar figure, and the racegoers are accustomed to seeing him walking on the inside of Matey, around the parade ring, at all the big race meetings. He flanks him, as well, in all the parades. Dave is always immaculately turned out and is a true professional. He never leaves anything to chance and is a most trustworthy individual with a brilliant sense of humour. In the yard, where he is always singing, he is known as the Magnet, although I have yet to understand the origins of this name.

He was the perfect choice to take Jackie's place at Matey's head before the First National Gold Cup Chase, but he did not have an easy task and his charge did not behave in his usual sensible way. Apparently, the journey to Ascot had been a nightmare and Returning, who was also in the horsebox, had taken it into her head to kick out violently all the way there. Both horses had arrived at the racecourse stables sweating profusely, and looking back on the day I think that this experience affected Best Mate, who is usually a brilliant traveller, because he continued to be on edge in the paddock and was worked up in the preliminaries. He was even sweating at the start. Jim Culloty maintains that it was just not his day and that he refused to relax, even during the race itself.

That race at Ascot was never going to be a straightforward task for Matey for another reason: he had to give 20lb to Wahiba Sands. The other jockeys would be sure to pile on the pressure. He was hot favourite but he never got into his usual rhythm, nor did he jump with his accustomed fluency. Mick Fitzgerald had Dusk Duel at his girth for much of the way, and as a result Matey probably did too much early on in the race. This, coupled with his refusal to settle, took a lot out of him. In the end, Wahiba Sands, ridden by Tony McCoy, beat him by half a length, but he bravely fought back in the closing stages. Jim Culloty considers it was the horse's state of mind, not the weight, which lost him the race, and nobody knows Best Mate better than this jockey. He is a strong horse and can carry big weights, but he did not show his true form that day. Ironically, Returning won her steeplechase that afternoon, yet she had probably brought about Matey's downfall through her unusual antics in the horsebox. She continued to be a difficult traveller from that day onwards, and in the future we were careful to keep her well away from other horses.

Back at Huntingdon, Jackie Jenner had her mobile phone and earphones in her coat pocket. She wore the latter as she led Edredon Bleu around in the paddock before his big race, which was scheduled to be run twenty minutes later than the Ascot contest. She was still listening intently to the commentary as we anxiously saddled up Bleu. She relayed the details to me and Fiona Hiscock as we tightened the girths and adjusted the rugs. Her face said it all as Best Mate passed the winning post: he had lost his unbeaten record over steeplechase fences. As we read it, weight had toppled the wonder horse from his pedestal. In due course, however, I would speak to Terry, who was at Ascot, and he would give me the lowdown, but at that moment it was imperative for Edredon Bleu to run well and rekindle Jackie's morale.

The result of the 2001 Peterborough Chase could not have been more welcome. Bleu kept the flag flying and yet again raced home with the trophy. It was his fourth win in a row in this race, and he had made history. No horse had ever won four consecutive Peterborough Chases. Norman Williamson was full of smiles; he'd enjoyed his armchair ride. He had been surprised by the horse's courage and by his quick jumping technique. Jim and Valerie Lewis had driven to Huntingdon to watch their star, and it was a memorable day for them too. The crowd gave their horse a wonderful reception, and he is tremendously popular on that Cambridgeshire course. I had not dared to watch the race and had hidden in the horsebox park. Throughout the race I had talked to Terry on my telephone. He watched the race on a screen at Ascot and helped to calm my nerves by telling me that Bleu was travelling well. I wanted something to lift my spirits during those desperately sad days, and it was a welcome victory on top of Best Mate's surprise reversal. Edredon Bleu is a real wonder. He tries his hardest and loves his racing. On top form, he is a hard horse to beat.

We eventually managed to get through that strange week in November 2001. Best Mate had not lost any of his admirers as a result of his defeat, and the King George VI Chase at Kempton on Boxing Day was now firmly on his agenda. We would give him a short rest and then train him, carefully, for the big day. Meanwhile, at Lockinge, we would prepare for my mother's funeral. There were a lot of arrangements to be made, and my head was reeling with a multitude of thoughts. I was surrounded by some wonderful people, however, and their support gave me the strength I needed to cope with the difficult days ahead. Terry's love was unfailing, but in the end it was the Queen Mother herself who gave me the greatest boost. On 28 November, she travelled from Windsor to the church in Lockinge to pay her last respects to my mother, and she sat beside me during that testing service. As I returned to my seat after reading a special poem, she turned, smiled at me and whispered, 'Well done.' It was a moment I will never forget.

CHAPTER THIRTEEN

A TENSE DAY AT KEMPTON

We gave Best Mate a two-week holiday following his defeat in the First National Gold Cup Chase at Ascot. He and Edredon Bleu spent some mornings together in their paddock, and this gave both horses a chance to unwind, which they always relish. They started afresh in December, and they were in good shape and had not left any food nor shown any ill effects since their November races. For Matey, the build-up to the King George VI at Kempton on Boxing Day would be crucial and would need to be carefully planned. It would be his most important race to date, and we had to get him there in peak condition.

Secretly, I was dreading that race. I wasn't sure that the course would suit him. Matey had shown his best form on tracks with stiff uphill finishes such as Cheltenham and Sandown, yet Kempton is a fast flat course. He had not yet run in a steeplechase on a course like this, although he had contested two hurdle races at Aintree, which is also a quick course without a hill. My next worry was that Matey would be running over three miles for the first time since his point-to-point days in Ireland. We were certain he would stay, but he hadn't raced over this distance under Rules and might need a race to readjust to the extra four furlongs. Then there was the record of the course itself, and its history. There had been some strange results in the King George over the years, and in the past, few horses had achieved the King George/Gold Cup double in the same year, probably because the two courses are so different. A Kempton specialist does not always adapt to the Cheltenham gradients, and vice versa.

For my part, I had a few bad memories of Kempton engraved on my mind. I had been present when one of my favourite horses, Dunkirk, had been killed at the last open ditch in 1965. Kempton had also ended Arkle's racing career in 1966 when he finished lame with a broken pedal bone. I prayed that no freak accident would befall our treasured horse. Even Terry had had his fair share of misfortunes on the London track. In the late 1960s he had suffered a bad fall on the last bend; he was trampled and kicked, and ended up losing the use of a kidney. Yet, while agreeing with me that it would not be the ideal course for Best Mate, he refused to share my pessimism. He told me to pull myself together; he was sure everything would be all right.

As we mapped out Best Mate's timetable for the days leading up to the King George, our plans fell apart. At Taunton on 28 November, Jim Culloty was unseated from one of our novice hurdlers, Abu Dancer, as she jinked and tried to run out at a hurdle. He landed awkwardly and was kicked by another horse on his right arm – he had broken the same arm two-and-a-half years earlier and this had necessitated the insertion of a metal pin. It was obvious that Jim was in considerable pain, and the X-ray revealed that he had chipped off a small fragment of bone close to the end of the pin. It would need a minimum of a month to heal, which made riding on Boxing Day a close call. He tried his hardest to get himself right and keep himself fit for that important day as he longed to ride Best Mate at Kempton, but, despite a trip to Dubai for extra swimming and the warmth of the sunshine, he was not happy with his arm. It still felt weak and was painful if he twisted it. We had stipulated that if Jim were to ride on 26 December he would have to demonstrate his fitness at Ascot on the 22nd, but on the morning of Thursday, 20 December he called me to say that, regrettably, he did not think he would be able to do Best Mate justice and that he would have to relinquish his longed-for ride. It was a sickening blow for him, especially as he knew that his favourite horse would now be offered to A. P. McCoy who had ridden Edredon Bleu, for Jim Lewis, to victory in that memorable Queen Mother Champion Chase at Cheltenham in 2000. Dave Roberts, Tony McCoy's agent, confirmed that he was available to take the ride, so now, with only four days left, we would have to ensure that he came to West Lockinge Farm to familiarise himself with his new partner. We wanted him to jump Best Mate over a fence, and we needed to discuss the best way to ride him in a race.

It is difficult to explain, but to me Tony McCoy is not the ideal jockey for Best Mate and never will be. His forceful way of riding, together with the extra effort he so often demands at a fence, does not suit our horse. He is a brilliant jockey, though, and this has been demonstrated by his record-breaking number of winners. However, a few horses do not adapt to his unique style and do not appreciate his strength. The Costello family educate their horses to a special pattern. They are taught to jump correctly from an early age, especially when loose, and all they need from the saddle is for a rider to sit quietly, maintain the balance, and keep the forward momentum. The jockeys must always allow the fences to come to them; they must not try to place their horses. Best Mate has an exceptionally good eye and sees his own strides; if he is continually asked to stand off at his fences, he gets confused and his ears flick backwards. He dislikes being asked to hurry into an obstacle, and if fired at a fence he loses his rhythm and fluency. He often puts in another little stride to set himself right. Best Mate trusts Jim, and since the spring of 1999 they have learnt together and developed a unique understanding. A. P. McCoy and Jim Culloty have two totally different riding styles, and with Kempton just four days away there was little time for Best Mate to forge a partnership with the champion jockey. Terry is an expert coach and was a superb tactical rider himself. He knows exactly how Best Mate should be ridden and has helped Jim Culloty right from the start. I hoped so much that Tony would listen to Terry's words of wisdom and adapt his style to suit the horse.

There was a big build-up to the 2001 King George VI Chase, and we hosted a special press day at West Lockinge Farm on the Thursday prior to Christmas. The media descended on us in force to watch Best Mate working, under Jackie Jenner, in a big grass field on the Downs. He was looking a million dollars and was clearly in excellent shape for the forthcoming race. Following that morning on the gallops there were numerous articles written in the national papers. The scribes were impressed by what they had seen. Jim Culloty's position was made public, and his replacement by A.P., the subject of much speculation already, was confirmed. On Christmas Eve, Tony McCoy turned up at West Lockinge Farm to sit on his new mount and to get used to the feel of him over a fence. The schooling went well and, as usual, Matey was accurate and obedient with his jumping. To our relief, the partnership looked good, and after some talks with the jockey there was plenty of optimism. Both Terry and Tony agreed that tactics would be vital on the big day.

Since he would be racing over a new distance on Boxing Day, the key would be to settle Best Mate for the first mile and conserve his energy. His natural speed could then be used on the second circuit. Provided that the race at Ascot had done him no harm and that he was easy to switch off in the early stages, the extra half mile would cause no problems. Terry was sure he would stay the distance well, and that his turn of foot would be decisive up the home straight. We had been longing to race him over three miles for some time. Terry planned to walk the course and assess the ground on the morning of the race before giving his final views to A.P. in the paddock. With the likes of First Gold, Bacchanal and Florida Pearl in the line-up, it would be an exciting race to watch – not that I would be viewing it live, of course. I would have to choose a quiet place to hide.

We did not move from West Lockinge Farm on Christmas Day. I cooked Terry a huge lunch, which included a turkey, and we guarded Matey carefully throughout the day. In the morning he had two easy canters up the four-furlong Eurotrack gallop at the back of the stables, and Jackie reported that he felt in top form. It would be a tense day at Kempton, but everything in the build-up had gone according to plan.

The horseboxes left at eight o'clock on Boxing Day morning. We had four runners at Kempton and three at Wincanton. Andy Fox would have a busy day at home with so many members of staff away at the races. It was a cold morning, and there had been an overnight frost; indeed, the temperature didn't rise much all day. When Terry walked the course at Kempton at around 11.30 he found that the ground was still bony with patches of frost in places. Fortunately, there was a slight change in the weather before racing, and when the first race went off at 12.40 the ground was described as good.

Our day began well, and there was plenty to keep us occupied, which helped to calm my nerves. Tony McCoy rode an inspired race on my sister's horse, Maximize, to win the Grade 1 Feltham Novices' Chase. His style of riding suited the horse extremely well and he jumped superbly to prevail by two and a half lengths from François Doumen's Innox. It was a thrilling race, and as I was standing with my sister, Ce, I felt compelled to watch the whole thing on television in order to help keep her in the picture. She was overjoyed, but had we used up our luck too soon?

Matey's race was run 80 minutes after Maximize's, and the tension was rising. We had two horses in the King George, the second being that evergreen old warrior Go Ballistic, who the previous spring had run so well to finish second to Marlborough in the Attheraces Chase at Sandown, when trained by Richard Phillips. He had been a very good horse on his day, but as there had been no rain we feared that the ground at Kempton would be too lively for him, which did indeed prove to be the case.

The racecourse was packed for that Boxing Day meeting. There were thousands of spectators at every turn, and an excellent atmosphere too. I was proud of our two horses as they walked round the paddock. Both Jackie Jenner and Jenny Turner, who led them up, looked like Michelin men in their huge red Pertemps jackets provided by the sponsors. As the runners set out for the parade in front of the stands, I began my lonely walk to the woods behind the stable yard. I reasoned that if I went far enough down a small leafy track I would not have to listen to any commentary.

It seemed like an age waiting on that footpath by the big trees on the left of the course, but I was soon to learn our fate. As I re-entered the racecourse proper, I noticed a host of cameras surrounding the red colours of Florida Pearl as he waited by the entrance to the track for his victory walk to the winners' enclosure. Best Mate had finished second, and had been beaten by three quarters of a length.

It was difficult to determine A.P.'s exact feelings after the race, but he was clearly disappointed not to have won. Terry spoke to him first and recalled that Tony's first words were, 'I should have won. They told me he wouldn't stay. But all this horse does is stay.'

'I told you he'd stay,' Terry replied. 'Forget it. It's gone.'

I have watched that race on many occasions since. Everything had gone according to plan until the last fence on the far side of the course. During the first part of the race Best Mate had been held up, but he was always in touch. He was in fourth or fifth position and had jumped economically, yet when he had made smooth headway four fences from home and was nicely on the bridle, instead of pulling out and giving him daylight, Tony kept him on the inside around the last bend. It was here that he got momentarily boxed in, on Bacchanal's right. He didn't get a clear run through, and Florida Pearl had made for home. The Irish horse jumped superbly and galloped on strongly right to the line. When Best Mate did get an opening he picked up well and pressed the winner from two out, but it was too late. He stayed on, but could find no more. It was his career-best effort and he lost little in defeat, but I'm sure that if the two horses met again on the same course under similar conditions the result would be different.

In his autobiography, A.P wrote: 'I was absolutely gutted when I pulled up because I knew I should have won. Walking back, I said to Mick Fitzgerald: "Next time I would pop him out and make loads of use round here. All he does is gallop." Henrietta, Terry and Jim were excellent in defeat, and I told them: "Look, I'm not saying he's slow, but he's not as quick as you think he is and he stays a lot better than you think as well." I watched the tape over and over again that night and I knew I was right.' Terry doesn't go along with A.P.'s interpretation of the correct tactics since he had anyway expected him to take up the running sooner and would never agree with the idea of 'popping him out and making loads of use of him'. In my opinion, Terry had given the correct advice, but when the jockey afterwards said to him 'they told me he wouldn't stay', it was obvious that Tony McCoy had expected the horse to run differently and had deviated from the original plan.

There was visible disappointment in the Lewis camp in the unsaddling enclosure after the race, but one cannot take it away from Florida Pearl. He looked superb that day, and Adrian Maguire gave him a brilliant ride. I congratulated Willie Mullins and was relieved that Matey had come back in one piece. There would be another day. A.P. made up for losing the big one by scoring again for us in the very next race. This time he rode Perfect Fellow and galvanised him from three fences out to snatch a well-deserved head victory. It was McCoy at his best. And so ended a day of mixed fortunes. I have cast my thoughts back to the 2001 King George VI Chase on many occasions. I have read most of the reports that appeared in the papers, and it seemed that Best Mate was still held in high esteem. Thankfully, he had not lost his fan club. The bookmakers were still keen on him for the 2002 Cheltenham Gold Cup, and this was our next goal.

Jim Culloty spent Christmas at his parents' home in Killarney. On Boxing Day he went out in the car and followed his girlfriend, Susie Samworth, on a local hunt in Co. Kerry. He drove along the narrow lanes to pass the time before stopping off at a pub in the little village of Myvane to watch the Kempton race. Half of those gathered in the pub recognised his face, but many didn't, and he watched intently from a secret hideout. There were eruptions when Florida Pearl won, on account of the Irish connections, but Jim's emotions were mixed. 'I was sorry for the horse, but to be honest, it was better for me that he didn't win. Obviously I thought he should have won, no two ways about it. It was a false-run race, but Florida Pearl got first run on him. A.P. rode the horse like a non-stayer. Watching the race, I thought Best

Mate would win, but Florida Pearl winged the last. Had he not done that, Best Mate might have won. I just watched the race in the pub and left.'

For the first time in his life, Best Mate did not trot up with his usual fluency on the day after that Boxing Day race. The ground had been fast enough for him but there might still have been some frost deep in the ground. He was sound but somewhat scratchy, and it took a while for him to recover from his exertions. The race had taken a lot out of him and he was not himself for a few weeks. Luckily, there was plenty of time for recovery, so we left him alone, and again he spent time in his field. The stiffness gradually dissipated from his shoulders, and around the third week in January his action returned. We now had seven full weeks to get him back on the Gold Cup trail.

CHAPTER FOURTEEN

THE RUN-UP TO
CHELTENHAM 2002

At the end of January, with Best Mate seeming a lot brighter, we began to step up his training programme so that he would reach peak fitness during the second week of March. The run-up to Cheltenham is always a tense time; every day and every piece of work counts, and there can be no hold-ups in the work schedule, no missed gallops or canters. I hadn't previously had a runner in the Gold Cup, so I was breaking fresh ice – three times, in fact, because it looked as if Lord Noelie and Go Ballistic would also be in the line-up at Cheltenham. It was a daunting prospect, but exciting too, exactly what you aim for all your life as a trainer.

There is always so much hype in the weeks leading up to the Cheltenham Festival. Most National Hunt enthusiasts plan their whole year around those three indescribable days. I found I could not get away from the Festival. Every newspaper and magazine was bursting with preview articles, and every time I allowed myself to think about the Gold Cup my heart missed a beat. I thought about those magical days in great depth, and everything else in my life seemed to fade into insignificance. For two whole months, Cheltenham was the only thing that really mattered, even though there were plenty of other horses to train who would not necessarily be Cheltenham-bound in 2002, and we still needed winners. The younger horses who were running in February and early March could well develop into the stars of the future, and their education was equally important. There were some lovely young embryo chasers among them, and it was important to treat all owners alike. I have some brilliant patrons and they are always full of enthusiasm, but if their horses are do not hog limelight they may feel neglected and it is so important that everybody is counted. Success is based on team effort.

It was about this time that I remember reading a particularly good article, written by Charlie Brooks, in the racing pages of the *Daily Telegraph*, which is the paper I tend to delve into each evening before I go to sleep. Charlie is a talented writer, though at times controversial. His early analysis of the Cheltenham Gold Cup was headed IT HAS TO BE BEST MATE AT THIS STAGE. It gave me great encouragement and made my heart beat even faster. At least somebody believed in our horse. I now had further reason to dream, and I read the article over and over again. I even hid the newspaper, for two months, under my bedside table and took a little peep at it every night before turning off my light. Could Matey really win a Cheltenham Gold Cup?

As February neared its end, one member of staff who was praying as hard as anybody that all the horses would remain fit and well for Cheltenham was Drew Miller. He has been my travelling head lad for a number of years and has worked in the yard for almost ten full seasons. He has never missed any of our Cheltenham victories, and the festival is always the highlight of his spring. In the early 1990s he looked after Easthorpe, whom we trained to win fifteen races, including seven in a row. Nobody enjoys a day out at the races more than Drew. He far prefers to travel than to stay at home and work in the yard. On a racecourse he meets plenty of friends and keeps closely in touch with important members of staff from other yards. He constantly informs Terry and me as to what is happening at the races and reports to us if anything is amiss with our horses in the racecourse stables. Having been with us for so long, Drew understands me well. I trust his judgement and he is extremely loyal. We have had some great days together, but he knows that emotions can run high both in triumph and disaster. Racing is full of ups and downs. There are never two days the same.

Drew started off in life as a diesel mechanic, which comes in handy since he is now our chief horsebox driver. He was born and bred in Scotland and his family live in Ayrshire, about twenty minutes away from Ayr racecourse. He has always enjoyed racing and has followed it closely for many years. Before he moved south in the 1980s, he rode in flapping races close to his home, and then worked for Robert Goldie, who trained nearby. When he came down to Oxfordshire, Drew spent fourteen months with Andy Turnell, arriving just one month before Maori Venture won the Grand National in 1987. He used to give me a hand at weekends during our busy point-to-point years, and often helped me to saddle up the runners. His wife, Liz, also rode out for us for a number of years before she started working full time as a legal executive. She is still in charge of our annual Five to Follow competition, and every month she updates the list of points scored. She remains closely connected to the yard.

One of the main responsibilities of a travelling head lad is to ensure that the correct racing equipment goes to the races with each horse. Drew must allocate the travelling boots and rugs together with the shiny leather headcollars and lead ropes to the lads and lasses for their horses to wear when they leave our yard. He also packs up the hampers with the smart paddock clothing and the racing boots, as well as the individual race bridles. Every horse has its own bridle on a race day, and we are adamant that these bridles are fitted correctly to match the horses' heads. It is important that the bits are the right size too: if they are too big they can slide through the horses' mouths, and if they are too small they can pinch the corners and cause considerable discomfort. Drew keeps all the leather supple and clean as well as checking that the reins and buckles are in good repair. If a rein were to break in a race, he might feel responsible had he not checked it over beforehand. Leather can easily snap with excessive use, and when it dries out after constant soaking in wet weather it becomes brittle. Owners' colours are also important, and Drew must ensure that the correct sets are taken to each race meeting. They must be clean and display the correct sponsors' logos. These colours, together with racing girths and saddle pads, are put into special bags. They are handed to the jockeys' valets in the weighing room. It is here, too, that Drew signs the declaration sheets to confirm that the horses have arrived at the races and are definite runners. When it's time for the horses to be saddled up, the travelling head lad checks that they are correctly attired and that everything fits. He accompanies them to the paddock and is available to lend a hand whenever he is needed.

All my owners accept Drew as an integral part of the team. His dry sense of humour helps to keep them calm before a race, but as he is also a mine of information they love to ask him questions. Yet it is not always an easy job, especially when dealing with other members of staff, who often suffer from nervous tension before their horses run, but Drew is competent to handle the different situations and copes extremely well. He also knows how to treat me when my own nerves take hold!

During the last weeks of January and through the month of February we didn't have too many runners, but Lord Noelie and Go Ballistic both ran in the Pillar Chase at Cheltenham on 26 January. The latter ran particularly well to finish third. The ground was fairly testing and did not suit Noelie, but he had been lightly raced and needed the outing. We had no plans for a prep race for Best Mate, despite the constant nagging of the press, who kept asking whether or not he would be seen out again before the Gold Cup. There were times when I became so fed up with the telephone calls that I hinted there was a possibility of giving him a run, but in reality we never considered any other race. I was particularly annoyed by a piece that

Hen holding Katday, Best Mate's mother, at Baroda Stud, June 2003

Best Mate, ridden by Tony Costello, winning his only point-to-point, at Tuam, March 1999. Only later did we discover it was a two-horse race © Healy

Tony Costello, Best Mate, Tom Costello Jnr © Healy

My loose jumping school

Running free: the new Gold Cup champion in the fields at Lockinge, summer 2002

Best Mate winning the Grade 2 Martell Mersey Novice Hurdle at Aintree, April 2000, with Jim Culloty © Healy

Best Mate and Jim Culloty jump the last on the way to winning the Haldon Gold Cup at Exeter, November 2001 © Press Association / John Bachelor

Home and dry: Best Mate clears the last fence ahead of Commanche Court and Marlborough (who finished fourth) on the way to victory, Gold Cup, March 2002

The perfect athlete: Best Mate and Jim Culloty in action during the Peterborough Chase at Huntingdon in November 2002, two months after his injury

*Best Mate returns victorious
after the 2002 Gold Cup
accompanied by Hen, Jackie
Jenner and Lucy Biddlecombe
© Steve Davies*

*A jubilant A.P. McCoy returns to
the winners' enclosure at Kempton,
2002, after winning the King
George VI Chase on Best Mate*

*Before the parade, 2003: Best Mate and Jim Culloty are smiling but
Dave Reddy and Jackie Jenner are preoccupied © Mark Johnston*

Making history: Best Mate jumps the last on the way to becoming the first horse since L'Escargot in 1971 to win back-to-back Gold Cups. Valley Henry is behind

An historic occasion. HM The Queen, having presented the Gold Cup in 2003

The hero returns: Best Mate back at Lockinge with HK after his second Gold Cup

HK with the Queen Mother at Lockinge, as photographed by Terry (2001)

Looking to the future: Elsa, HK and Terry © Gerry Cranham

appeared in the *Pacemaker* magazine in early March entitled MATE CHECKED which insinuated that he should have run in February, and that since he had not had a prep race it was unlikely we would be able to get him fully fit for the Gold Cup. 'Let's sincerely hope,' it said, 'we hear no excuses from Henrietta Knight or any other trainer whose horse appears to blow up on the famous Prestbury Park hill. They're not called prep races for nothing.' I've yet to discover the author of this patronising little gem, but whoever it was obviously has little knowledge of training racehorses. I was unusually aggravated by the sneering tone.

Terry and I attended very few point-to-points in Ireland at the beginning of 2002. We watched Supreme Catch run second at Lisgoold, Co. Cork, on 6 January and were able to buy him as a result of his good showing, but we didn't purchase any other point-to-pointers that spring. Instead, we were extremely busy at home, and I spent most of my spare time studying the form of the other horses likely to run in the Gold Cup. I began to make regular visits to the local bookmaker to place my ante-post bets on the opposition. My superstitions always run high when the tension mounts, and I decided it would be an insurance to back most of the other runners. If Best Mate did not win, at least there might be some money to come back from Ladbrokes. In the end, I laid out £274 in the run-up to the festival. I am not a gambler and hardly ever have bets on horses, but this was no ordinary race. I have never had money on a horse of my own since I started training, and I was certainly not going to back Best Mate.

The training programme for Best Mate went smoothly during those weeks leading up to Cheltenham. It helps that he enjoys his exercise and is therefore a straightforward horse to get fit. Yet, sometimes on the gallops he tends to find the work too easy and switches off more than is necessary. On these occasions, when he does not exert himself, we wonder whether we have given him enough to do, but he is always clean in his wind and recovers so quickly. During February, we were indebted to Mick Channon, who allowed us to use his grass gallops. These are designed on beautiful old downland turf and they are always on the collar, which means that they gently rise uphill all the way. Matey loved those outings and was always taken over to West Ilsley in the horsebox with several other West Lockinge Farm inmates. I know the gallops well, as Dick Hern allowed me to use them when I trained the point-to-point horses. They are as good as any other gallops in the country, but the horses must not be allowed to go too fast in the first two furlongs lest they tire too early and run out of steam at the top. From previous experience, I am able to gauge the exact fitness of my charges on these gallops, provided that the work riders obey their instructions. Mick has always been a good friend of Terry's, and he is a welcome new neighbour. His enthusiasm, sense of humour and tremendous generosity are great qualities. Fortunately, apart from being a highly successful flat-race trainer, he enjoys National Hunt racing as well. During Cheltenham week, he holds parties every day at his home. The whole of West Ilsley would be shouting for Best Mate on Gold Cup day, and Mick would be glued to his television.

As the final weeks approached and the month of March began, my nerves started to fray badly. The day-to-day running of the yard went on as usual, but my temper was short and Terry said I was noticeably on edge. He referred to me as being 'toey', and if people annoyed me they received the sharp end of my tongue. Jim and Valerie Lewis had returned from a holiday in Tenerife and the faxes, our main means of communication, were flying between their home and West Lockinge Farm. No doubt their nerves were in tatters too. We received a number of visits from journalists and photographers as well. There was plenty to read about in the press, and Best Mate got wide coverage. Both Channel 4, led by John Francome, and Central Television, under the guidance of Tim Russon, visited the yard on 5 March to film the horses at work. It was an unusual morning, and I remember it well. A fox had attempted to kill my newborn ducklings at 5.30 a.m. but Terry had spotted him on top of their cage when he'd ventured outside to start his early-morning feeding rounds. He had swiftly returned to the house and grabbed his shotgun. The fox was dealt with at once and the mother duck ceased her panic quacking. Saving my precious ducklings was so important because they had hatched out a week before the festival and I regarded them as a good omen for Cheltenham. We could not let a fox ruin the good luck.

Terry and I always feed at that hour of the morning. It means we can check every horse individually and satisfy ourselves that all is well. We have seven alarm clocks in our bedroom and they start ringing from five o'clock onwards, but it still doesn't get any easier when the time comes to get out of bed and brace oneself for the cold dark dawn. Terry is usually five minutes ahead of me, which is how he saw that fox, but I am never far behind. We work together and discuss what we find, despite the distractions of the noisy cockerels crowing from their perches on the beams in the rafters of the barn.

It was an extremely busy pre-Festival week which also included a Cheltenham Preview Evening on Newbury racecourse organised by the West Berkshire Racing Club. Terry and I were on the panel, which was chaired by Richard Pitman. I would not discuss any of our horses and picked out Like a Butterfly as my banker. On the Friday, it was the Grand Military Meeting at Sandown followed by the traditional cocktail party at the Royal Lodge, hosted by the Queen Mother. The guest list included many of the amateur jockeys who had ridden in the special military races that day and a range of other people with racing links. It was a privilege to be there, and I will never forget my last visit to that house in Windsor Great Park. Although she was exceedingly frail, the Queen Mother spent time talking to Terry and me. She asked, in particular, 'How is Matey?' I never saw her again, but I did speak to her on the telephone on the evening of the Gold Cup. I had been given a message to ring her. She told me that she had watched the race and that Best Mate was wonderful; she added that my mother, Hester, would have been so proud. Queen Elizabeth the Queen Mother was a special lady.

As the final countdown began, we watched the weather forecast avidly. It looked like a reasonable week ahead with the going likely to be on the soft side of good. Terry walked the course at Cheltenham on the Sunday, which he does every year, and always alone. He tests the ground and reports back to me and the owners. He was happy with what he found. At home, the horses all seemed well, though Jim Culloty, who had been riding Best Mate a lot, would need to give him his final school and this he would do on the Tuesday, on the morning of the first day of the festival. I prayed that nothing would go wrong, but it was important to leave no stone unturned. Showjumpers use practice fences before they enter the ring; surely a racehorse should have jumping fresh in its mind before tackling one of the most important steeplechases of the year? Many trainers would consider that schooling two days before the Gold Cup represents too great a risk, but on big occasions I revert to my earlier experiences with the three-day event teams at the Olympics. Why should there be any difference? To my mind, it is all about accurate jumping and fine tuning.

Then it was Monday, 11 March, and the stage was now set. There was little more to be done at home. Best Mate was in brilliant form. We had moved a caravan into his yard and Bob Bullock, one of our lads, watched him after dark. All the usual spotlights would be on at night in the yard and our fingers were crossed. Our number one mascot, Andrew Coonan, the noted Irish solicitor, flew in from Heathrow and we followed another tradition by dining with one of my best owners, Charles Cadogan, at his home in the next-door village of Ardington. We had been there before during Cheltenham week and had enjoyed some successes afterwards, so I was delighted that we had been asked again. Jim McGrath and Reg Griffin from Timeform always stay there for that special week. They are two of my greatest friends and really make me laugh, which is so important when my nerves are at breaking point. Terry always enjoys this dinner as well, since Brian and Rose Jenks are the other regular guests and Terry rode over 90 winners for Brian in the 1960s and 1970s on horses trained by Fred Rimell. These included Normandy, Domacorn, Coral Diver and Fearless Fred. Dorothy Cadogan organised a wonderful dinner. We enjoyed having Andrew in our midst as he never stops talking and provides plenty of amusement. I felt much better afterwards, but I knew we were still facing a tough week.

CHAPTER FIFTEEN

A GOLDEN AFTERNOON

When Terry and I ventured into the stable yard at 5.30 a.m. on Thursday, 14 March, the dawn had not even broken. We were about to begin our regular breakfast feeding rounds, and to check over the 75 racehorses stabled at West Lockinge Farm. For once, I had needed no persuading to leave the warmth of the sheets and blankets and brace myself against the raw chill of the bedroom air (we always sleep with open windows). It had not been a good night; too many thoughts, and too many dreams. I'd even ridden the Gold Cup myself by the time I woke up. Once awake, I lay there with my head on the pillow, waiting for the first alarm clock to pierce the deadly silence. As soon as it rang, just after five a.m., I switched on the light, turned off all the other alarms and sprang out of bed. Terry followed suit. We both knew there was work to be done and that a full programme lay ahead. It would be a testing day, and it would put a premium on nerves. I prayed that luck would be on our side and that the horses would come back safe and sound. It would be better still if we had a winner.

We fed all the horses and there were no problems. Best Mate was alert and hungry. As soon as he heard the feeding trolley at the gate he started his usual banging on his door. He even gave Terry a playful nip on his coat sleeve as he bent down to unfasten the bottom bolt. He polished off his breakfast in twenty minutes and was clearly ready for the big day. His neck was hard and his coat was shining, even under the dim light bulb in his stable. Two doors along, Lord Noelie also looked well. Both horses were at peak fitness. Our team for the day would be completed by our third Gold Cup runner, Go Ballistic, who was thirteen years old and possibly past his best, and Juralan, who had an entry in the Cathcart Challenge Cup Chase.

Bob Bullock, our highly dependable senior lad who had volunteered to stand in as nightwatchman, had survived his night in the caravan with his six collies and a spotlight torch – it was a nerve-racking experience, he said, and not one he wanted to repeat. For most of the night he had strained his eyes on Matey's box and tiptoed round the barns with a dog. Not an enviable task. Bob is far happier training his dogs for agility contests or busying himself in the schooling field, where he replaces the divots or mends the fences when the horses have been jumping. He says, now, that he would never apply for a job with a security company.

The atmosphere in the yard was tense that morning. The staff knew the routine would be different. This was no ordinary day and there would be fewer hands on deck. Debbie Bollard, who manages the day-to-day running of the yard, would have to devise new work sheets. There would be a lot of spare horses to look after. Nine people were due to accompany the four horses to Cheltenham, and Andy Fox, together with his wife Vicky, would pick up our farrier, Mervyn Richings, from his home in Uffington and take him to the races as well. Mervyn is a valued member of our team, a top man who has assisted my family for nearly 40 years. He began working for my mother in the 1960s and clearly remembers shoeing my event ponies and horses during their competition days. He also shod that famous Tim Forster-trained hunter chaser Baulking Green, who spent his summers close to Mervyn's home. He is an excellent farrier and takes a great deal of care, especially with difficult feet. Best Mate is one of Mervyn's favourites, and he jealously guards him, having looked after him from the day he came over from Ireland. He takes spare sets of shoes with him to Cheltenham and is always on call for us if needed. Racehorses can so easily lose or spread a plate at the most unexpected times. There are good racecourse farriers too, but Best Mate is special and we feel happier when we know that Mervyn is around. Tim Morrissey, another hard-working farrier who assists Mervyn at West Lockinge Farm, was also determined not to miss the big day. He set forth independently, with several friends, and a handful of complimentary badges I had given him the previous day.

The horsebox for Cheltenham was due to depart at eight o'clock. We like to use Merrick Francis's boxes for the festival. His transport company, Lambourn Racehorse Transport (LRT), has served us well over the years and his drivers have brought us plenty of luck. They know our staff and are always invited to our yard parties. My own horsebox holds only three horses and there is a shortage of space for extra handlers, but the LRT boxes are huge and can easily accommodate extra racegoers.

At 7.30 a.m., Jackie Jenner began to prepare Best Mate for his big day. He knew something was up. When she tied him to the ring on the wall, he kept moving as she put on his travelling boots and special rugs. He was fidgety and restless, similar to ourselves. Indeed, most of the horses sense they are about to go somewhere different once their routine is disturbed. Some of them sweat up and shake. Their own nerves come to the fore, and they can become extremely worked up. A few horses cannot handle the tension associated with a day at the races and they waste far too much energy in the preliminaries. As a rule, Matey is a cool horse; he is laid back and takes life as it comes. The one exception was that day in the autumn of 2000 when he went to Ascot for the First National Gold Cup Chase and was upset by his companion's behaviour in the horsebox. Today, we prayed that he would stay calm. Gary Poynton was the boxdriver, and as he guided the huge transporter through the gates of our yard on that crisp March morning, I wonder what thoughts were going through his mind. Would he be bringing home a Gold Cup winner that night?

The early departure of the horsebox was carefully planned. It was essential to miss the long queues of traffic and give the horses a stress-free journey. It would be better for them to spend longer in the racecourse stables than to stand on a horsebox in a traffic jam. Every horse had two minders that day, and Drew was the overseer. It was his job to ensure that the horses were never left unguarded at any time, even allowing for the supposed security of the stable yard. The staff would take it in turns to keep watch and see that their charges were relaxed and settled. Jackie Jenner hardly left Best Mate's stable – her nerves were also running high. The atmosphere was electric, and the wait seemed unending.

Back at Lockinge, more good luck cards had arrived in the post and the telephone continued to ring. People were anxious to send their good wishes. My own nerves were close to breaking point and there were times when I could barely think straight. My head felt fit to burst. How many times had Terry said 'Steady down; take a pull'? How I wished I could stay at home and go to sleep for the next six hours. I could then wake up when it was all over and tentatively ask somebody, 'What happened today at Cheltenham? How did Best Mate run?' Yet I knew that I must face up to the day ahead. It would soon be over and we would all know our fate. I wandered around in a daze until it was time to leave, but I was deep in thought and had not yet finished my dream. This was the day I had lived for. It was Cheltenham Gold Cup day, and my lifelong ambition had always been to win this race. I knew that sometimes dreams can come true.

Terry and I were prepared for our departure at ten o'clock. I am notoriously unpunctual, but for once I had allowed myself plenty of time. I could not be late for Cheltenham. I decided to wear a blue suit and a shirt of blue and maroon to match Best Mate's colours. I'd given the suit a trial run because it's unlucky to wear anything new, and fortunately we'd had a winner when I was wearing it. It had already brought me good luck. Terry had unearthed his old trilby hat, which he too had worn on special winning occasions. It is very much the worse for wear and looks as if it has been run over by a train, but Terry loves it. He is becoming as stupidly superstitious as I am. We dispatched Andrew Coonan back to Ireland, via Heathrow, and were almost ready to roll. Poor Andrew, we never allow him to accompany us to the festival on day three because in 1997 he had brought us luck for Karshi in the Stayers' Hurdle by not being with us. He had travelled home on the Thursday that year and his support from across the Irish Sea had been of far greater use. He has still never witnessed any of our festival successes first hand.

We had a good journey to Cheltenham and arrived with ample time to spare. Terry set off to walk the course, for the third time in five days, and I kept myself occupied by wandering around the shops in the tented village. I tried to keep my mind off the big race and avoid meeting people, but it is hard to do when there are so many friends at every corner. Everywhere I went I met somebody I knew, but I kept my head down and managed to buy several souvenirs. Best Mate was a fancied runner for the big race, but fortunately not the favourite. There were eighteen runners, and to me the opposition looked formidable. I had covered most of them with my ante-post bets but they were still to be feared. I could make out a case for the majority, and Looks Like Trouble, who headed the market, was a known Cheltenham specialist. If his setbacks were behind him, he posed a huge threat, having won the Royal & SunAlliance Chase in 1999 and the Gold Cup in 2000.

Most of Terry's family had turned up to support us. He has five children from his previous marriages, but since I have none he calls me the barren mare! Libba and Laura, who both live and work in London, come down to the festival every year. They are great enthusiasts and enjoy their racing. James, Terry's eldest son, has plenty of friends in the Cheltenham area and has farming interests close to Gloucester. He never misses out on the Gold Cup. Robert,

Terry's second son, is himself a jockey, and in 2002, as a promising amateur, had several rides at that meeting. He had started his career from our yard after a spell at the British Racing School in Newmarket, and had been introduced to racing through point-to-pointing on a lovely old chaser called Rectory Garden given to him by Charles Cadogan. He won nine point-to-points on 'Rex' and is currently attached to his godfather Nigel Twiston Davies's yard, where he continues to ride winners in a professional capacity. He has also had several wins on horses from our stables. However, the greatest of all the Biddlecombe supporters is Lucy. She was only thirteen in 2002 but already knew more about racing than any of her brothers and sisters. She studies the form intently and watches as many videos as she can find when she comes to stay with us. She knows our staff and feels closely connected to the yard. She adores Best Mate, too.

As well as Terry's supporters, I, too, had good family back-up that day at Cheltenham. In particular, my sister Ce and brother-in-law Sam Vestey (chairman of the Cheltenham racecourse) were rooting for our runners. They both have horses in our yard. Sam bred and owned Karshi and proudly led him into the winners' enclosure at the festival in 1997. Ce had a Gold Cup runner herself in 1985 when her Drumadowney, trained by Tim Forster, finished fourth. She worries about my horses almost as much as I do, but is tremendously proud of them. She lives for the winter racing and our National Hunt season.

After my wanderings around the shopping area, I found my way to the steps beside the weighing room and it was almost time for the first race. Once racing began the time would go faster. I spoke to Drew several times on the mobile phone and he assured me that all was well in the stable yard. It would be fairly hectic with three horses to saddle for a single race, but we had lined up plenty of helpers. Andy and Drew were due to assist Terry and I together with Bridget Nicholls, whom we had employed for the last eighteen months as our trainee assistant. As a lover of fast cars, she had chauffeured us to a large number of race meetings. She knew Cheltenham well and had previously experienced the thrill of being in the limelight when her ex-husband, Paul Nicholls, had trained a number of big race winners at the festival. Jonathan Hatch (Hatchy) would help Terry get the saddles. He is a good friend and has known Terry for many years. He stays with us several nights each week during the winter as he is an expert work rider and is also responsible for the yard's clipping programme. Indeed, he had reclipped Best Mate just three weeks earlier. He is never fully clipped as he has a very light coat, so the hair is left over his loins for extra warmth. Hatchy had done a good job, and all three horses looked superb as they walked round the pre-parade ring.

There is little more a trainer can do once the saddling is complete, and apart from talking to the owners in the paddock and ensuring that all jockeys are efficiently legged up on to their horses, the responsibility then passes to the riders themselves. Occasionally a trainer is needed at the start to encourage a reluctant horse to join the line-up, but this happens only in rare cases.

As ever, the paddock at Cheltenham was seething with people prior to the Gold Cup. All our horses had numerous representatives. Jim and Valerie Lewis had mustered a huge group of supporters, and it was obvious that Jim was extremely nervous. Neither he nor I felt inclined to do much talking. Executive Racing, which owns Lord Noelie, were also well supported, and Sheila Lockhart, Go Ballistic's owner, had also assembled her friends. You could feel the tension all round, and it could be seen on the anxious faces of the jockeys as they ventured forth from the weighing room. I did not speak to Jim Culloty. I had not spoken to Tony McCoy when he won the Queen Mother Champion Chase on Edredon Bleu, so I decided to give Best Mate's jockey an equally wide berth. After all, it's Terry who gives the advice and decides the tactics. He is the Cheltenham expert and has ridden numerous winners on the course.

All three jockeys – Richard Guest rode Lord Noelie and Carl Llewellyn rode Go Ballistic – were united with their horses and began to sort themselves out into programme order for the parade. Dave Reddy walked beside Matey, on his off side, while Jackie looked anxious as she held on to the leading rein on her side. Lord Noelie, with Matt Jackson at his head, had Claire Hart on his right, while Jenny Turner, Go Ballistic's lass, had the extra assistance of Lucy Adams. Drew followed the three horses down the walkway to the course, and the parade began.

It was at this point that I conveniently found Edgy and we set off for a little press tent behind the paddock which Jonathan Powell had so kindly offered to me as a quiet place to hide, well away from the crowds. I watched the parade from the television in that tent, and took up my position on a white plastic chair. I am not a great supporter of parades before big races. It is important that horses stay relaxed during the preliminaries and conserve their energy, but a parade can produce the opposite effect. Many horses become agitated and react adversely. They often sweat up and behave badly; some even blow their minds completely, which is not surprising considering the noise of the commentators and the vast crowds. It is extremely unnerving for the attendants and jockeys, let alone for the super-fit racehorses, who have been trained to the minute and are ready to run for their lives but the spectators love to watch their favourites walk in front of the stands.

It seemed like an eternity as I sat there waiting for the horses to start. I was not used to watching these big races live and it was a heart-stopping experience. At times I grabbed the arms of the plastic chair; at other times I could not bear to watch at all and turned my head away. Yet I could not turn down the sound, nor turn off Edgy, who was certain that Best Mate would win from some way out.

I did not relax until every fence had been jumped. There were only two mistakes, when Jim 'dropped' Matey's head at the fence at the top of the hill on each circuit, but they were only minor and the horse had adjusted himself accordingly. They were the only noticeable hiccups in an otherwise faultless display of jumping. At the last, he produced one final, immaculate leap and sprinted up the hill to the line to claim the Gold Cup crown by one and three quarter lengths from Commanche Court, with the gallant See More Business eight lengths further back in third. Lord Noelie finished a disappointing tenth, and Go Ballistic pulled up. In 6 minutes 50.2 seconds our champion had turned my dreams into reality. He had silenced his critics and was undoubtedly the best three-mile chaser in the country, yet he was only seven years old. What a horse! What a race!

I leapt to my feet and threw open the door of the tent. I ran out into the open air and squeezed myself under the white railings. I wanted to head for the course and find Terry and the two new heroes. My mobile telephone was vibrating in my pocket and I fumbled to get it out and answer the ring. It was Michael Moore – he was almost speechless. He had watched from his home in Ireland and was nearly lost for words. It was fitting that he was the first person I spoke to. Had we not met Michael some years before we would never have attended the Irish point-to-points nor seen Best Mate. He has brought us plenty of luck over the past seasons and had also helped us to buy Lord Noelie from a point-to-point in Co. Cork. Unhappily for his owners, this was not Noelie's day, but he'd had his glory in the Sun Alliance Chase in 2000.

When I reached Terry he was sobbing with joy, and his daughter Lucy was close by his side. They had watched on a television under the Tote building, close to the course. I flung my arms round Terry, and for a couple of seconds I did not speak, still in a state of semi-disbelief. Had it really happened to us? It seemed a long time ago that the alarm clock had rung that morning, but those last hours had been hell and now this was pure magic. The greeting of the horse and jockey, the walk to the unsaddling enclosure, the endless string of congratulations and cheers are hard to describe. There was a sea of faces around the winners' area and genuine delight abounded. Jim Lewis was on cloud nine as he walked proudly beside his wonder horse; the colour had returned to Jackie's face and she was beaming as she held the reins on Matey's bridle; Jim Culloty, who had given our horse such a perfect ride, was ecstatic. The cameras flashed, television crews made their recordings, and that famous enclosure went wild. Ce grabbed my arm. She, too, was in tears and could not believe that Matey had won. The occasion deeply moved us, and we so wished that Mum could have lived longer and been part of that memorable day.

Several members of the Costello family were also present in the winners' enclosure to welcome the horse they had bought as an undersized yearling in 1995. It was the sixth Gold Cup winner Tom had sold – a fair record by any standards, and justification of his special eye for a chaser. The Princess Royal presented the Gold Cup to Jim Lewis as well as prizes to me, Jim Culloty and Jackie Jenner. Terry and I felt extremely proud as we stood there on the podium amid the endlessly clicking cameras. It was an experience I will never forget. Princess Anne, a talented rider, knows the thrill of an important victory and has successfully ridden in races herself; she also won the European 2 Day Event Championship at Burghley in 1971. I have known her for many years, especially during her eventing days. She is a good judge of a horse, and was taken with Best Mate. It is always a privilege to receive a prize from somebody with knowledge.

The rest of that day resembled a fairy story, except that it was real. When we left the racecourse it was dark; there had been so many interviews and so much to do. Best Mate's fans were over the moon, and we enjoyed talking to many of them as we left the course. The time just flew past. The drive home was memorable too. I had never felt so happy. Telephones rang and rang; I was almost hoarse by the time I reached West Lockinge. It was from the car that I spoke to Queen Elizabeth the Queen Mother, at Clarence House. She was delighted with the Gold Cup result and asked a number of questions. She told me she had watched it from her home.

We finally returned to the farm amid waving welcome banners, balloons and flags. Decorations had been attached to every possible gatepost and fence. Best Mate's stable door was festooned in streamers, and even more balloons hung outside it. There were congratulatory cards everywhere and the lights were shining. The atmosphere was indescribable. The team members at home had excelled themselves. It was a victory for the yard as well as for the horse. There was jubilation everywhere. Best Mate, too, looked happy as he stood there munching his hay. He might have been weary, but he didn't show it. I was once told that good men and good horses never get tired. He was certainly good, but he deserved a rest, and he would get one in the months that followed. People were now recognising him as a true champion and pinning their hopes on him for the future. His fan club would grow, but I was sure that he would take stardom in his stride.

However, there was no time for complacency. That night, Terry and I began planning for the next year.

CHAPTER SIXTEEN

THE PEOPLE'S HORSE

Best Mate's win at Cheltenham in March 2002 marked the dawning of a new era. Racegoers love a rising star, and Best Mate, at the tender age of seven, had put himself into that category. It was certainly a memorable day for Terry and me, as well as for all the team at West Lockinge Farm, but there were many other contributors to that brilliant victory, and in particular Jim Culloty deserves special mention. He had most probably been a nervous wreck in the weeks leading up to the race and was definitely 'on trial' as he rode out from the paddock on to that famous Prestbury Park turf. Yet he rose to the occasion and kept his cool. Victory was the fulfilment of so many dreams.

Jim Culloty has been with us since 1995 and has experienced most of the ups and downs of racing in those seven years. At the beginning of 2002 he was finally given the green light by Jim Lewis to ride his star horse in the one race that really mattered. This gave him so much confidence, and he adored Best Mate. He has always held him in high regard since the first day he sat on him. By skilfully riding Best Mate to lift chasing's most coveted crown he had managed to repay the faith that had been placed in him by Terry and I. He called winning the blue riband of steeplechasing 'the pinnacle', and described his feelings as unreal. 'It was like a dream come true,' he said. 'From childhood every jockey dreams of winning this race.'

Jim Lewis, Best Mate's ebullient and colourful owner, took many weeks to come back down to earth after leading his champion into the winners' enclosure. He has had some great days at the Cheltenham Festival, but Best Mate's win had put the icing on the cake. Jim is a popular owner and the crowds enjoy his enthusiasm. He likes sharing his fortunes with members of the public and he likes Best Mate's supporters to enjoy the glory to the full. Jim maintains that he never believed, for a minute, that Best Mate would win that first Gold Cup. 'He was a bit inexperienced and he had never been that far. We didn't know whether he would get up the hill, but he did everything, didn't he? He jumped and won it, and from then on I was totally in awe of him. Now I think he is a great horse. Only after that Gold Cup did I seriously start to realise what a horse he was. Now I believe that if he stays fit he can win another and that he will stand alongside Desert Orchid and Arkle. Hen and Terry have a daunting responsibility ahead of them.'

It was understandable and typical of the man that after the thrill of the Cheltenham victory he should wish to celebrate that win by generously hosting a stable party, for the home team, at nearby Lains Barn. It was a brilliant evening, and the videos of the Cheltenham race together with abundant champagne and sumptuous food made it one to remember. The atmosphere was excellent, and everybody connected to Best Mate was made most welcome. We never dared to dream that in twelve months' time we would be back there for a repeat celebration.

In the ratings review, published in the *Racing Post* on 19 March, Steve Mason stated that Best Mate's quality performance was the best at a vintage festival. He regarded him as the top chaser in training following his impressive win. It was good to read, but we did not need reminding of Matey's excellence. The fan mail had already begun, and many hundreds of congratulatory cards and letters continued to swell the postman's bag each morning. This lasted for several weeks. He was beginning to be called 'the people's horse' on account of his amazing popularity. He had captured the imagination of the public, and his ardent fans had taken him to their hearts. Racing enthusiasts love a worthy champion, and they appreciate a proper horse. Best Mate was the ideal candidate for their adoration: not only is he an exceptionally talented racehorse, he is also stunningly beautiful. His classic head and floating stride make him easy to single out. He does everything right and loves the attention. He enjoys playing to the crowd and flaunting his good looks. On top of all this, he has the right name. Graham Greene once wrote, 'There is a magical quality in names – to change the name is to change the character.' Nobody would ever want to change Best Mate's name.

Shortly after the Gold Cup win, I asked Jackie Jenner, Best Mate's devoted lass, to describe him in her own words, since she knows him so well and maybe sees him in a different light to other people. 'I often liken Matey to Robbie Williams [the singer],' she began. 'He is talented and good-looking. He is also arrogant, but in a pleasant way. Everything comes easy to him; if he were human all the girls would be after him. He would definitely be a party animal and burn the candle at both ends. I can picture him surrounded by females everywhere he went.' She went on to say that 'he is a natural athlete who would be good at all sports without having to try very hard. He finds his work easy and loves to show off.' Jackie also cares for Edredon Bleu, who has been Best Mate's companion for the last four years, but she finds the two horses decidedly different in character. 'Edredon Bleu is the quiet lad,' she pointed out. 'He would be good at school but shy and sensitive. He would enjoy running, especially on sports say, but would worry about what people thought of him. In his class lessons he would be especially conscientious and frightened about doing anything wrong. Most probably he would be the teacher's pet, but he would have his mischievous days as well and his little games – like the times when he plays about in the paddock and refuses to be caught and tries to prove to Matey that he is not always the model pupil.'

I was deeply touched by all the wonderful letters, cards and faxes after Best Mate's Cheltenham win. I badly wanted to answer them all and acknowledge the kindness of our supporters. In the end, I decided to pack an extra suitcase when we went on holiday in June, and I filled it with fan mail. We took our break in Co. Kerry, and while Terry sat fishing on the river banks in Kenmare, I stayed indoors and answered the letters. I managed to send small individual photographs of Matey at Cheltenham to everybody who had sent their congratulations, the only exceptions being those who had not included their addresses.

We did not spend long away from West Lockinge Farm during the summer of 2002 because we didn't fancy the prospect of leaving our champion. Our lifestyle was beginning to change and we needed to watch over our star. It was important to monitor his condition throughout the quieter months and ensure that he put on weight in the right places for the season ahead. He needed to build up extra muscle, especially over his hindquarters and on his neck. A three-mile chaser requires plenty of strength, and Best Mate was still unfurnished. After all, he was only seven years old, but a most striking specimen. Ed Whitaker from the *Racing Post* came down to West Lockinge Farm at the end of June and photographed Matey cantering across his home paddock. The very next day a superb picture adorned the front page of the paper. Best Mate looked magnificent, and we were so proud of him. By coincidence, Ed had driven down to see us before, in 2000, and had used Edredon Bleu as his subject after his win in the Queen Mother Champion Chase. At the time of that visit Matey had again been turned out in the field with Bleu, and I remember saying, 'By all means photograph Edredon Bleu, but take a look at his companion as well. He's called Best Mate, and one day he too will be very good. Everybody will know his name.'

It was about this time too, in the summer of 2002, that Channel 4 approached me with a view to filming Matey at various stages through the next nine months, in the build-up to the 2003 Cheltenham Gold Cup. I was hesitant at first, thinking that the filming might jeopardise a second win, but eventually I relented and allowed the crew to move in. It was the beginning of an extremely happy association with Channel 4, and the producer, Stephen Burn. The filming crew came to West Lockinge Farm on numerous occasions and were quickly accepted by the staff and everybody connected with the farm. They brought us plenty of luck, and we enjoyed their company. They never got in our way. Their filming produced some wonderful shots and we now have lasting memories on video. The ducks, too, received plenty of publicity, and several people rang up with offers to buy some black Cayugas. However, Terry and I are far too sentimental and we could not bear the thought of letting any of them go. We much prefer to see them at home, either splashing around in the pond or trailing around the yard.

June and July passed by in a flash. In what seemed no time at all, the horses were back in work and we were once more starting to get them fit for the busy season ahead. We do not like to give them too much time lazing in the fields as they lose their muscle tone and it takes longer to rebuild their fitness, and we always allow a minimum of twelve weeks in work before we consider entering any horse for a race. Racehorses are athletes and should not be allowed long holidays during their competitive years. Best Mate looked in fine shape when he restarted his exercise. Terry said that he believed he would improve a stone in the months to follow. I remember being highly sceptical of this remark, but he was not far wrong and we were amazed by his increased stature. He would not race until November, but my owners would see him during the open day in September.

By the beginning of that month all the horses had begun their steady cantering, and soon all hands were on deck to prepare them for our important annual event. It is always a popular day, and we prayed for fine weather to parade the reigning champion in front of the assembled guests. Excitement was mounting, and the proper National Hunt season was not far away. Best Mate had started on another gold trail and I was already starting to worry, especially as the second time round promised to be an even greater test for my nerves.

CHAPTER SEVENTEEN

THE AUTUMN SCARE

The training of racehorses is known to be a precarious occupation, but nothing could have prepared us for the huge fright Best Mate gave us during the month of September 2002. Even now it sends a shudder down my spine whenever I think about it, and I still find it difficult to describe the exact nature of my feelings.

We held our annual owners' open day on Sunday, 15 September. This has become an extremely popular event at West Lockinge Farm, and every year we make sure all the horses in training are paraded in front of the visitors, in the paddock behind the house. The parade is accompanied by my own comments on the tannoy, and there are always plenty of laughs. The staff put in a number of extra hours to help prepare the horses, the stables and the yards; and we ensure that they are made as neat and tidy as possible. Roger Huggins, our handyman and gardener, takes special care to perfect the colourful hanging baskets and flower tubs that adorn the walls and walkways. He does a superb job, and deserves a medal for the time he spends with the watering can and hosepipe. He is a great supporter of our yard and has joined us in the winners' enclosure at Cheltenham in both 2002 and 2003.

We had a perfect open day and the weather was kind. The racehorses looked good and I was proud of them. We had a wonderful bunch on show, but Best Mate stood out, gleaming in the sunlight as he was photographed beneath the autumn leaves that still clung to the trees around the duck pond. He enjoyed his day and the assembled company were delighted to see him. He was on show for all to admire and everybody was happy. On the Monday morning, Matey's picture appeared in the *Racing Post* and his well-being was made public. I had outlined our plans for the coming season and some exciting months lay ahead.

It was the very next day, Tuesday, 17 September, that disaster struck. As usual, Terry and I started our regular breakfast rounds at 5.30 a.m., but on this day the routine was not straightforward. When we reached Best Mate's stable we got an unwelcome shock. It is usually Terry's privilege to take the bucket of food to the horse's manger, and he is familiar with all Matey's feed-time habits, but on that day there was no impatient banging on Best Mate's door. In fact, it was unusually quiet in the middle yard. The silence was only broken by Terry's sudden cry of horror: 'Hen, come here quickly and take a look. Something's wrong with this horse.'

I dropped my feed measure and hurried to the open doorway of Best Mate's box. He was obviously ill at ease. His head had blood on the off side and he'd sustained a number of cuts and grazes. The hair above his right eye was missing and there was considerable swelling in this area. He looked more like a boxer at the end of a tough fight than the horse our owners had seen two days earlier. There were no marks on his legs or on any other parts of his body, but he had hurt his head badly. He stood quietly in the middle of the stable and looked a sorry sight. He didn't go to his manger and showed no interest in his breakfast, which is most unusual for Matey.

We looked round the stable but could see nothing out of the ordinary. Best Mate always has plenty of bedding on top of his rubberised floor, but there had been little disturbance to the arrangement of the shavings. The light was dim so we could not see the walls clearly, but we were convinced that at some time during the night he had rolled and hit his head. We later discovered distinct hoof marks across the brickwork on the back wall.

As dawn broke, Jackie Jenner arrived for work, and with the onset of daylight and the appearance too of Andy Fox, we all took a further look at our number one star. He was led out of his stable and on to the gravel drive. Thankfully he walked with even steps, but he was carrying his tail to the left and looked uncomfortable. Jackie asked him for a few trot strides, and although he was stiff, he was sound. This was a big relief. We had telephoned our veterinary surgeon, Roger Betteridge, and he soon arrived on the scene. He gave him a thorough check and tested all his reflexes. There was bruising on the right side of his head, especially in the region of his sinuses, and a small trickle of blood from his right nostril, but Roger was satisfied that he had not broken any facial bones, though we were sure he was slightly concussed. He was certainly in a daze. His body seemed fine except for a small area of soreness in his right hindquarter. All he needed was rest and some quiet days. A few lead-outs in hand were also prescribed to help his stiffness and restore him to normal. Fortunately, his appetite soon returned, and we gave him plenty of arnica, a wonderful herb well known for its healing properties. It is especially good for bruising.

My main concern then was how to tell Jim Lewis. I rang him at breakfast time. He knows I never ring unless I have something vital to say, so a call from me always puts him on edge, and he dreads bad news. He was most understanding, but clearly shocked. I told him that the next few days would tell us more and that I would keep him in touch through constant bulletins on the fax machine. Terry and I were still extremely worried. In fact, I remember feeling distinctly sick. All sorts of thoughts raced through my mind. What if Matey had suffered more serious injuries than we had initially thought? What if he could not, after all, race that season? There is such a narrow dividing line between success and failure, and an alarming uncertainty in the training of racehorses. We would just have to sit and wait. We would watch for further developments.

Over the next couple of days, Best Mate's condition worsened, yet it was essential to keep his injury quiet. He was the country's biggest hope for more chasing honours and was already ante-post favourite for the 2003 Cheltenham Gold Cup. Fortunately, a number of journalists had seen him at our open day a few days before, when he was in perfect health, so there would be no further reason for them to call me. The last time they had seen Best Mate, he was fine. I always like to be straight with the press, but in this case I saw no reason to alert them until we knew more.

The big worry now was not the state of Matey's head but his strange behaviour. When he was led out of his stable for short walks, he would suddenly try to dart forward with his tail clamped down and his ears back. It was as though he was trying to escape pain. Andy took over the responsibility of leading him but found that it was an alarming experience and he was hard to hold. Roger watched him on several occasions with Terry and I, and the three of us tried to determine the reason for these unnatural movements. It was most disturbing, because in all other respects he was mending well. The cuts were healing and the swelling had gone down from above his eye.

Roger Betteridge is a top-class vet and has treated horses for my family since the beginning of the 1970s. On many occasions he helped my mother with her Shetland ponies, and then with her Connemara stud. He also attended my event horses and point-to-pointers before I began training in 1989. There is nobody better in dealing with emergencies or diagnosing injuries, yet he is notoriously pessimistic and his bedside manner is rather abrupt, which can be upsetting for those who do not know him well. However, his loyalty to my yard is well known, and both Terry and I trust him implicitly and have the highest regard for his judgement. Not only that, but he has followed Best Mate from the day he arrived at West Lockinge Farm so he knows exactly how much he means to us all, and to Jim Lewis. It was essential that he got it right when assessing the current setback.

When we analysed Best Mate's sudden panic attacks, we noticed that it was movement to his right hindquarter that agitated him most.

He would sweat in one particular area on this part of his body and resented pressure. After a great deal of thought, Roger diagnosed the problem as being trochanteric bursitis. The horse was getting twinges from his sciatic nerve, which runs from his hindquarters and down his hind leg. When this nerve was aggravated by movement of the leg, Matey experienced excruciating pain, similar to that which a human encounters with sciatica. This condition in horses is most commonly seen in the USA in the quarter horses used in barrel racing. In these races they are required to do sharp turns around barrels, and this places enormous pressure on their hindquarter regions. The horses often pull muscles and tear the nerves. The only remedy is rest. I faxed Roger's views to Jim Lewis and copied some diagrams of a horse's hind leg from a veterinary book to demonstrate to him the position of the sciatic nerve. The diagnosis made perfect sense, but how long would it take to heal? How long would Best Mate be out of action?

It was fortunate that Best Mate was well forward in his work schedule and was already doing steady canters on David Gandolfo's gallops. He is an easy horse to get fit and a short break would not do him any harm, except that his muscles would be sure to waste away to some degree if he stood in for too long. We had planned his first race as the Haldon Gold Cup at Exeter on 5 November, but it was barely six weeks away. Most people in our yard knew he was on the easy list and had cut his head when rolling, but apart from Roger, Jim Lewis, Andy, Jackie and ourselves no one else knew anything about the severity of his injuries.

Best Mate was a wonderful patient, and after seven days of rest we once again dared to take him out of his stable. We watched with bated breath as Andy led him forward, but the improvement was considerable. He was virtually normal. Nevertheless, Roger was adamant that his return to work should be gradual. He needed exercise, but it had to be carefully controlled. He was very fresh, and it would only be safe to lead him in a confined area. We chose the all-weather arena beside my garden as his daily exercise ground. Andy Fox would be in charge, and it was now that Andy's past experience in leading stallions for hours and hours around the Lockinge estate came in so useful. He is extremely skilful when it comes to handling strong and wilful horses. He is calm and talks to them, but his is also extremely positive.

For two whole weeks Andy Fox led out Best Mate twice daily around our arena; he built up the walking to a total of two hours by the end of this time. Andy himself ended up so fit that he could have tackled a marathon! After this spell of rehabilitation, which also involved some trotting and plenty of changes of rein, we once more introduced our champion to the weight of a rider. Alexia Buckwell, an event rider who knew Matey and had ridden him before during his 'dressage' sessions, was asked to give him some quiet schooling on the flat. Everything went according to plan and Alex did a good job, but she never knew the full extent of his original injury. He was soon back in normal work, and Jackie began cantering him on the all-weather gallop behind the yard.

Channel 4 came to West Lockinge Farm on 8 October to continue the filming they had begun during the summer when Best Mate was at grass. He was in great shape on that pleasant autumn morning and looked good as he trotted and cantered around a big grass paddock on the farm. He had recovered quickly, and we could at last breathe again. He was back on course for his new campaign, but Exeter was still in doubt because of the persistent firm ground and lack of rain. We would have to keep an alternative up our sleeve. We decided upon the Peterborough Chase at Huntingdon on 23 November as our second choice and, as it happened, this was where Best Mate made his seasonal reappearance. In many ways it suited us to give him an extra eighteen days, and he did not let us down. He returned to the fray stronger and better than ever.

Those last weeks of September had been tough, but we never lost faith in Roger Betteridge. Jim Lewis, too, had shown the greatest possible patience and trust. It must have been very hard for him, especially living, as he does, just two hours from our farm. He never interfered with what we did, yet we consulted him on every move. He knew we were doing everything possible to get his horse right so he never applied any pressure. I would like to thank him for his extreme consideration and support. He is a model owner. There were times when Terry and I felt so low that we believed the bottom had dropped out of our world, yet horses are animals – flesh and blood – and there is a huge element of risk and uncertainty when working with them. They are not machines, and nothing can ever be taken for granted. When everything goes right, we should truly rejoice since life in the horse world is finely balanced, and no two days are ever the same. There are frequent ups and downs, but one has to learn to live with these changes of fortune. The good days are usually worth all the anxious hours in between.

CHAPTER EIGHTEEN

THE PETERBOROUGH CHASE

After giving us such an unwelcome scare, Best Mate was now back in top form. Indeed, on 21 October, the BBC cameras, led by Clare Balding, spent a whole morning filming him at Lockinge, and they all agreed that he looked superb. The plan now was definitely to take him to Huntingdon on 23 November for the Peterborough Chase; we decided to bypass Exeter on 5 November due to lack of rain and the quick ground: two miles two furlongs on a fast surface would not be ideal for a comeback race against proven two-milers. The distance at Huntingdon was still short enough, but by running Best Mate over two miles four furlongs, instead of three miles, it would give him a less taxing reintroduction to racing and, hopefully, help to sharpen him up for Kempton on Boxing Day, where we had pencilled him in for another tilt at the King George VI Chase. Kempton is a quick track and right-handed, therefore his preparation via the Peterborough Chase seemed logical.

The Peterborough race has been a lucky race for our horses over the past years. Edredon Bleu won it on four consecutive occasions from 1998 onwards, and as a result his name has been placed on a special board. In many ways it would have been tempting to take him back there for his fifth bite of the cherry, but since both he and Best Mate are owned by Jim Lewis it was up to the owner to decide, and his younger horse got the vote. We sent Edredon Bleu to Exeter instead and he scampered home to win the Haldon Gold Cup, so it cannot be said that we disappointed him by leaving him at home on Peterborough Chase day. He'd already had his taste of autumn glory.

Huntingdon, like Kempton, is a flat right-handed track and the fences are inviting. They are well built but possibly look a little too easy. A few horses take liberties and brush through the tops, but they soon find that they are caught out and end up on the floor. Although we like the course, it has to be said that the chasers do not always back off enough at the obstacles. Of course, this suited Edredon Bleu to a tee, but I hoped that Best Mate would not pick up any bad habits. The fences are so different to the ones at Cheltenham and we did not want him to become flippant. Jim Culloty gave Best Mate a couple of good schools in November to refresh his memory about jumping, and he seemed in explosive form.

We are always well looked after at Huntingdon; it is a friendly course with a lovely atmosphere. Mike Newman, the head groundsman, keeps us well informed as to the state of the going and is most helpful. He is always accurate with his reports and goes out of his way to accommodate owners and trainers. The ground on 23 November was returned as good to soft and soft in places. As it turned out the jockeys reported it was slightly sticky to ride on – not ideal for Best Mate – but perfectly safe.

Our horsebox, driven by Drew Miller, left West Lockinge Farm early on that Saturday morning. The Channel 4 crew arrived at 7.30 and filmed Best Mate's departure. They also watched Jackie as she prepared him in his stable. They followed Matey to the races and filmed him again on his arrival there – it was all part of their 2002/03 package. We had two runners at Huntingdon that day as Supreme Catch had also been declared for the two-mile four-furlong novice chase. It would be a busy afternoon, and I anticipated plenty of tension. I knew it would be nerve-racking as it was Best Mate's reappearance race and everyone expected him to do well. Anxious thoughts kept flashing through my mind. Was he totally normal after his accident in the stable? Would he be able to pick up the threads from where he left off in March? I prayed that he would not let us down and that his fans, who had flocked to the course, would be happy with their favourite. As usual I was biting my nails with anxiety, but I was glad Terry was there to support me. He was, as always, a calming influence. Fortunately, I had seen a huge load of straw on the A14 and this had put me in a good mood.

We turned down all invitations for lunch – I didn't feel like eating – and instead Supreme Catch's race helped to focus my mind in other directions. He put up an excellent display and won his novice chase that day. Was this a good omen? It was certainly a bonus, but the big race was still to come.

There is no pre-parade ring at Huntingdon, and, as Alastair Down wrote in the *Racing Post*, 'there seemed something interminable about the proceedings as the five runners went round and round more times than a carousel horse at a funfair'. Poor Jackie and Dave Reddy seemed to walk round for ever as they paraded Best Mate in front of the hundreds of fans who flanked the dual-purpose paddock. The railings and the grassy bank were packed solid. Best Mate walked so fast that Jackie almost wore out the soles of her shoes on the gravel pathway, but Dave was more fortunate: he chose the inside berth and walked on the grass. He always accompanies Matey on the off side. Our champion seemed delighted to be back on a racecourse, and he stepped out proudly in all the preliminaries, looking magnificent and champing the bit with his impatience. The atmosphere was electric.

The race would be no walkover. Best Mate's four opponents were there to be counted, not least the French challenger, Douze Douze, the one horse who could upset the apple cart. I watched him in the paddock. He is a huge animal, tall – well over seventeen hands – and narrow but not particularly handsome. He has a disappointing walk and is not my type of horse, but his record in France reads impressively. His trainer, Guillaume Macaire, is a shrewd man, and he obviously thought highly of his charge. He was also preparing him for a crack at the King George, and this was his first venture over English fences. Judging by the size of him, he would be able to step over them! Geos was also in the line-up. This attractive ex-French horse, trained by Nicky Henderson, was sure to run well. He had been fourth in the Champion Hurdle, but two and a half miles could suit him better. He has a lot of class. Tresor de Mai and Castle Prince completed the field. I didn't regard them as threats to Best Mate.

As the horses finally left the paddock, my nerves once more took over and I made for the racecourse exit. The horsebox park had been a lucky hiding place for me in 2001 when Edredon Bleu had been victorious, so I hoped it would again serve as a good bolt-hole in 2002. Terry made off into the crowds and I was once more on my own. My heart was beating fast, and with clenched fists and crossed legs I sat down on the wheel hub of an old trailer. I could hear distant mumblings on the loudspeakers but I never watched any part of the race. I was completely alone, and it was amazingly quiet. I timed my re-entry to the racecourse on my wristwatch, and for once I got it right. I returned to the action amid roars from the crowd and an announcement that Best Mate had won. He had apparently sparkled on his reappearance and had toyed with the opposition. Douze Douze had finished second following a series of untidy jumps, but Matey had won comfortably in the best time of the day. It had been a most pleasing comeback run, and his adoring public gave their idol a hero's welcome as he returned to the unsaddling enclosure.

What a relief! It was all over, and Best Mate had come through his race with flying colours. The joy on Jim Lewis's face was immense; he was exceptionally happy. His Mate was back! Jim Culloty was just as delighted. Best Mate had given him a good feeling on ground that was a shade stickier than his ideal. He thought he was even stronger than the year before. There was, however, a small amount of whiteish mucus in his right nostril that I quickly wiped away with my handkerchief. It was a reminder of his autumn accident and the earlier damage to his sinuses. This nasal discharge would continue to be visible throughout the season, at the end of each race, and it may never completely disappear. It certainly does not affect him, but the bones on the side of his face were slightly dented on that horrific September night and his sinuses may never return to their former shape. Now, thankfully, the pressure was off for a few weeks before Best Mate needed to begin his preparation for a second run in the King George.

In the meantime, we had a couple of social functions to attend in London. Firstly, on 9 December, the Horserace Writers' and Photographers' Association held their annual Derby Awards luncheon, and to my utter amazement I was presented with the National Hunt Trainer of the Year award. It was totally unexpected and a great honour – all thanks to Best Mate. Then, on 12 December, Terry and I attended the ROA (Racehorse Owners' Association) dinner as guests of Jim Lewis and were able to witness him receiving the Outstanding Chaser award for 2002 for his brilliant horse as well as the Owner of the Year award for himself. What a double! It was a memorable evening, and a moving one too. Matey had certainly changed all our lives, and he had attracted many followers.

CHAPTER NINETEEN

SECOND TIME LUCKY

It was Friday the 13th, a day in the calendar I always dread. Yet when Jim Culloty came out to join me in the car park at Doncaster racecourse on that miserable grey December evening, I could hardly believe what he was telling me. History was repeating itself: for the second time in the space of twelve months, Jim announced that it was unlikely that he would be able to ride Best Mate in the King George.

We had driven to the races together that day, and Jim had won the novice chase on Over the Storm. He had given the horse an excellent ride. The last race had been a run-of-the-mill National Hunt flat race and he had finished fourth on Beechwood. After the race I had gone straight back to the car and was intent on starting my work list for the following morning. I had not noticed the time, nor had I been worried about Jim's lateness. Jockeys often seem to take an age changing their clothes and gathering up their kit before leaving for home. It never occurred to me that something was wrong.

The light was fading when Jim opened the car door. I did not see his face, but I presume that it was pale. The stewards had called an inquiry after the bumper and Jim had been asked to go in front of the officials for supposedly dropping his hands before the finishing post. Beechwood had lost third place by a short head. As a result of the hearing, Jim had been given a three-day suspension, and one of those days coincided with the Boxing Day meeting at Kempton. Of course, at first, I did not agree with the stewards since I had not noticed Jim doing anything wrong. Beechwood was only a four-year-old and still green; he has always had a tendency to hang. At the time I thought Jim had ridden a lovely race: he had nursed him all the way and had not abused him with the whip when he tired close to the line. Jim knows that I never like my young horses to be knocked about; it is so important that they have good memories from those formative days in their racing careers. Jim was devastated by his suspension and talked about an appeal, but I sensed that this would prove futile. Jockeys have to abide by the rules.

We were all shattered by the news from Doncaster and the prospect of finding another jockey for Best Mate for the second successive year. And it looked as though the partnership of Matey and Jim would definitely have to be changed for Kempton. Every avenue was explored regarding postponement of the penalty, or getting the officials to take a more lenient line, but Andrew Coonan, considered by many as the best solicitor in Ireland, told Jim Culloty that he held little hope of the findings being reversed. Therefore, the appeal was withdrawn. After much consultation with Terry and me, Jim Lewis nominated A.P. McCoy as his chosen substitute jockey, but even that booking was not straight forward as A.P. already had a ride in the race and needed permission from his boss, Martin Pipe, to switch to another horse. Fortunately his owners were understanding, and after 24 hours Dave Roberts, A.P.'s agent, was able to confirm the booking. Tony was the obvious choice for Best Mate as he already knew the horse having ridden him into second place in the King George the previous year. He was sure to want to go one better in 2002 and put the record book straight.

Best Mate had been going extremely well in the build-up to Kempton and he seemed in excellent shape. The media were bullish about his chances and he was the clear favourite, but yet again I dreaded the day. I had not enjoyed seeing the replay of the 2001 race, and my vibes for 2002 were not good. I just hoped that the champion jockey would listen to Terry's advice, but he tends to have his own views when he rides our horses and I could see another reversal. Fortunately, however, I would not have to attend the meeting in person, as I could go with Edredon Bleu to Wetherby. I always see Bleu run, and I tie his tongue strap before each race. It was just the excuse I needed.

Boxing Day was quickly upon us. As in 2001, Terry and I had spent Christmas Day at home and watched over the horses. Jackie was getting used to working over the holiday and happily cantered both Edredon Bleu and Matey on the Eurotrack gallop. Everything looked good and all the horses were on top form. We had runners at four separate meetings on 26 December. Edredon Bleu had originally been going to Wetherby for the Castleford Chase, but there was an inspection at the course after heavy rain so he was re-routed to Wincanton, which suited me better as it's only an hour and a half down the road. Richard Guest, his jockey for the day, was fortunately also able to make the change as well.

The LRT box left for Kempton at 8.15, and we sent four horses and six members of staff. Lord Noelie, with J. P. McNamara, was also a planned runner in the King George. As well as Best Mate and Lord Noelie, Lucky Bay and One Nation were also included in the quartet. For once, Terry remembered his telephone and we were able to keep in close contact throughout the day, but I had a lot on my plate that afternoon and I was already feeling the pressure. I was delighted when Ce rang up at breakfast time and suggested that I be driven to Wincanton by her loyal chauffeur Marrick Dzendrowski; she would accompany him to West Lockinge Farm and lend her support at the races as well.

Edredon Bleu had not been to Wincanton before. Clare Thorner, a loyal member of our team and daughter of the ex-champion jockey Graham, would be in charge and would be assisted by Helena Brend. They set off early to avoid the traffic, and Bleu's race was at two o'clock – twenty minutes earlier than the King George. Everything went according to plan on the Somerset course, and the former two-mile champion relished the extra distance. The Dick Reynolds Chase was run over two miles five furlongs and Edredon Bleu jumped round for fun. It was more like a stroll in the park for him and he made all the running, eventually beating Fadalko by an easy seven lengths in a good time. He had acquired many West Country fans after his scintillating display at Exeter in November, where he'd won the Haldon Gold Cup by a wide margin, so there were plenty of admirers to welcome him back into the winners' enclosure. Though in his eleventh year, his enthusiasm for racing was showing no signs of decline. He is a tough and determined racehorse.

After the excitements of the Wincanton race, I did not know whether or not I would be brave enough to watch the King George live on television. It had been bad enough trying to follow Edredon Bleu's race and keep Terry informed on the mobile. During the race I had hidden behind a hedge close to the stables with my sister at my side, but I'd listened to the commentary and had been able to come up with a few details as the race had unfolded. With one win on the board perhaps I would glance at the Kempton race after all. In the end, I decided to walk to the trainers' car park and listen to the commentary from there. The big screen in front of the lawn was showing the whole race. A couple of times I peeped over the car-park fence and glanced at this screen, but I found it too nerve-racking to watch and could barely distinguish which horse was in front. I did know, however, that it was Best Mate and Marlborough who were together at the last, and they looked horribly close.

I was told afterwards by Jackie Jenner that a whole group of lads and lasses with interests in the King George had gathered to watch the race unfold on a television beside the entrance to the weighing room. She said that the screams for Matey coupled with the shouts for

Marlborough from Nicky Henderson's staff must have been heard as far away as Sunbury itself. 'The atmosphere was unbelievable,' she said when she reflected on her day at Kempton.

Best Mate's win in the King George took a huge weight off my shoulders, and Terry was over the moon when I spoke to him on his telephone. It had been a hard slog, but Matey had shown another side of his character, taking up the running fully five fences from home and having to battle bravely all the way to the line. He does little in front and he was there to be shot at on soft and testing ground, but at the line he had one and a half lengths to spare over the equally gallant Marlborough. He might have pricked his ears at the line, but there was little left in the tank. His expression merely disguised his tiredness; he was most probably listening to the cheers of the crowds who were willing him home.

So A.P. had done it; he'd won the race that until that day had always eluded him. Timmy Murphy had given Marlborough a superb ride, but Tony's genius and strength together with Matey's huge heart had eventually prevailed. Bachanal ended up third a further four lengths back, and the 2001 victor, Florida Pearl, was another twenty lengths away in fourth. Muddy and weary, Best Mate returned to the unsaddling enclosure and there was relief all round amongst his supporters. I spoke to Tony McCoy that evening and he was unusually chatty, full of praise for our horse which he told me had been a delight to ride. He told me that he had been particularly impressed by his courage, and that he would always be there on standby, in the future, if for some reason Jim Culloty was unable to be in the saddle. Tony agreed that he had just ridden a special horse.

Jim Lewis was proud of his superstar and, needless to say, ecstatic after the victory. Although on the surface Jim looks jovial and calm, underneath he endures agonies during the long pre-race build-ups. During that day he had been followed for much of the time by TV cameras. Not only did Channel 4 film him on the grandstand during the running of the King George, capturing some brilliant facial expressions, they also covered many of the runners in the pre-parade ring and followed Jim to the saddling boxes. When the Lewis team arrived there, Terry was putting the saddle on Lord Noelie. Jim proudly strutted up to the box, thinking that Terry would be with Best Mate. 'Hello, Matey,' said Jim, and gave his head a stroke 'The wrong horse,' said Terry. 'Go and have another Guinness. This horse has a star on his head and a white strip; your horse has no white.' Poor Jim, he will not be allowed to live down that case of mistaken identity. Yet it can be put down to the pressure of the moment.

As for Jim Culloty, he once again spent Christmas in Ireland with his parents in Killarney. On Boxing Day he went out hunting with the Kingdom Hounds in an attempt to switch off and take his mind off the day's racing. The meet was at Rathmore on the Cork/Kerry border and Jim enjoyed his day. He negotiated plenty of strange obstacles but could never properly eradicate Matey from his thoughts. He knew the race was at 2.20 and plenty of people enjoyed telling him the result, but he did not see the replay until he returned home that evening. It must have been bittersweet viewing, especially when he was forced to watch Tony McCoy hugging Best Mate in the winners' enclosure and saying that he wanted to marry him. He admits to feeling aggrieved and likens his feelings to that of a man watching someone else pinch his girlfriend. He adores Best Mate and guards him jealousy, but at least he knew that the horse had only been lent to his rival for the day. He was still Jim's ride for the Gold Cup, and that was the ultimate goal.

After the King George, it appeared that Best Mate had suffered no ill effects, and he trotted up well the following morning. His action was fluent and his steps true, which contrasted strongly with the previous year. He was in good form, and he clearly knew that he'd done well. It might have looked a gruelling race, but he had recovered quickly. There were almost eleven full weeks to Cheltenham, but the build-up would not be easy. Matey would start off with a good rest in January, but from the middle of that month the pressure would begin to grow. The country expected so much from the champion now, and the team at West Lockinge Farm could not afford to buckle under the strain. The people's horse would dominate the racing pages of the newspapers right up until Gold Cup day on 13 March. It is an honour to have a horse of Best Mate's calibre in the yard, but it is also a huge responsibility. Terry and I knew it was our duty to produce him at his very best for his supreme test at Cheltenham.

CHAPTER TWENTY

MAKING HISTORY

From the beginning of the year until the Cheltenham Festival in mid-March, every week counted in our schedule to prepare Best Mate for his second run in the Gold Cup. We did not go to Ireland after January as it was too risky to leave the yard, though we did attend one Irish point-to-point in the first month of the year, but more than anything we tried to do everything exactly the same as we had done in 2002. Still, somehow the build-up was different. Of course, no two years are ever alike where horses are concerned, and there is also the unpredictability of the weather, but in 2003 we definitely encountered greater pressures and I found the months decidedly stressful. We knew Matey was popular with the public but I never envisaged so much publicity and attention as that which we received over those vital preparatory weeks. In the past, I have always worked well under pressure and my best results have been produced when the cards were down, but somehow those days were different. It was hard to relax for any length of time.

Despite Best Mate's brilliance in his races prior to 2003, he was not the finished article. He was still immature and open to further improvement. Terry told the press in November 2002 that he had come on a stone since the previous season. I had been cynical about this remark, but I did know that he was a stronger horse going into the run-up to the second Gold Cup than he had been a year before. Yet there were huge mountains to climb. We mus prepare him for March in the best way possible. No stone could be left unturned, yet this preparation must not involve any extra stress for the horse. It was of vital importance to retain his enthusiasm and nuture his high spirits. He must not be over-trained. There is always a danger of doing too much and a horse going over the top.

In those difficult and trying weeks during which I worried more than usual, I am well aware that I must have been hard to work with. For a lot of the time I was decidedly on edge, and I was easily irritated by people who did not do things my way. As Terry put it, I was more determined than ever to get everything right. I am particularly grateful for the support I received from my loyal staff, and especially from my long-suffering secretary, Christine Douglas-Home, and her assistant, Sarah Griffiths. Without them and without Christine's endless patience, the weeks of February and early March would not have passed as smoothly as they did. During that time, the telephones never stopped ringing and we were inundated with visits from journalists and photographers as well as film crews and local radio personnel. Sometimes it is difficult to fit everyone into our busy schedule, but we never turned anyone away. The media interest acted as a catalyst and spurred me on. Best Mate's popularity continued to grow.

Christine is one of my greatest friends. She is utterly indispensable in the office and advises me on numerous important matters. Luckily, she is on my wavelength and understands my fluctuating moods. She never panics and is known by many as 'Mrs Cool'. It was during the 1980s, when I ran a livery yard, that Christine first agreed to help me, and this coincided with our busy point-to-pointing days. She has tolerated me for many years and I am at sea with all the paperwork when she is away. Her loyalty and sense of humour are impossible to define. They are second to none.

Christine was brought up in the world of horseracing. Her father was Willie Stephenson, a much-loved racing character who trained Arctic Prince to win the Derby in 1951 and Oxo to win the Grand National in 1959 (Vincent O'Brien is the only other trainer to have saddled a winner in each of these races). Christine came to this area in the 1970s and was, for a time, secretary to Peter Walwyn at Seven Barrows in Lambourn. It was there that she met her husband, Jamie, who was at that time the trainer's assistant. Nowadays, with their daughter Emily at university, Chris spends long hours in my office while Jamie concentrates on his journalistic skills in their home at the other end of the village. She is extremely popular with the staff and enjoys talking to my owners when they come to see their horses or ring her on the telephone. She copes so well with pressure and keeps all the different issues in the correct perspective. Nobody understands the workings of a busy racing yard better than Christine, and I would find it hard to run my business without her. She is a key figure in the West Lockinge Farm team, and the part she played in the 2003 Cheltenham build-up can never be underestimated.

Best Mate's work programme was relatively straightforward, and the build up to full fitness went according to plan. Terry and I knew him so well, and with the help of Andy Fox, Jackie Jenner and Jim Culloty we gradually covered all the relevant ground on our way to Cheltenham. It helps that Matey is such an intelligent and co-operative horse to train. We took several blood tests to confirm his well-being and Mia White, our physiotherapist, kept a close eye on the correct workings of the muscles along his back. Mike Field, the noted equine dentist, had already attended to his teeth in November. Most of the time we worked him on grass, but in order to reach the special big field on the Downs, known as Butterbushes, he had to cross several stony pathways, and closer to the race I became paranoid and kept imagining that he might tread on a stone or flint thus cutting or bruising the soles of his feet. We could not afford for him to have any days on the sidelines with poultices on his hooves. So in the end, we decided it was safer to box him to his main work areas. We made several trips to Mick Channon's beautiful grass gallops in West Ilsley and a couple of visits to David Gandolfo's woodchip track. David kindly allowed us to unbox in his yard and could not have been more helpful.

We have known David Gandolfo for many years; Terry even rode a winner for him, Coral Cluster, at the Cheltenham Festival in 1965. He is one of the great characters in racing and is an excellent neighbour. We have had some good laughs together over the years and have never had any seriously cross words. We value his loyalty. David is a shrewd man and has trained many winners; what's more, he has stood the test of time. In the days when I had a livery yard, he used to send me horses to put round the loose school. He still uses it now to teach his young horses to jump, and his daughters, Sarah and Fred, frequently bring their charges across to Lockinge. David knows how much Best Mate means to us all and takes a keen interest in our training. His gallop has proved invaluable to us; its steep climb helps to increase a horse's fitness and to clear its wind. We could not have trained our winners without it. The Gandolfos have subsequently attended all Best Mate's parties and we regard them as part of the team.

As the days went by, and March approached, I again placed my ante-post bets for the Gold Cup with the local bookmaker, singling out Matey's most dangerous-looking opponents and gradually covering them with twenty-pound notes. Beef Or Salmon, Hussard Collonges, See More Business, Behrajan and Marlborough were all well backed! There was a constant stream of letters and good luck cards, and more statistics appeared in the papers by the day. My nerves continually took a further battering, since most of those statistics were stacked against Best Mate. Despite L'Escargot, Arkle, Cottage Rake, Golden Miller and Easter Hero all winning a Gold Cup more than once, it had been 32 years since the last back-to-back win.

Terry once again walked the course on the Sunday prior to the Festival and was happy with the ground and the fences. Much to the surprise of a number of people, he was photographed standing on top of the fence at the top of the hill. It must have been stiffly built to have held his weight! Although we would go racing on the Tuesday and Wednesday, with runners on both days, I was already sorting out my clothes for the Thursday. I carefully studied the photographs from 2002 and laid out my blue suit on the bed in the spare room. I also unearthed the same shirt and the same hat, and I would wear my lucky pearls. Terry's old hat was removed from a shelf in his cupboard and prepared for its annual day out. It needed a good dusting. Valerie Lewis tells me that Jim is equally superstitious when it comes to clothes, and that he has a special tie for each horse. It is a good job that the horses are not as cranky as their owners.

Andrew Coonan arrived from Ireland on the Monday afternoon, and we were delighted to welcome him back. We again dined with the Cadogans on the Monday night, where we found the same guests staying. It was a good tonic to see Rose and Brian Jenks together with Reg Griffin and Jim McGrath, and it was an excellent evening with plenty of laughs. So far so good – everything was going the same way it had gone in 2002. I hoped it would continue in the same vein. Best Mate was in tremendous form and we had enlisted a security firm to guard him round the clock. The nightwatchmen did us proud. Everything was in order, and he had his customary final school with Jim Culloty on the Tuesday morning. He jumped impeccably.

We had no winners on the first two days of the festival, but several of the horses ran well: Impek was second in the Arkle Chase, and Maximize was fourth in the National Hunt Handicap Chase. Thursday was quickly upon us. The day of reckoning had arrived.

Our morning routine on Gold Cup day was much the same as in 2002, except that the faithful cameramen from Channel 4 turned up at seven o'clock and once more filmed our big hope as he left the yard and walked up the ramp into the horsebox. We again used Merrick Francis's transport, but this time Dougie Ball was at the wheel. Chives accompanied Matey to the course as he too was running in the big race. The two horses were attended by six members of staff. Jackie Jenner once more had Dave Reddy to assist her, while Laura Nichol, who cares for Chives, chose Katie Clark as her escort for the parade. Tory Tremlett and Drew Miller completed the numbers. Tory is a most competent member of our team, and in the months to come she will accompany us to the races more often. Terry and I left home at ten a.m. in our car which had been given a special polish by Malcolm Lumb. Andrew Coonan was once again sent packing to Ireland, though he desperately wanted to stay.

There was little left of my nails by the time we arrived at the racecourse, and the thought of lunching with the Tote filled me with horror. Apparently it is always the Tote's custom to invite the winning trainer from the previous year's Gold Cup to their annual luncheon. They are the official sponsors of the big race, and we knew they would be pleased if we accepted their invitation. As it happened, it was a most enjoyable lunch and helped to steady me down. I did not have to face up to meeting so many people in the crowds outside, but the time still dragged. Would the ordeal ever be over?

When the moment came to prepare our two runners for the feature race, I waited patiently at the edge of a stable for Terry to appear with the saddles. I distinctly remember that my legs felt like jelly and that my knees were knocking together with nerves. At one moment it was almost as though I was frozen to the spot with fright, like a rabbit at the sight of a weasel. There were so many people staring at Best Mate and his connections that I wanted the ground to swallow me up. We saddled Chives first, and both horses were beautifully behaved. The atmosphere was electric.

It was much the same in the paddock, where the crowds were packed in like sardines in a tin. It was a sea of faces, but I knew where to find Jim Lewis and Trevor Hemmings, my two owners, as we always stand in the same place close to the weighing-room steps. Our patch of grass has brought us luck in the past, maybe it would be lucky again. I didn't speak to many people, and fortunately there was little time before the bell rang and the jockeys met up with their horses. Jim Lewis looked worried and must have suffered agonies during the long build-up. The public expected so much from Best Mate. I didn't speak to Jim Culloty at all, but instead talked to Richard Guest concerning his riding plans for Chives. I thought I knew how he was going to ride him, but as the race unfolded I wondered if I had heard him correctly. It had not been the plan to take up the running at the top of the hill, and I still believe that if his energy had been conserved for a little longer he would have lasted home up the run-in and filled one of the placings. He is a very good horse.

When the jockeys were mounted and the horses began to make their final rounds of the paddock, I once again latched on to Edgy and made my way to the press tent behind the weighing room, from where I had watched the 2002 Gold Cup. Terry was slower to leave the crowded parade ring and had walked beside Best Mate in order to recheck the girths and continue talking to Jim Culloty. He wanted to give Jim plenty of confidence and help relax him at this notoriously tense time. Yet, once the horses reached the pathway to the course, there was little more anybody could do.

I reached the tent and watched the parade from a white plastic chair close to the canvas on the right-hand side. I had done this the previous year, and I hoped it was the same chair. Matey looked magnificent. He walked, as he always does, proudly and positively. His manners were impeccable, and his two minders, Jackie and Dave, were not let down. Chives, too, showed himself off well. He is a polite, sensible horse with an imposing air, and is a pleasure to handle. Both horses moved well to the post, but afterwards the whole field seemed to walk around for an age before a line was formed and the tapes were raised.

By the time the runners started, the press tent had become noticeably crowded. It was no longer the secluded hideaway I remembered from 2002. During the race, it was not the voice of Edgy that rang in my ears; instead, I was conscious of a running commentary from my old friend Mick Easterby. He has always been a great help to me since I began my training career, so I resigned myself to his dulcet tones, even though at times I'd have given anything for complete silence and to have been anywhere else but Cheltenham.

As the race unfolded, I strained to focus my eyes on the two emerald-green breast girths we always use for our horses, and which help us so much to pick out our runners from everybody else's. They are first and foremost worn for safety reasons – lest the saddles slip backwards during a race – but my owners and many members of the public have learnt to appreciate the distinctive green colour.

The first circuit seemed to go smoothly enough. Both Lockinge horses travelled comfortably behind the leaders and jumped well. The commentator seemed happy with Matey's position (as did Mick Easterby), and Chives was also running an excellent race. I could hardly bear to watch the second part of the race and kept covering my face with my hands, occasionally peeping at the television through the gaps in my fingers. The atmosphere was unbelievably tense, and when Chives was pushed into the lead five fences from home, with Best Mate tracking him, I could hardly believe my eyes. The two home-trained horses briefly led the field before the third last, and my heart almost missed a beat. It was a sight I shall never forget. A few strides later, when Best Mate hit the front, the crowd erupted – one could hear it even through the walls of the tent. I cannot imagine what the noise must have been like in the grandstand or on the lawn. Terry says it was sensational, that 'the stands took off just like the horse. There was a huge roar and the crowds went wild.' They continued to scream and shout for the champion all the way to the winning line. As soon as I knew the result, I leapt to my feet and barged my way out into the open to make my now famous run down to the course and into Terry's arms. I couldn't wait to see him and to welcome Best Mate as he returned to the enclosures. What a day! What a horse!

The story of the race is best told by Jim Culloty, who had excelled himself in the saddle. 'If I was confident he would win last year, I was absolutely certain that he would win in 2003,' Jim said. 'I was on a Cheltenham Festival preview panel in Ireland with Michael Hourigan, trainer of Beef Or Salmon, the brilliant Irish chaser, and he was raving about his horse. I said, "I'm very sorry to disappoint you, but Best Mate will not be beaten. It's quite simple." The ground was better for him today. He jumped brilliantly, he travelled brilliantly, and he just loved it. It was as easy a winner as I've ridden, and that's saying something when you're talking about the Gold Cup.

'We went some speed in the race too. I promise you, I rode in the Queen Mother Champion Chase and we definitely went as fast as we did on that day. We were travelling for the whole three miles and two furlongs. The only thing I said all race was when Guesty [Richard

Guest] allowed Valley Henry to come up his inner. He was in front on Chives, our stablemate, and he should have been on the rails as we turned to go down the hill. I shouted at him: "Guesty, yer man's coming up the inner! Keep in!" But he just stayed where he was and let him come up the inside. So I had to come round the two of them.

'But for me, this victory was better, emotionally, than last year. I was able to enjoy every moment of it because I'd done it the year before.'

It had also been an emotional day back at home. Debbie Bollard was in charge of the yard, but she had been left with only a skeleton work force. She is a well-established member of our team and has known me since the point-to-point days. It was Debbie who cared for Matt Murphy when he won his first point-to-point at Tweseldown with Richard Dunwoody in 1981. After a short spell running her own yard, she returned to help me with the racehorses in the early 1990s. Debbie has many unenviable tasks and is known as the yard manager. She is good with the staff, has an excellent sense of humour, and deals with the daily programme. She vividly recalls that Gold Cup morning.

From the moment she arrived in the yard she was conscious of the extreme tension. She said that the staff were unusually quiet, but that they gave a cheer when Terry and I departed down the drive. They tried to keep off the subject of the big race until the morning's work was done, but it wasn't easy. The pressure was getting to them all, and Debbie recalled that on many occasions in the preceding weeks they had tiptoed around the yard as if walking on eggshells, constantly whispering to one another, 'Keep out of Hen's way.' With only a few hours to go before the start of the Gold Cup, they gathered in their respective cottages and sat glued to the television screens. They would not miss a minute of the action. Jo Castle, who looks after my own horse, Red Blazer, and who has supported me for nine seasons, reported that everybody was screaming and shaking. They were even more excited when Best Mate and Chives were upsides, three fences from home.

Evening stables started later that day and everybody was overjoyed. Even Brian Dale, our senior lad, was smiling. Christine, who had hidden under her desk during the closing stages of the race, handed round the champagne, and I'm told that the celebrations in the yard needed to be seen to be believed. It had been a great team effort, and the staff had been so supportive for many months. I will forever treasure my memory of the expressions on their faces when we returned home that evening. They are a close-knit, loyal band and were genuinely delighted. They might have stayed at home, but they still felt part of the action on that very special day and they were determined not to miss out on the party that night in Luke Harvey's pub, the Blowing Stone at Kingston Lisle. By all accounts, the celebrations lasted until the early hours and the atmosphere was euphoric.

CHAPTER
TWENTY ONE

DREAMING AWAY

The following morning, a beautiful basket of flowers was placed on my table in the kitchen. They were predominantly dark red and blue and were accompanied by a little card which read 'From Your Best Mate'. Jim Lewis had sent them, just as he had twelve months before.

There was barely time to reflect on what Best Mate had achieved, or on what we had all achieved. Best Mate had made light of all those pessimistic statisticians and put up a display of real class. What were the emotions this time? A huge relief, for sure, and immense pride in the horse, who had proved himself worthy of the acclaim, as well as in the jockey, Jim Culloty, who has not always been given the recognition his skill deserves. There was relief, too, for Jackie Jenner, his faithful lass, and for all those involved in the particular tension of that special day. There was further relief for Jim and Valerie Lewis, and, above all, for Terry and I, not to mention the growing army of fans who had cheered their champion every step of the way.

'It's an incredible romance, isn't it?' Jim Lewis said. 'I always refer to Henrietta as the Weaver of Dreams, and the romance of the whole story includes Terry, her mother Hester, the horse and so many others. I didn't believe for a minute that we'd win one Gold Cup, but the second was an exhibition. Now some people say, "Oh, don't worry, he'll win four Gold Cups," but you wouldn't think about that in your wildest dreams.

'I've always been totally extrovert about all my horses. I like to express the joy of winning, and all the stuff with Aston Villa colours lends itself to that. The message that comes across is that you can share these moments, you don't have to own the horse. If you like racing and you think Best Mate is a great horse, then go and enjoy it. You can love or hate David Beckham, but you don't have to buy him, do you?'

Jim Lewis had toasted Best Mate at Cheltenham racecourse, with his South African connections, in the tented village where Marcus Jooste, one of his best friends, had taken a box. By the end of the day, he had virtually lost his voice. After the prize giving, the interviews and an audience with the Queen, we had said goodbye to him and Valerie before we finally made our way home. Jim celebrated for most of the night and was quite exhausted, but his faxes were superb and his gratitude immense. From Cheltenham, he'd returned to the Old Bush pub at Callow End, his home village, where the television cameras and 250 people were waiting to greet him. It is hardly surprising that his throat was playing up. A few choruses of the Best Mate anthem, to the tune of 'Amazing Grace', were sung that night. But his greatest thrill was yet to come. On Saturday, he was invited to Aston Villa for the match against Manchester United where he paraded round the ground with the Cheltenham Gold Cup. A huge banner was emblazoned across the balcony at the Holte End of the pitch, where he had stood as a boy. It read BEST MATE IS A VILLA FAN.

At Lockinge, the impromptu Friday-morning party was held on the garden lawn, a unique occasion during which the champagne flowed – for everyone except Terry and I – and many of the local community joined in the celebrations. The media were well represented and there were plenty more photographs of the champion. We would not come down to earth for several days; we were too busy enjoying ourselves on cloud nine.

In the weeks that followed there was another stream of faxes, congratulatory cards, telephone calls and letters. Numerous people called at the yard to get a glimpse of the hero, and I fielded several enquiries from artists and sculptors who wanted to paint and model him. He was asked to parade at horse shows and race meetings as well as to perform a dressage 'pas de deux' at Burghley Horse Trials in September alongside Pippa Funnell and Supreme Rock. Very politely, we refused all invitations. Firstly, Best Mate needed a rest and a stress-free summer; secondly, he still has a job to do as a racehorse. There would be plenty of time to play the celebrity circuit in his retirement. As the mailbag grew by the day, I enlisted Clare Richmond-Watson, who rides out for us every day, to become fan club manager. Together, we sent out over 500 photographs as tokens of gratitude for the wonderful messages. I could not have done it without her.

In April, Matey was given special recognition when he recorded the greatest number of votes in a Channel 4 poll and received the Horse of the Year award on the last day of the National Hunt season. It was a great honour, a source of real pride. In May, Jim Lewis hosted another wonderful party at Lains Barn and, as in 2002, he invited all our staff and everybody else connected with Best Mate. It was an even better celebration than the previous year, and the Lewises stayed the night with my uncle, Larch Loyd, who is such a loyal supporter of ours. I am so pleased that he has been able to witness two Gold Cup victories. He knows a number of my owners and painted a lovely picture of Best Mate and Edredon Bleu resting in their field, which he gave to Terry and me as a Christmas present. I can't hang it at the moment in case it brings bad luck. None of the horses is given wall space until their racing careers are finished.

Once again, we encouraged Best Mate to unwind gradually after the exertions and excitement of the Gold Cup. He deserved a long rest to recharge his batteries before starting out on his third Gold Cup trail, this time for March 2004. My ambition had been to train one Gold Cup winner; now we are aiming to make it three. It seems unreal. Best Mate has changed our lives completely. Jim Culloty expressed it well when he said, 'My life does revolve around Best Mate. I maybe take twenty-five per cent fewer rides because I want to stay in one piece so that I can ride him. I'm just very proud to be associated with him and I hope he goes on to win a third and, dare we say it, even a fourth. People say he can't keep going, but why can't he? Firstly, he only has three races a year, and secondly, who's going to beat him? And he's in the right hands too.'

Jim Lewis no longer talks of owning just a horse but a priceless Ming vase or a Koh-i-noor diamond. He says that if it doesn't break, it might win another Gold Cup. 'I always say I'm living in a dream, but if we don't win and the dream is all over, then it's somebody else's turn and I'll envy those people and the experience they will have. I'm quite prepared for the dream to go on and on and to end one day. If he's fit for the next Gold Cup, it'll be one helluva horse that will beat him because I don't think we've seen the best of Best Mate. I think he saves a bit for himself.' Luckily, at the time of writing, the dream does continue.

In June, Terry and I managed a short holiday on Lake Garda, this time with no letters to write. But our rest did not last long. We were soon planning for Best Mate's open day in September. We also made additions to his stable, and rubberised all the walls in case he rolled and hit his head again. One scare was enough for my nerves. Our faithful builder Stuart Ackrill and his skilled team made the necessary alterations and Terry now says that all Best Mate needs to make his box a bit more cosy is an electric blanket! It's a thought. Terry also believes that Best Mate has improved further during the summer.

In rare moments of peace, there is time to reflect on how far we have come, and on the incredible turns our journey has taken. What if Terry and I had not met and had not gone to the Lismore Point-to-Point that rainy afternoon? Would I have driven straight to Tom Costello when Best Mate was on offer? If Jim Lewis had not read a copy of *The Field* with my portrait on the front, would I ever have met him? Would I ever have been asked to train his horses? There are so many twists and turns to the story. I've quoted it before, but I find those lines from *Julius Caesar* so apt: 'There is a tide in the affairs of men which, taken at the flood, leads on to fortune...' Terry still wonders where our fortune is, but Best Mate's there, out in our yard, already a great champion and still chasing gold.

*orough Chase at **Hu**ntingdon r du Cochet sprints **to** victory*

*Back to form **in** the Ericsson Cha**s**e at Leopardstow**n** in December 20**0**3. Best Mate puts in **an** exhibition rou**n**d of jumping*

CHAPTER TWENTY TWO

BACK TO REALITY

Following Best Mate's second Gold Cup win, the racing experts considered that everything else ahead of us would be easy. The pressure would be off and there would be ample time for Terry and I to enjoy the months leading up to Matey's third crack at the most prestigious steeplechase in jump racing's calendar. Yet their assumption was totally wrong. Although we had broken one hoodoo, by keeping hold of the crown, we were now beginning to eye an even bigger prize. No horse since Arkle had won three Gold Cups and Arkle was incomparable, wasn't he? All through the year the spectre of the great horse loomed over our preparations and though Terry once jokingly dismissed Arkle's rivals as 'slow old boats', I was keen to distance myself from the pressures of such an exalted comparison. I had enough to worry about. My first aim was to get our champion fit and ready for another season.

Certainly, we did have a few weeks in which to savour the magic of March 2003's historic win. Gradually, and it was only gradually,

the importance of that victory sunk in. However, with
and racing there is never time for reflection, let alone co
Nor is there ever time for complete relaxation. As a tra
measured every day by the statistical table which peers
racing pages – the number of winners, prize money and
There is no hiding place. If one is fortunate enough to
pinnacle in a particular sphere, there is only one way to gc
frighteningly easy fall. I am full of admiration for Martin l
has been at the top for nearly twenty years now. He has wor
trainers' titles and yet he is still hungry for success, still r
his enthusiasm and his standards. The uncertainties conne
horses, and indeed with all sporting events, mean that t
constant feeling of living close to the edge of a cliff. I try no
about falling over this edge and not to allow mysel
overwhelmed by a natural pessimism. It is important to
optimistic when striving for even more glory, but, inevitabl
are moments of doubt especially for someone as superstil
myself. Fortunately, I have wonderful family support and pl
encouragement from friends, but there were still times dur
build-up to March 2004 when I felt completely alone.

After an all too brief summer break, the season began
wonderful reminder of the champion's ever increasing popu
Best Mate's Charity Open Day, which was staged at West Loc
Farm on 21 September 2003, was an overwhelming succes
seemed to have become something of an idol in the eyes c
public.

There had been continual planning for the Open Day sinc
end of April. Sandy Thwaites and Becci Berry, of Sporting E
Promotions, put in hours of work and did a great job. Fortunatel
were blessed with fine weather and to our amazement close on 5
people turned up to see the champion. They filled the farmyard
the stable areas almost to capacity. All the horses were on view
the staff spent many hours talking to the enthusiastic visitors. I
Mate's stable and its surroundings were always packed with w
wishers and although all of the horses had been paraded in a specia

*Best Mate tastes defeat in the Peterb
in November 2003 as Ja*

*Safely over
the last fence.
Best Mate
records his first
success on
Irish soil*

Happily cantering in a paddock at West Lockinge following a dressage lesson with Annabel Scrimgeour in the autumn of 2003 © Bill Selwyn

Right: *HK with Edredon Bleu and Best Mate having just caught them in their paddock after some morning exercise in the rain*

Left: *Walking home along a quiet lane beside the fields at West Lockinge Farm. Best Mate and Jackie Jenner are accompanied by Claire Masiak and Stars Out Tonight*

Left: *Terry sits pensively on one of the Cheltenham steeplechase fences following his walk round the course on the Wednesday prior to the 2004 Gold Cup. He is not wearing his lucky old hat as that is reserved for Gold Cup day © Grossick Racing Photography*

Above: *Best Mate, flanked by Dave Reddy, makes his way onto the course for the parade prior to the 2004 Cheltenham Gold Cup © Alan Wright*

Right: *Jim Culloty looks solemn as he and Best Mate examine the first fence prior to the start*

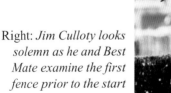

Left: *Best Mate shows his economical jumping style en route to victory © Healy Racing Photos*

Below: *Best Mate jumping alongside Sir Rembrandt (left) and Harbour Pilot in the closing stages of the race © Healy Racing Photos*

Making history – Best Mate forges ahead of Harbour Pilot to win his third Cheltenham Gold Cup. The second horse, Sir Rembrandt, is obscured but was making rapid ground up the stand rails © Healy Racing Photos

Jim Culloty's face says it all as Best Mate proudly stands at the top end of the course and surveys the ecstatic Cheltenham crowds © Alan Wright

Left: *Terry and HK walk excitedly up the side of the course to greet Best Mate and Jim Culloty as they make their way back to the winners' enclosure*
© *Alan Wright*

Below: *Returning to the hallowed unsaddling and winners' enclosure, Best Mate received a hero's welcome*

Below: *Smiles and hugs all round. Jackie Jenner proudly holds Best Mate in front of his adoring fans*
© *Matthew Webb*

Best Mate poses beside a copy of HK's book at
West Lockinge Farm in November 2003

designated paddock during the morning, it was fortunate that we had decided to take out Best Mate again, in the afternoon, for further adoration by his fans. He enjoyed the extra attention and played to his audience. He was extremely fresh and cheeky during the morning but the afternoon outing gave him another opportunity to show off and demonstrate his extreme well-being.

It was certainly an amazing day and the crowds were infectiously enthusiastic. Not only had they turned up to catch a glimpse of Best Mate but many seemed anxious to talk to Terry and myself as well as to Jim Lewis, Jim Culloty and Best Mate's lass, Jackie Jenner. I don't think any of us have ever signed so many autographs in such a short space of time. The visitors had travelled from far and wide but they were not disappointed. There was something for everybody and the many tradestands were well supported whilst a number of children enjoyed the Aintree Simulator and the mechanical Bucking Bronco.

As a result of the successful Open Day it became clear that the next months would not be straightforward. We had a lot to live up to and the public expected even more wins to come from Best Mate but the road to Cheltenham 2004 was unlikely to be smooth all the way. Certainly, we had the third Gold Cup as a major goal but we also had over 70 other horses to train. Most of the up-and-coming youngsters needed education and introductory races. Somewhere in their midst another future champion could be waiting to come through the ranks. When mapping out a programme for Matey it was important not to lose sight of opportunities for the other horses. I was reminded of the saying: 'One swallow does not make a summer'.

The media attention on West Lockinge had been steadily growing but we were determined not to let the increased interest of the press and Best Mate's fans lead us away from the path we had always followed. Terry and I had a job to do – to train our racehorses – and it was all the more important to keep a healthy balance between media demands and the daily workload. It was particularly important that Best Mate's routine should continue in exactly the same way as it had done in previous years and that he, himself, should feel unaffected by the growing attention of the public.

Little did Terry and I know what a difficult season this would prove to be, from Best Mate's defeat in his first race of the year at Huntingdon through to his triumph at Leopardstown and to ultimate glory on that forbidding day at Cheltenham. Many times along the way there were moments when we could have doubted ourselves, but we never doubted the strength of the team at West Lockinge Farm and we never doubted the brilliance of Best Mate in his quest to win Triple Gold.

CHAPTER
TWENTY THREE

DEFEATED BY
THE FRENCHMAN

Although it is now well known that Best Mate's owner – Jim Lewis – does not, due to his superstitions, visit West Lockinge Farm once the season has started in earnest, we decided nevertheless that it was important for him to come over to the stables shortly after the 2003 Open Day. We needed a proper discussion to clarify our plans for Matey's races in the build-up to Cheltenham 2004. Terry and I wanted to discuss our ideas and sometimes there is not enough room on the fax paper for me to write all of them down. My faxes to Jim are often three or four pages long but at the end of September there were a lot of points to debate. Best Mate's programme for the coming months would be all-important and we could not afford wrong moves.

One of the problems is that the opportunities for horses of Gold Cup calibre are extremely limited, particularly in the first half of the season. There are very few suitable races to choose from and we always have to bear in mind that Best Mate needs time between one race and the next. We know that he runs better when he is fresh – a factor which seems applicable to many horses by his sire, Un Desperado. Some horses thrive on racing: the more often they run the fitter and better they seem to be, but Matey puts so much into his races that the edge is usually taken off him for some weeks afterwards. Many a time we have been criticised for not running him enough but what is the point of running him if he is not right? The public want to see Best Mate for sure but they also want to see him at his best, and so do we. So we resisted the calls from various quarters for Best Mate to add another race to his schedule. We were still adamant that, unlike Arkle, he should not be asked to lump huge weights round tough courses in handicap chases.

After putting all our cards on the table, we decided upon two races for Best Mate prior to the March 2004 Gold Cup. Our first choice was the Peterborough Chase at Huntingdon on 22 November since Matey had been successful in this race in 2002. The course and distance were not ideal but there was no attractive alternative. The second race would rest between the King George VI Chase at Kempton on Boxing Day and the Ericsson Chase at Leopardstown on 28 December. A lot would depend upon the weather and the underfoot ground conditions. We knew that our champion had shown his best form on a sound surface but we would not risk ground with any jar. The only possible limited handicaps or conditions chases which could be looked at as alternatives to the Peterborough Chase were the Haldon Gold Cup at Exeter on 4 November – the race which Best Mate had won in 2001 – but it was only 2 miles 2 furlongs and staying was becoming more and more his forte, or the Charlie Hall Chase at Wetherby over 3 miles 1 furlong on 1 November, a tough race which would come quite early on in the season on ground that could easily be too quick. I have never been one for statistics, but I am told that no past Gold Cup winner has ever won the Charlie Hall and the Cheltenham race in the same season.

Once the stage was set for the new campaign Best Mate's training began in earnest. He had summered well and we were happy with his overall condition. Terry thought that he was stronger than he had been in the autumn of 2002 but I did not totally agree with him. Yes, he had a bull-like neck but there were also days when I thought that his hindquarters were not as round as they had been in the previous year. Perhaps this was due to the accident that he had had rolling in his box after the 2002 Open Day. On that occasion he had damaged his sciatic nerve and had shown a degree of muscle wastage afterwards. Admittedly, he had won his second Gold Cup since then but maybe, as he gets older, he needs more flat work and hill climbing to build up his muscles. We do not have a weighing machine in our yard which means that we leave everything to the eye. It could have been that Matey was exactly the same but my own eye had changed!

The autumn of 2003 was an extremely dry one. The grass fields were tinged with yellow and desperately in need of rain. The soil had baked hard during the months of drought. At West Lockinge we were fortunate to have put down a new all-weather gallop during August. This Ecotrack surface proved invaluable and the synthetic materials, comprised of polypropylene fibres, industrial silica sand and a wax coating, produced a beautiful surface upon which to work our horses. The new gallop stretched across the farm for almost a mile with a gradual incline uphill. Terry and I watched the horses work from an old double-decker bus which we had bought off the internet and which had been towed to a strategic viewing spot on the edge of one of the fields. The horses loved the new gallop but they found it easy. Would it be stiff enough to get a horse like Best Mate fully fit for his first outing of the season?

As the weeks passed by, and the dry weather continued, we increased his workload until he barely blew at the end of each gallop on the Ecotrack surface. However, he has always been a clear-winded horse and I still worried about his fitness since we could not use any grass hills and banks due to the unusually firm ground. Even Mick Channon's autumn/winter gallops rode too fast for a steeplechaser and despite Mick's generosity in reopening his hallowed summer ones especially for Best Mate, we still did not dare to stretch him even on the famous downland turf. The gallops did make him blow and were a huge help to us but we longed for rain.

The jumping practice for Best Mate's first run was less of a worry. He had several mornings in the loose jumping school in order to get his eye in and then, when we did school him outdoors, he was ridden over a couple of steeplechase fences at a steady cross-country speed. He jumped accurately and enthusiastically on every occasion.

The days leading up to the Peterborough Chase passed quickly. Best Mate looked superb and his blood tests were spot on. The race appeared to be unfolding as a duel between him and Jair du Cochet – that imposing and talented French chaser who had finished a good second to One Knight in the 2003 Royal & SunAlliance Chase at the Cheltenham Festival. He was a top-class horse on his day and had already had the benefit of a win in an earlier race in October in France. Since that race he had reportedly been training exceptionally well at home on the soft French turf. His trainer, Guillaume Macaire, a burly man with a volatile temperament by reputation and a love of opera, did not apparently expect him to beat Best Mate – according to reports in the press, that is – but he was obviously optimistic. He stated: 'I have huge respect for Best Mate – I've nicknamed him "The Lion".'

Prior to Huntingdon, the racing pages of the newspapers were full of this feature race. Racegoers eagerly awaited the seasonal reappearance of the champion. He would be sure to start a warm favourite. For my part, I foresaw an extremely busy and nerve-racking day ahead of us. Not only would I be saddling Best Mate, but I had also agreed to sign copies of the new book which had been launched four weeks earlier at Cheltenham racecourse but which had only been on sale since the beginning of November. In addition, Sandy Thwaites and Becci Berry had set up a special Best Mate stand in order to sell off surplus merchandise from our Open Day. Best Mate mugs, posters and T-shirts would all be on sale to bring in more money for our chosen charities.

On the morning of the race, Terry and I set off from home in good time. I decided to do the driving as it would concentrate my mind on the road rather than on the race. I had done the same in 2002. The journey went remarkably quickly as we had the accompaniment of a radio commentary on the World Cup final – England versus Australia. I knew nothing about rugby when we set out from Lockinge but it was a nail-biting affair and when we arrived at Huntingdon racecourse everybody seemed emotionally drained by the outcome. I soon realised that Jonny Wilkinson was the new hero. The result of the World Cup may have been good for England but the steady rain was not a happy sight for our eyes. The more I worried, the more it rained. After all those dry weeks and months why should God decide to change the weather on Peterborough Chase day?

We had two runners that day, Inca Trail had been declared for the novice chase as well as Best Mate for the Peterborough. Unfortunately, the main race was scheduled as race six and there were two steeplechases before it, on the same ground. As I sat with Dave Jones in his Classic Racing Books tent signing books and talking to numerous Best Mate fans, I could not help feeling how different everything was to that same day at Huntingdon in November 2002. On that day everything was in our favour: fine weather and good racing ground – just on the soft side. This time, as the rain continued to beat relentlessly on the canvas of the tent, it seemed that the fates had turned against us. My vibes were bad – the ground had been watered and now the heavens were opening, surely the going would soon change to soft or even heavy. I knew that Matey would not be at his best on the churned-up soft ground – he has always preferred a sound surface – but there was never any question of withdrawing him although, in retrospect, I wish we had never run him.

Inca Trail ran in the second race, the novice chase, but was clearly unhappy with the conditions. He made several mistakes and was not himself. Jim Culloty pulled him up before the last fence. This horse is Best Mate's full brother. After the race several people came up to me and asked if Best Mate was still running. I knew he had been beaten by Barton in 2001 in heavy ground at Aintree but surely the ground at Huntingdon could not be as bad as it was on that day. After all, Matey had won the Scilly Isles Chase at Sandown as a novice in 2000 and parts of the course there had been heavy yet he'd coped with the situation. Terry went out onto the track to look at the ground. He was noticeably concerned and reported back that it was very soft and, in places, slippery where the rain had been falling since the early morning. There was plenty of anxiety.

We sheltered from the pouring rain in the saddling boxes after we had prepared Best Mate for the task ahead of him. He had been unusually quiet to saddle; not his customary boisterous self. Terry put it down to the weather and to him being older and wiser but it was nevertheless a little worrying. Then, as we watched him walk round and round that small paddock, which also serves as a pre-parade ring, we noticed that his manner of walking was different to the previous year. In 2002 he had been alert and proud. This time, he was clearly ill at ease in the soggy conditions. He was not tugging at the leading rein or throwing his head up and down in his normal fashion. Rather than appearing to say 'look at me', he walked politely and resignedly beside Jackie Jenner with Dave Reddy flanking him, as usual, on his off side. In contrast, Jair du Cochet looked outstanding. He seemed unfazed by the rain and walked positively. He looked an imposing horse and I said to Drew Miller, our travelling head lad, that he was definitely the one we had to beat. Of the others, Valley Henry and La Landiere looked much the same as they always did. Strong Magic and Venn Ottery made little appeal to me.

The Channel 4 cameras were always to the fore even in the centre of the paddock and Jim Lewis gave his customary interview, but when I talked to him before the race he was extremely edgy and the unpleasant weather had definitely got to him. We were both feeling horribly nervous. To me it seemed like the beginning of a bad dream. I wished that I could wake up and all would be well but unfortunately the dream went from bad to worse.

As is usual at Huntingdon, I took myself to the horsebox area, once the horses had left the paddock, so that I did not have to see any of the action, but Terry positioned himself in front of a television screen behind the stands and apparently watched helplessly as the race unfolded to our disadvantage. After an uncharacteristic mistake at the ditch on the far side of the course and several other indifferent jumps from Best Mate, Terry knew that the writing was on the wall. Matey was not running his usual race, he was unhappy and was not in command. Indeed, right from the beginning he was struggling and his usual jumping fluency was missing. In contrast, Jair du Cochet was relishing the conditions and thoroughly enjoying himself. Despite jumping left at the last two fences he was well in command from a long way out. He deserved to win, he was definitely the best horse on the day.

Thus our champion tasted defeat for the first time in 23 months. It came as a huge shock to his connections and to his fans but there would have to be reasons for this lacklustre display and the uncharacteristic jumping errors. The press went to town, exploring every avenue of explanation and asking every conceivable question about his defeat. Was there a genuine excuse or was Best Mate just not as good as everybody thought? Was he over the hill, under-prepared, injured, unfit or was there a more simple reason for his substandard performance?

Jim Culloty was visibly shaken and disappointed by Matey's run yet he blamed the ground for his defeat and maintained that the horse had given him the same feel when he ran so disappointingly over hurdles in similar ground at Liverpool in 2001. Nor has Jim ever changed this opinion since that day. He is adamant that the underfoot conditions were responsible for the horse's downfall. The ground was officially described as good to soft but this description is so misleading. Officials so often mark down the going as X but the jockeys claim it rides like Y and they are usually right. On that day at Huntingdon, Jim Culloty maintains that the ground was heavy in places and that Best Mate did not trust himself to jump off the looser surface.

Yet, the jockey's explanation was not enough for the racing scribes. All sorts of theories were put forward to explain Best Mate's surprise defeat. As for myself, I was obviously bitterly disappointed and, in retrospect, if conditions came up like that again we would probably not even start our champion since we now know that he does not handle that sort of ground. Yet, in the heat of the moment, I tried to find something positive to say to the press and in order to keep off the topic that hurt I told them that at least I'd had a bet on Jair du Cochet. One reporter, rather mischieviously, took this as indicating that I was a gambler. He suggested that I had laid Best Mate and he even contacted the Jockey Club for their views on my bet! As I have explained earlier in this book, I always place bets on most of the opponents in all of Best Mate's races. I have such a poor strike rate with my bets that by backing a horse it usually means that it will lose. My small investments are entirely through superstition and are used as a form of insurance. I never back the horses which I train myself as I consider that I might jeopardise their chances and bring them bad luck. A number of people laugh at me but we all have our eccentricities.

The weeks that followed the Peterborough Chase were not easy. Best Mate was thoroughly checked over after breaking his winning streak but he appeared fine on all counts. His blood was normal, he kept on eating and he was fresh when turned out in the paddock each day for a buck and a roll. We could not pinpoint anything wrong with him and we still maintain that he went to Huntingdon as a fit horse ready to do his best. With humans, it is sometimes said that in top sporting events, if two out of three factors are wrong, success is still possible but I suppose that in Best Mate's case, in the Peterborough Chase, three out of three factors were against him. Firstly, the ground; secondly, the lack of a previous race that autumn; and thirdly, the distance. It could be argued that two and a half miles is not his ideal trip. Jair du Cochet's performance was certainly good but he relished the ground and had already been given a prep race in France just three weeks earlier. I am not in the habit of making excuses but I like to analyse a race. Suffice to say that perhaps Matey was a little ring rusty and, racing on ground that was not to his liking, he was beaten by the Frenchman fair and square.

Interestingly, despite defeat in the Peterborough Chase and many cruel remarks in the press, the bookmakers still kept Best Mate as favourite for the 2004 Gold Cup. It was therefore all the more important to look forward in a positive manner and ensure that the next step taken towards this goal was the right one. Jim Lewis was typically ebullient and eloquent in defeat: 'There was the feeling like the ice cream had just dropped off the stick. We wanted, almost expected, two victories that day – England to win the World Cup followed by Matey's Peterborough Chase win which would give him five wins in a row. We had joked about doing the Best Mate Anthem to the tune of "Sweet Chariot", to compliment England's victory. I thought about Damon Runyon's book, about Broadway (New York) in times of the prohibition. There is a lovely story about a horse, Governor Hicks, who was an impossible nag. The trainer always believed that the horse could win – especially if it came up mud! I thought to myself Jair du Cochet – especially if it comes up mud. I said to Valerie on the way home: "Every horse has his day and today it was the turn of the Frenchman" – and in the light of his final fate, I'm glad he had his day when he beat the mighty Best Mate.'

CHAPTER
TWENTY FOUR

THE IRISH QUESTION

After the disappointments of Huntingdon and Best Mate's defeat in the Peterborough Chase, we needed a little time for a rethink. We had discovered, for certain, that he was not at his best on soft/heavy ground and we decided that he would not be risked again on that type of going. Of course, if it came up heavy at Cheltenham he would probably have to take his chance as there is only one Gold Cup each year. His next race would be crucial. Another slip-up and everybody's confidence would be shaken. Indeed, even Best Mate could lose heart. On the plus side, a race in December would mean that he should be in top form. We should be able to have him at peak fitness by Christmas and the race in November would have sharpened him up. He may not have enjoyed his Huntingdon experience but he'd have had plenty of time to recharge his batteries and rekindle his enthusiasm. We planned to give him steady work on the grass hills. It had rained at last, and the ground was beginning to improve. There was a lot to look forward to but picking the right race was so important.

The King George VI Chase at Kempton had for a long while been pencilled in as the most probable reappearance race for Best Mate over the Christmas week. He had already won the race in 2002 and been second there in 2001 but despite his highly respectable record on the Sunbury course, I had never felt happy about him running there. To me, he had never shown his best form at Kempton – maybe the course is too quick for him and he needs a hill? It is certainly very different to Cheltenham and I also have a personal belief that he is a better horse going left-handed. Terry disagrees with me and argues that he has won impressively around Exeter and Sandown, both of which are right-handed. Admittedly, Best Mate always jumps straight but I do not think that he is at his best on a course with sharp right-hand bends.

The main concern about Kempton was the ground. It is a free-draining course and rides extremely quick. The going had been on the firm side in the autumn of 2003 and even the heavy rain which fell on Peterborough Chase day was lighter in the London area. It had done little to change the ground. Added to our worries about the lack of rain at Kempton there were also concerns regarding the lack of grass cover. The geese on the lake in the middle of the course tend to cause havoc along the left-hand side of the track mainly in the region of the water jump and the two following fences. They devour the grass wherever it grows and must be a nightmare for the groundsmen, who have our sympathy as I know how much our own farmyard geese can eat! Terry and I expressed our worries to Jim Lewis in early December and it was decided that I would investigate the possibilities of sending Best Mate to Leopardstown, as an alternative to Kempton, if the ground remained unsuitable in England. Of course, there was a strong chance that the going on the Irish course would be too soft so there were worries on both fronts.

During December, we kept close tabs on the underfoot conditions both at Kempton and at Leopardstown. I was beginning to seriously favour Ireland and we had already made one successful raid across the Irish Sea to Co. Tipperary in November when Edredon Bleu had lifted the Clonmel Oil Chase in his customary brave fashion on ground which rode yielding to soft by our standards. In the autumn of 2003, Ireland was not experiencing its usual heavy rain for the time of year and I talked to a number of people over there concerning the likely ground conditions at Leopardstown around Christmas. We kept in close touch with the officials at the course and in particular, Matt O'Dwyer, its manager, gave us plenty of encouragement. Everybody was extremely helpful but our personal Irish guru was Franny Woods – the ex-jockey who had won the Queen Mother Champion Chase at Cheltenham in 1996 on Klairon Davis but who had been forced to retire prematurely from the saddle due to a shoulder injury and damaged nerves incurred in a car crash. He is still close to the racing scene and successfully buys and sells store horses each year. He is a most knowledgeable and reliable person as well as being a good friend. Both Terry and I trust him implicitly. From the beginning of December onwards, Franny made regular visits to Leopardstown and kept walking the course. He would report back to us in England and we rang him on many occasions for an update on the weather and the ground. He knew the course so well from his riding days. We felt that nobody would give us a better assessment of the Irish situation than Franny. His judgement is sound – almost as good as Terry's when he walks the course at Cheltenham.

As the weeks passed by it suddenly dawned upon us that Christmas was only just around the corner and concrete plans would have to be made. On Monday 15 December, Johnno Spence organised Kempton Park's Press Day at West Lockinge Farm. We had hosted the same type of morning in 2001. Both Terry and I knew the majority of the journalists and cameramen. Many had become our friends over the years and we were used to having some good laughs with them. It is important not to make these days too serious but nevertheless those attending wanted facts. Best Mate was the ante-post favourite for the 2003 King George VI Chase but we made no secret of our fears regarding the ground and we explained, right from the start, that he was by no means a certain runner. It would depend upon the weather and our own assessment of the course conditions. We told the assembled guests that we would walk round Kempton on Friday 19 December and inform them of our decision afterwards. We also stated that if Matey was withdrawn Edredon Bleu would take his place. If the ground was too quick for the champion maybe it would be just right for Bleu. They did not seem to take much notice and nobody believed that Edredon Bleu, who had been beaten in the Kempton race in 2000 behind First Gold, would truly stay the three miles, even on fast ground. We had an excellent morning with our guests and joined them afterwards whilst they lunched in the Boar's Head, in the neighbouring village of Ardington. I was presented with a magnificent birthday cake, with lettering on the icing mentioning the King George VI Chase, yet I made it quite clear that we could not be bribed by a cake to run Best Mate in that prestigious race.

Whilst the Kempton deliberations continued, we made parallel plans for Leopardstown. Michael Hinchliffe, whose horsebox had already taken Edredon Bleu to Clonmel, was asked to book the necessary places on the ferries. The Irish race was on the Sunday after Christmas and it would be necessary for Matey to sail from Holyhead on the Friday night. We had also entered Rosslea for the three-mile novice chase. The two horses could travel together to keep each other company. Franny Woods was put in charge of arrangements on the other side of the Irish Sea. Best Mate would not be stabled at the racecourse but at a secret hideout – chosen by Franny – within a reasonable distance of Leopardstown.

According to plan, on Friday 19 December Terry and I drove from Ascot racecourse, where we had had a runner, to Kempton Park in order to walk the course. Equipped with two special sticks we set off on our exploratory mission. The further we walked, the deeper our concern – the ground did not feel right for our champion. There was definitely some jar beneath the surface and no real prospects of any significant rain. We were sure that the course would ride fast and our minds flashed back to the King George of 2001 which was also run on quick ground. For a number of weeks after that race Best Mate had been visibly jarred up. He lost his action and was sore in his shoulder muscles. We returned to the racecourse office and explained to Brian Clifford, the clerk of the course, that we would be unlikely to start our horse but I was still surprised to see the *Racing Post* headlines on Monday 22 December which said: 'Best Mate all set to take King George route as ground fears ease'. We never stated that he was a definite starter and told all the journalists that they would have our final decision on Tuesday 23 December.

After a weekend of lengthy discussions and many faxes passing backwards and forwards between Jim Lewis and myself it was decided to run Best Mate in Ireland. We all knew that we would be treading on new ground and changing our usual routine from previous years but there seemed to be no alternative. We would surprise the British press and we would surprise the Irish, in particular Ted Walsh, who had apparently stated on Irish television that he believed 'Henrietta Knight would never bring Best Mate to Ireland'. It was not an easy decision and we prayed that we had made up our minds correctly. There was no point in waiting any longer and there was no point in dithering – everybody needed to be positive.

Christmas Day was quickly upon us and, as in previous years, both Terry and I anchored ourselves to West Lockinge Farm. We never left the village all day. A number of the horses cantered on Christmas morning including Best Mate, Edredon Bleu and Rosslea, all of whom had been declared for races later in the week. On Boxing Day, Jackie Jenner decided that she would like to lead up Edredon Bleu at Kempton but special arrangements would have to be made to get her back home again by five o'clock as the horsebox was leaving for Ireland, with Matey and Ross, at a quarter to six.

On arriving at Kempton, Terry and I once again ventured out onto the course and made our way past the water jump to the far side of the track. How relieved we were that Best Mate had stayed at home. In places I could feel the jar in the ground through my ankles. We watched the three-mile Feltham Novices' Chase from the edge of the track. The horses, especially the favourite Strong Flow, did not jump particularly well. Had we brought Matey, I doubt whether we'd have allowed him to start but the conditions were fine for the evergreen Bleu.

It was drizzling a little and I wore a long cream-coloured mackintosh which I had never before worn on a racecourse – it was not classified as a 'lucky mac' and I had not singled out special clothes for this Boxing Day meeting as I did not expect to be saddling a winner. There was no pressure on our team. When I go to Cheltenham, I am extremely superstitious and wear the same clothes every year. I was quite relaxed at Kempton and even changed my normal race routine as well. I ventured out onto the course to watch the big race from the stables bend from where I could hear the commentary, and at times, watch the big screen. There were some good horses in the field and Jair du Cochet had once more made the journey over from France. Not surprisingly, he was the favourite. Edredon Bleu's price varied from 33/1 to 25/1. He was one of the outsiders in the field. Terry was sure that he would stay the three miles, even as an eleven-year-old, but I have to admit, I had my doubts. Certainly he had been bouncing at home and had already won his first three races that autumn – the Desert Orchid Chase at Wincanton, the Haldon Gold Cup at Exeter, and the Clonmel Oil Chase in Ireland. He was on the crest of a wave and was as good as ever but he had a lot on his plate at Kempton.

I watched the first circuit intently and was happy to see our little fellow jumping away at the head of affairs but I never believed that he would be able to hold his position once they turned into the straight for the last time. Sure enough, he was headed after the fourteenth fence and it looked as though history was repeating itself. He had run a similar race in 2000 but then, just as I started to accept the inevitable, unbelievably, he rallied to regain the lead. All of a sudden he was back in front and three brilliant jumps put his opponents in trouble. I was leaning on the white railings and pumping them with my arms: 'Go on Bleu, go on Bleu'. On he went, keeping his proud head in front, all the way to the line, to lift the coveted crown. What a star!

Jim Culloty could hardly believe the victory nor could Jackie Jenner. Jim had missed riding Matey at Kempton in the very same race in 2001 and 2002 and had been much looking forward to riding him – the ante-post favourite – in 2003. Yet we'd rerouted his Gold Cup horse to Ireland and left him to do his best on the second string,

Edredon Bleu. He rode a superb race and his partner's jumping was outstanding. He judged the pace so well that he was even able to give Bleu a breather before that final surge up the straight. Jim and Valerie Lewis were ecstatic but the result had stunned them. What an incredible race; even the press were silent. Their open day at West Lockinge Farm on 15 December had not been a waste of time and the journalists had seen their winner after all. Perhaps the birthday cake had done the trick. But there was little time for Jackie to enjoy the Kempton celebrations as only half her job had been done. Our loyal friend, Colin Donald, drove her back to Lockinge and the horsebox that was waiting to take Best Mate to Ireland. That day marked the beginning of an incredible weekend and a Christmas that Terry and I will never forget.

Rachel Geary, who had taken Edredon Bleu to Clonmel in November, drove Michael Hinchliffe's horsebox. Having already worked with Jackie and Dave Reddy on that earlier trip, she knew them well. She is a most reliable driver and a good friend. Tori Tremlett was the other passenger as she was in charge of Rosslea. We kept in constant contact with the horsebox and from all accounts, they had an excellent journey. Both horses travelled perfectly and neither sweated up even when they crossed the Irish Sea. The boat sailed overnight from Holyhead and the valuable cargo arrived on Irish soil at 7am. From then on Franny Woods took over and escorted the vehicle to its secret destination. Not even Terry or I knew where they went. Franny also laid on a special security guard so that Best Mate was never left unattended in his Irish stable. As well, he organised for him to canter in a special field and watched over him whilst he exercised on Irish turf.

On the Saturday, in between the King George and the Ericsson, Terry travelled to Chepstow to support Chives who ran disappointingly in the Welsh National. I went to Kempton to watch Stars Out Tonight. I met Jim and Valerie Lewis there and I drove them to Heathrow where we then met up with Terry and took a flight to Dublin. It had rained hard all day in Wales and my other half was not in the best of humour with the weather when he eventually met up with us at the Aer Lingus check-in desk. He had got very wet on the Welsh course. There had been rain, too, at Kempton on the Saturday and plenty of people had tried to unnerve me by telling me that Leopardstown would be heavy ground, but I kept in touch with Franny Woods and he reassured me that conditions were not too bad. Leopardstown was a four-day meeting and our race was on the third day. I was worried that considerable damage would have been done to the ground on the previous two days but Michael Moore, another of our loyal Irish supporters, told me that he had watched Saturday's racing on the television and that the horses were finishing well. The weather forecast for Sunday was fine, so we could only hope and pray.

At Dublin airport the four of us were met by Franny Woods and driven to our accommodation – Kingswood Country House, on the Naas road. Terry and I always stay there when we attend functions in the Dublin area. In particular, we go there every June for the Fairyhouse Sales and for Punchestown races in April. It is a most friendly place and we get on well with the owners, Sheila O'Byrne and her father, Tommy. They are racing enthusiasts and big supporters. When we arrived they knew all about Best Mate's long-awaited race the following day. The food at Kingswood is outstanding and we had a quiet evening discussing the horses and the racing with Jim and Val but we were all apprehensive. Our plan for the next morning was for Michael Moore to collect Terry and I at 8am and drive us to the racecourse so that we could be there in good time to walk the course. The Lewises would leave a little later with Franny as their chauffeur and guide.

Sunday morning dawned cold and grey. I woke up early. It was hard to sleep with so much on my mind and my head was ready to burst. Michael was punctual and we set off on our journey. There was hardly any traffic on the road but to my amazement it started to snow and we drove through several snowstorms en route to the course. Unless one knows the short cuts, the last couple of miles are quite confusing and the course is not well signposted. Needless to say we made several unsuccessful forays up the wrong roads close to the racecourse but we eventually arrived there and were able to digest the enormity of the day ahead of us. Best Mate and Rosslea had arrived on the course at about the same time and were settling into the racecourse stables, Jackie and Tori reporting both horses to be in good order. They had eaten well and were raring to go.

Shortly after our arrival at Leopardstown we met up with Jim Culloty beside the weighing room, and, together with Michael, set off to walk the course. Surprisingly, this was an enjoyable experience and we were delighted with the underfoot conditions. There was a lot of grass and overall it was good jumping ground with a few soft patches. I fell in love with the place and felt sure that it would suit Best Mate. It is an expansive, left-handed galloping track with well-presented fences. They are big but inviting. An Irish radio station rang me whilst we were walking round and, although somewhat breathless, I told them that I could not be more happy with what I was seeing. Terry was also enthusiastic and together with Jim Culloty discussed race tactics as well as carefully examining the ground.

After completing our course walk, Terry and I stopped off at the racecourse stables to see the horses. It was lucky that we did so since Matey had been allocated a loosebox in the top corner of the yard, which was close to the loudspeakers and gave him too much vision of the course. It was a lovely stable but not in a quiet enough area. He had become very lit up. Jackie was having a job to keep him calm: he had even begun to sweat and was weaving feverishly over the door. Immediate action was necessary and we organised for him to be moved to a different position. He needed to see his friend, Rosslea, and he did not need a view. No doubt the racecourse stable staff thought we were crazy – moving the champion from a big, airy box to a smaller, darker one – but it was so important that we kept him relaxed during the long wait until his race. If he had spent any longer in the first stable he could have used up all his energy before the Ericsson Chase began. We put Rosslea into the box beside him and they talked over their doors. Jackie was relieved that we had turned up in time as she had been worried by Matey's frenzied state. Dave and Tori lost no time in carting the extra bales of shavings to the newly designated area. It was an excellent piece of teamwork.

Relieved that the horses and staff were safely settled into the racecourse stables, we made our way back to the enclosures. We were superbly looked after and a special table had been allocated to us for lunch in the restaurant. We were joined by the Lewises together with Michael, Franny, and Niamh Cashman, who is the daughter of Liam Cashman, the owner of Rathbarry Stud and another good supporter. However, neither Terry nor I felt like eating and we quickly decided that it was preferable to be on ground level around the weighing room and paddock. We needed to be close to the action. Michael was a brilliant support and kept me company as I drank cupful after cupful of cappuccino from the mobile coffee units. It was so cold that despite wearing long boots and socks my feet felt like icebergs and I held the cardboard cups of coffee tightly to keep my hands warm. The wind was bitter but once the racing began it was still preferable to remain outside and watch the horses in the parade ring. There were plenty of people to talk to and the time flew by. It was easy to watch the races from the big screen beside the paddock. We had a lot of Irish supporters. There was certainly a big crowd. The Costello family, from whom we had bought Best Mate, was well represented. On one occasion, as I tottered back to the food stall for my fourth cappuccino, the girl behind the counter recognised me and asked me for my autograph. She had no paper so I duly signed my name on a crumpled white paper napkin.

The novice chase was a good contest with some interesting SunAlliance type horses taking their place in the line-up. Rosslea, a beautiful horse and a real chasing stamp, ran his usual sound race. As in his previous runs, he jumped well and stayed on strongly from the last fence to take second place behind Edward O'Grady's promising young chaser, Pizarro, who won in emphatic style. Hi Cloy was third. Everybody was pleased with Ross and the race had given Jim Culloty a good opportunity to ride round the course to get the feel of it before the Ericsson Chase.

As the feature race loomed, my nerves tightened and my feet went numb. Michael and I watched intently for Best Mate to make his way up from the racecourse stables to the pre-parade ring and I was relieved when he appeared. He looked very bouncy and full of himself. There was plenty of space for the horses to walk around under the trees by the saddling boxes on a special woodchip surface and it did not take long before huge crowds lined up along the adjoining fence to watch the contenders for the big race. Dave Reddy carried the kitbag that contained brushes, sponges, a green racing breast girth and certain items of spare tack. He placed it in a saddling box and we made our way over to the entrance of the stable. Michael and I waited nervously for Terry to appear with the saddle. Jim and Valerie joined us but none of us felt much like talking. The atmosphere was electric and we were all feeling the tension. When Terry reappeared, Dave called to Jackie so that we could saddle Best Mate and prepare him for his task ahead. He was extremely fresh and fractious – like an overexcited schoolchild waiting for sports day to begin, fidgeting and keen to get on with his race. He had been the exact opposite at Huntingdon so we were delighted to see him alert and in such good form.

As Jackie and Dave accompanied Best Mate to the parade ring proper, I felt immensely proud to be associated with such a magnificent-looking horse. He stood out and as he walked round in front of his many supporters who'd gathered to watch him, he seemed to say: 'Look at me, I'm the champ'. On occasions like this he is a real show-off – he would sell himself to anybody. His charisma reminded me of the first day we saw him, on the rain sodden turf, at the Lismore point-to-point in 1999. In contrast, Beef Or Salmon is not a particularly eye-catching horse in the preliminaries. This is partly due to his short, somewhat wispy-looking tail and partly to the carriage of his head. He has a longer, lower outline than Best Mate and sticks his neck out, whereas, Matey carries his head high when he is walked around. Rince Ri is another good-looking horse and looked very well. Le Coudray is huge but looked to be carrying a bit more of a tummy.

Once we were all in the paddock the time seemed to drag and I wanted the ground to swallow me up. There is a large tree and a bank at one end and I sat on this bank for six or seven minutes until Terry told me to 'Brace up and pull myself together'. I returned to the centre of the parade ring and mingled with the assembled crowds but I was relieved to hear the bell ring for the jockeys to mount; and even more relieved to see Jim Culloty on Matey's back. Although he does not show it outwardly, I knew that Terry was just as nervous as I was and afterwards he admitted that he had been even more anxious than before the last Gold Cup. Yet he remained in the paddock and watched the race on the big screen with Alastair Down, Colin Mackenzie, Cornelius Lysaght and Aussie Jim McGrath. In contrast, I made a quick exit from the paddock and went out of the racecourse gates past a gypsy lady and her table of chocolates. I stopped to talk to her and she wished me luck. She pressed some sweets into my hand and I gave her a few euros in exchange before walking out towards the crowded car parks from where the commentary would be muffled and virtually inaudible. By now I was feeling almost sick with worry and the walk did me good. I wandered around several car parks but kept a close eye on my watch. I would not dare walk back towards the course for at least eight minutes. When I plucked up courage to retrace my steps I picked up the commentary from the loudspeaker just as Best Mate was nearing the finishing line. It was a huge relief to hear that he had won but all details of the race would have to wait. There was a roar from the crowd and I ran down to the course to meet the horses as they pulled up and to walk with Best Mate as he made his way back to the winner's enclosure. It was a long walk but a brilliant one and Jim Culloty was ecstatic with his ride. Everybody rushed to greet the winner and we were able to breathe normally once again. This was the Best Mate that we knew so well. He had returned to form. Jim Lewis was quick to be at his head and as Matey was led back to the unsaddling area, the applause echoed through the air. He deserved a hero's reception and the Irish, who love a champion, gave him full honours. They welcomed him with open arms. He had treated everybody to an immaculate performance.

Only then did we have the luxury of thinking about our decision. How fortunate that we'd taken the plunge and allowed Best Mate to cross the Irish Sea and compete on his home soil. After all, he'd been foaled within an hour of Leopardstown racecourse and the Irish could rightly treat him as their own even though he is trained in England. They love class horses and they deserved to see him in their home ground. Maybe Beef Or Salmon wasn't at his best on that December day and, in time, he may turn the tables on our horse, but Ericsson day was Best Mate's day and one that we will never forget. The racing press now had to eat humble pie. Perhaps they would apologise for the unkind words they'd written about the dual Gold Cup winner after the Peterborough Chase. Certainly he had impressed the journalists but they were still cagey regarding the value of the form. The assessments of two experts meant rather more to me than what I read in the papers. Arthur Moore was quoted as saying: 'He was poetry on Sunday and seems to have it all. He is a fluent natural jumper and a beautiful specimen. He doesn't seem to have any flaws.' Tom Taaffe stated: 'I was highly impressed by him. He has a smashing physique and conformation. He oozes sheer class.'

After his scintillating display at Leopardstown Best Mate was ready to make his way home to England. He left the racecourse two hours after his race and the horsebox joined the ferry at Dun Laoghaire that evening. He seemed in excellent shape and had taken his race well. He would now be able to enjoy a few easy weeks before the build-up to Cheltenham 2004. Terry and I were driven back to Dublin airport but Jim and Valerie, who were in less of a rush, stayed on in Ireland for an extra day. It was a good flight home but we still worried about Matey on the boat that night. We prayed that Jim Lewis's 'priceless Ming vase' would have a safe trip but we need not have had any anxiety as both horses travelled home like well behaved children and by 5.15am they were back in their own stables at West Lockinge Farm. That Monday morning everybody was tired but there was a feeling of elation. It had certainly been a Christmas weekend for the record books.

CHAPTER
TWENTY FIVE

PRESSURE RISING

After Best Mate's emphatic win in the Ericsson Chase there was a feeling of great relief on the home side. He had forced the press to retract some of their unkind words and they were now offering different opinions. His price for the Cheltenham Gold Cup shortened further, yet for a couple of weeks the tension was reduced and the pressure was less obvious. I even began to enjoy the early part of January, especially when I looked back at the achievements of our horses over Christmas. The Leopardstown race had restored everybody's faith and it was great to have Matey back home – all in one piece and having notched up plenty of gold stars in Ireland. Sending him across the Irish Sea had been a bit like launching a satellite into space. Fortunately his journey into the unknown was successful and ended up with a safe landing.

Inevitably, however, my days of semi-relaxation did not last for long and thoughts of the Cheltenham Gold Cup were never far away – 18 March was our red-letter day. In many of my dreams aspects of the big race would creep in. I tried to focus on day-to-day happenings at West Lockinge Farm but there were plenty of distractions. Most certainly the other horses in the yard were a tremendous help to me and training them kept me going but the build-up to the Festival was a definite strain. Fortunately, we had more winners than usual in January but the media attention never diminished and there was hardly a day when Best Mate was not mentioned, somewhere, in the racing pages.

It was during January that I began to watch the progress of Matey's Gold Cup rivals. He had been favourite for the race for a long time, but on occasions, his ante-post price was so short that it sent a shiver down my spine whenever I thought about it. Presumably, people had been backing him steadily since March 2003. What a responsibility to be training the horse who carried the expectations of so many. The weight on my shoulders felt heavier by the day but I was still convinced that there were other good horses entered in the Gold Cup. I had enormous respect for them. Why should we beat Jair du Cochet when he'd already put Best Mate firmly in his place at Huntingdon? Admittedly, he had run badly in the King George on Boxing Day but he returned to Cheltenham on 24 January for the Pillar Chase and once again demonstrated his liking for the course by putting up a workmanlike performance and winning comfortably. Therealbandit fell in the same race but was still strongly fancied in ante-post lists. Personally, I was never worried about this horse as I considered him too much of a novice to be pitched in at the deep end in a Gold Cup. He had not clocked up enough miles over steeplechase fences and needed more time to learn to fiddle his fences when meeting them on the wrong stride. A talented horse, yes – but not a Gold Cup horse for 2004.

Sir Rembrandt and Kingscliff are two horses that I like a great deal. The former is a magnificent individual and had shown some very good form in previous races even though he had been uncharacteristically on the floor in the Hennessy at Newbury in November. His second placing in the Welsh National at the end of December stamped him as a worthy contender for the Gold Cup.

Kingscliff's win in the 2003 Foxhunters' Chase at the Festival had been most impressive and he had further confirmed his liking for Cheltenham by winning there, once more, in November 2003. Beef Or Salmon had not been himself in the Ericsson Chase but I always believed that he could revert to his best form if one hundred per cent right in March. His Irish compatriot, Harbour Pilot, was deemed an unlucky loser when parting with his jockey at the second last fence in the Irish Hennessy at Leopardstown in early February. Terry and I had travelled to Ireland to watch that race and had been impressed by him and his way of running. He would most probably have beaten Florida Pearl that day had he not unseated Paul Carberry; and so it went on. By the time I'd finished thinking about them, they were all champions.

In mid-February, there were further worries with which to contend. A number of our younger horses contracted sore throats and needed antibiotic treatment. They seemed off-colour and, although only a few had coughs as well, we were forced to ease off with their work and give them time to recover. I was desperately worried that Best Mate might pick up this bug and become similarly afflicted but fortunately there were no younger horses stabled in his yard as we always try to separate the older horses from their juniors. It is so often the case that the four- and five-year-olds behave like children in nursery schools; they react to all the germs which are doing the rounds and are particularly susceptible to infections. When children or young horses mix with a number of others of the same age they need to build immunities in order to prevent them from being attacked by viruses and bacteria. We find that the older horses are much tougher and usually escape the day-to-day germs. Best Mate only ever went out on exercise with a horse from his own yard and no horses were allowed near his stable bar those housed on either side of him. Edredon Bleu was on his right and Inca Trail on his left. Much to our relief these two remained healthy. We kept buckets of anti-viral solutions in all the yards and made certain that all the horses' bits were dipped into these after exercise but there was still the risk that the wind might carry an infection from one area to another. My mind would have been more at rest if all our horses had been healthy but it was not to be. We took every day as it came and I prayed to the gods!

The weather in February was fairly dry and the month was relatively frost-free. We worked the horses regularly on the grass hills as well as on our new all-weather gallop but we only made one trip to Mick Channon's winter gallop, known as Gilbert's, as we felt that the turf still rode too fast and that our work riders might go quicker than we wanted them to. Best Mate tended to take a strong hold on the Ilsley gallops and it was not easy to work him at a steady pace. He was very competitive on the grass – he has a different attitude when his feet touch the turf but he has never liked woodchip surfaces which is why we avoid them. If the horses work too quickly there is always the risk of incurring unnecessary injuries. Fortunately, Mick agreed with us about the ground and, being the generous friend that he is, unbelievably allowed Best Mate to set foot once more on the summer gallops – which as a rule are not used until April or May. We made several trips to work on this beautiful turf and Sue Huntingdon used her video camera to record Matey's visits. We viewed the tapes afterwards and they are now treasured possessions kept in my Best Mate cupboard. They could prove valuable one day, even though on the first journey Sue was seriously hampered by fog.

Gradually, the weeks moved on in the run-up to the Gold Cup. Despite some scares with the younger horses we were happy with Best Mate's progress and his work schedule. He seemed perky and well. He looked like getting to his peak on target.

His special gallops were punctuated with days of hacking on the Downs, cantering on our all-weather surfaces or quiet flat work in our arena, where Annabel Scrimgeour added the finishing touches and checked that he was using all his muscles correctly. She is a talented dressage rider who regularly rides a number of the horses. It is so important that they carry themselves in balance and with the right outline.

Terry and I had attempted to take our minds off Cheltenham by travelling on Sundays to several point-to-points both in England and

Ireland. On 22 February we attended the Duhallow point-to-point at Kildorrery in Co. Cork, where Cheltenham racecourse had taken a hospitality tent. We did a number of book signings from the back of a trailer, which was most entertaining and enabled us to meet a variety of different supporters and fans. We also saw a number of friends including the Channel 4 racing crew who were busy recording for English television. It was a good day out and even though the word 'Cheltenham' cropped up on many occasions, we had plenty of laughs and were made to feel especially welcome. Unfortunately the horses running that day were a mixed bunch. We did not see a new Best Mate.

In the middle of February, I decided to restart my exercises with my fitness trainer, Lee Hogan. He is well known in this area and has been responsible for keeping Jenny Pitman on her toes over the years as well as a number of other individuals connected to the racing world. I forced myself to have weekly workouts in the late Chris Brasher's gym at Chaddleworth, which is approximately five miles away from Lockinge. On most occasions, Shirley Brasher shared these lessons with me and was a tremendous support over those difficult weeks leading up to the Gold Cup. She is well used to pressure in sport, having been a top-class tennis player, and her husband, Chris, had so much experience in the athletics world. He was always fascinated by training methods and we would often compare racehorses with athletes. He had many interesting theories and I gleaned an enormous amount from him. Both Terry and I miss him a lot. I always enjoy Shirley's company too and she has a wonderful sense of humour. During those weeks leading up to the Gold Cup, her words of wisdom greatly helped to unwind me; I would never have believed that preparing one horse for a particular race could cause me to become so uptight.

The pressure associated with the build-up to Best Mate's race in March 2004 was worse than anything I had experienced in the previous two years. I did not enjoy my own work-outs but I knew they were good for me. I would be a difficult horse to train and not like too much galloping. I would probably need blinkers since I found the exercises more difficult than I had expected and I often felt like shirking the issue. In contrast to myself, Terry kept amazingly calm. If he worried, he did not show it. He has always believed in Best Mate. He kept telling everybody that the horse would win a third Gold Cup. I am told by those who knew him in his days as a jockey that he never got worked up before big races. It is probably one of the reasons for his past record as a jockey – three times National Hunt champion – since temperament plays such an important role, both with humans and horses, when striving for success. Terry's ability to stay cool has always been a great help not only to me but also to Jim Culloty. His faith in the horses we train gives everybody extra confidence.

Following the pattern which they had adopted in 2002 and 2003, Jim and Valerie Lewis wisely went on a two-week holiday towards the end of February. Understandably, they like to get out of the country and away from the pressure as the Cheltenham Festival draws closer. It was during this time that we were inundated by press visits. The telephone seemed red-hot and we had numerous camera crews filming in our yard as well as on the gallops. Much of the material would then be shown live on different television channels during the run-up to the Gold Cup. I was constantly asked: 'How do you cope with all those reporters and television crews? They must drive you mad.' Yet strangely, we got used to their visits and their interest in Best Mate. It would have been far worse if nobody had telephoned; at least we knew that we were wanted and that the country was following our horse. Many of the visitors were most helpful and we felt honoured to have them in our midst. On some of the days, I became almost oblivious to their presence and there were times when we had some good laughs. I had forgiven them for the unkind words which they had written after the Peterborough Chase.

On 3 March 2004, Cheltenham racecourse staged its Press Day at West Lockinge Farm. All our likely Festival runners were paraded in the paddock behind the house. The morning went well and everybody seemed happy. We answered numerous questions whilst feeling proud of the horses and the way in which the staff had turned them out. The Kempton Press Day in December had brought us luck in the King George VI Chase; would Cheltenham's 'day out' help us to win the Gold Cup?

On 10 March there was a pre-Cheltenham evening at Newbury racecourse staged by the West Berkshire Racing Club. Terry and I were on the panel together with Emma Lavelle, Noel Fehily and Rishi Persad, the latter being responsible for introducing the programme and chairing the panel. There was an excellent turnout and plenty of jokes. We enjoyed the outing but our tips were useless and I would not give a selection for the Gold Cup.

The pre-Cheltenham week ended with a Channel 4 invasion. We were asked by Stephen Burn to host "The Morning Line" from West Lockinge Farm on the Sunday morning. This was a new venture on Channel 4's behalf but we agreed to co-operate and the programme went out live at 8am from the drawing room in our farmhouse. The house had been turned upside down during the previous afternoon, in order to set the stage for the filming session. Indeed, it was hardly recognisable – sofas, armchairs, tables, lamps, ornaments and rugs had been moved into new places but the final set looked good with an abundance of tripods and extra lights. John McCririck, John Francome and Lesley Graham moved in during the early hours of Sunday to inspect their new surroundings. Their back-up team had done a good job and they were happy with what they found. The programme went off extremely well. We enjoyed it immensely and so did the dogs who lay obediently at our feet during the filming. Even Best Mate's early- morning canter on the gallops was shown on the programme and we did not antagonise Big Mac as I was able to give him a large cup of tea from a teapot – he detests tea bags!

In the racing days prior to Cheltenham we had been encouraged by the performances of our horses. There had been five winners in nine days and most of these had been in steeplechases. We even had a winner at Stratford on the day before the Festival – Creative Time's victory looked like a good omen for the week ahead. Stable morale was high and Best Mate was in great form. On Thursday 11 March, I had driven home with Jim Culloty from Wincanton where he'd ridden a double for us on Alvino and Zaffamore. He said to me: 'A week today we'll know our fate and one way or another I intend to get drunk either on our victory or to drown my sorrows.' This remark stuck firmly in my mind. I sincerely hoped he would be having plenty of drinks to mark Best Mate's win – anything different and I might have to return to alcohol myself!

CHAPTER
TWENTY SIX

CRESCENDO AND
ANOTHER MAGICAL DAY

From the Sunday of Festival week onwards, I felt totally committed to the task ahead. Gold Cup day would be upon us in a flash and the noose was tightening around my neck. I did not want any distractions. As in previous years, Terry walked the course on that Sunday morning. As soon as the ' The Morning Line' team had left our yard, he set off, equipped with his long walking stick. He returned home drenched to the skin as he'd been unprepared for the steady rain that had fallen during his recce. At that stage, he was reasonably happy with the ground but reported that there was a strip of grass, on the inside of Thursday's track, which had not been used during the winter months. If the weather deteriorated it might be necessary for Best Mate to race on this fresh turf. It would not be ideal for Matey to run his race down the inner, but we might have to adopt plan B if the going became any softer. Jim Culloty would need to walk the course carefully and Terry would take a look at it several more times himself. In 2003 he walked the track three times and his findings paid off handsomely. He was prepared for further mileage in 2004 and fortunately was not suffering from his customary gout so would be able to stride out better than usual.

Whilst Terry had been reconnoitring around Cheltenham racecourse in the rain, I had been keeping dry just down the road, signing copies of my book at various shops. I also made an unusual appearance in a betting office to place a charity bet for the week ahead. Needless to say it lost – I had chosen Baracouda. Before venturing to Cheltenham that Sunday, I had been somewhat dubious about deviating from tradition. I had not ventured over there on any of the previous Sundays prior to any Festival but I realised the importance of promoting my book and took a chance.

Yet my superstitions were rife in the final run-up to the Gold Cup and I watched for omens wherever I went. Best Mate and I had been sent a whole host of good-luck cards; many were accompanied by touching messages. I also received a number of lucky charms that included four-leaved clovers and pieces of white heather. One well-wisher posted me a bottle of lavender oil and I was assured that it would help to calm my nerves if I regularly put some drops into the bath. I also received some lavender essence that I was directed to sprinkle onto my pillow for a good night's sleep. It smelt strongly and Terry was not impressed but I religiously followed all the instructions. Miraculously, as well, I managed to nurture an Amaryllis bulb during the months of February and March and the beautiful yellow flower bloomed during Festival week – indeed it was at its best on the Thursday. This made me extremely happy as my other Amaryllis had flowered on the same day in 2003. Ladybirds returned to the warmth of my bathroom, just as they had done during previous Cheltenham Festivals. These little insects are supposed to bring one luck and I enjoyed watching them as, from time to time, they opened their tiny wings and flew over the basin to the edge of the bath. I walked carefully across the carpeted floor for fear of squashing any of them. I needed them badly.

In contrast to the ladybirds, I was also fascinated by a huge red kite that constantly took my eye when I watched the horses cantering on the Downs. This beautiful bird of prey was so majestic and graceful. He looked like a king amongst the other birds as he glided gracefully and effortlessly over the valleys. I adopted him as the Best Mate of the skies and hoped that Matey would be able to fly across his kingdom at Prestbury with similar ease on Gold Cup day.

In keeping with tradition, Andrew Coonan, our lucky leprechaun, emerged from the Emerald Isle on Monday afternoon. He is an exceptional spirit raiser and we were thrilled to welcome him back to base. I gave him a big hug and showed him to the same spare room that he had occupied in previous years but warned him that he'd be unlikely to get much sleep due to the disruption caused by the security guards each night. We had enlisted their help for almost ten days in the run-up to Cheltenham. Two men were on duty from 7pm and patrolled the yard at regular intervals; they had done the same in 2003. Unfortunately, when they came into the house for cups of coffee, our dogs went wild and barked aggressively. They never got used to these guards and we were forced to suffer a number of noisy broken nights. Indeed, the hours of dark were extremely tiring and our sleep was constantly interrupted. Each morning I felt exhausted when it was time to get up.

On the Monday night, we had our traditional dinner with Charles and Dorothy Cadogan. The atmosphere was, as always, extremely good and on several occasions Jim McGrath's jokes even managed to keep my mind off the Gold Cup. The whole week was put into perspective and we were given plenty of encouragement.

Jim Culloty arrived at West Lockinge Farm at 7am on Tuesday morning to give Best Mate his final school. He had done the same in previous years. It is always a risk to jump a horse over an obstacle so close to a race but it was important to check that he was properly focussed and concentrating on his jumping. We could afford no errors on Thursday and we would feel happier once we'd seen him jump at home. It was like putting the icing on the cake – Jim and Terry needed to put the finishing touches to Matey's work programme. Although he had jumped several times in the loose school during February and March, he had not been over a steeplechase fence since his race at Leopardstown in December. His accuracy on Tuesday morning was spot on and Terry was delighted with his charge. He looked a fresh, happy horse who was ready to do his best when the chips were down.

After Best Mate's jumping practice, we began to prepare for day one of the Festival but we had no runners that day. The weather was kind and the ground rode well. The racing was, as always, highly competitive. There were two unexpected results. Hardy Eustace beat Rooster Booster in the Champion Hurdle and Maximize, once owned by my sister, won the Fulke Walwyn Kim Muir Handicap Chase. Terry and I spent a lot of time signing books in a special tent and talking to well-wishers. We were amazed to meet so many genuine supporters and they raised our spirits with their enthusiasm. Also during the day on Tuesday, I was presented with the Guinness Festival Award for 2003 and received a fine glass bowl from the rostrum in the winner's enclosure. I thought to myself that it would be nice to be back on this platform again on Thursday afternoon.

Wednesday was a different day and we had three runners, Yardbird, Foly Pleasant and Inca Trail – all in hurdle races. They did not fare particularly well which was disappointing but at least they all came back home safely. The ground remained good despite the threat of rain. Cheltenham had escaped this rain on the Wednesday but the forecast for Thursday was not so good. Once again we talked to numerous Best Mate fans and received plenty of encouragement. I kept telling myself that in 24 hours' time we would know our fate. The agonising wait would be over.

The big day was fast approaching and I was beginning to feel increasingly nervous. I could not bear to read the racing pages of any newspapers as I did not want to be told anything more about Best Mate. On Wednesday evening, Andrew and I watched the Cheltenham highlights from the first two days but the best distraction was my favourite video on the life of a Meerkat family that I had taped from a previous television programme. I adore these little animals and tried to interest my guest in them as well. He was very patient and pretended to enjoy the video but I know he was being ultra polite. Terry had already gone to bed as he sensed what was in store.

Thursday 18 March 2004 dawned at last and I woke up early. As usual Terry and I fed all the horses in the yard at 5.30am. It was a dull, damp morning but Best Mate looked great; both he and Tusk, who was stabled in the same yard, would leave the farm at 7.30. Tusk was scheduled to run in the first race, the JCB Triumph Hurdle. Impek would also travel in the same horsebox but his race, the Cathcart, was not due to start until 5.10pm. A Channel 4 film crew arrived soon after 7am and filmed Matey's departure just like they had done in 2003, thus maintaining another ritual. When the LRT box with our lucky driver, Dougie Ball, disappeared up the road I kept thinking about all those horses that Best Mate would have to beat if he was going to equal Arkle's record of three Gold Cup wins in a row. There had been a few drop-outs since the beginning of the year, and the absence of Jair du Cochet, who was so tragically killed on his home gallops a week or so before Cheltenham, had been a cruel blow to Guillaume Macaire and to all the supporters of this talented French chaser. Indeed, I had felt a shiver run down my spine when I'd been told of the disaster during a day's racing at Exeter on 9 March. The news quite stunned me. There is such a narrow dividing line between success and disaster. All I wanted was for Best Mate to come back home again – sound and well. It would be unthinkable to do our morning rounds and be confronted by an empty box. Kingscliff was another Gold Cup absentee, due to a muscular problem, but there were still ten declared runners and plenty of good horses left in the field. I was reminded of my ante-post bets; I had invested just over £300 on Matey's opponents. I termed this my insurance money and I had done the same in previous years.

After breakfast, which I did not eat, I went upstairs to change into my racing clothes. The old blue suit came out of its plastic bag and my pearls were taken out of the safe. I laid out Terry's suit on the bed in his dressing room together with his special yellow silk tie and his battered old Trilby hat, which nowadays only sees daylight once a year. I turned on the television whilst preparing for the day ahead and caught the end of "The Morning Line". It showed the LRT horsebox and the arrival of Best Mate at the racecourse. It was a relief to know that he'd reached the racecourse stables and had not been held up in a traffic jam. I still had a little time to fill in. Andrew Coonan was packing his suitcase, so I picked up some shoe polish to clean his shoes. He was amazed and, thinking back on it, it was as much a surprise for me as for him, since, in a normal week, I never even clean my own shoes. Malcolm Lumb always removes them from me and smartly polishes them for my next day at the races. I'd be lost without him as it's a job I hate – it is almost as bad as ironing which I cannot do at all.

The weather forecast for the day was mixed. There had been 15.4ml of rain at Cheltenham between 7 and 15 March but none on the 16 or 17 March. The clouds were ominously low and grey so there was every chance that the heavens might open in the hours before the Gold Cup. There was plenty of moisture in the air. The times had still been fast on the first two days of the Festival but rain would alter everything. We planned to arrive at the racecourse in plenty of time as Terry wanted to carefully reassess the ground conditions. A load of straw duly arrived in the yard before our departure and Andrew Coonan was once more despatched to Heathrow. We left on time and Tori Tremlett drove our car. My nerves were decidedly on edge and I remember being irritated when she accidently hit and broke a wing mirror as we negotiated a narrow lane in Wantage that had parked cars and lorries on either side. I was ready to jump at anybody and noticed that the staff back at home had kept well out of my way that morning. It was almost as though I was suffering from an infectious disease.

We arrived at Cheltenham at about 11.30. The traffic was very heavy but we took our usual short cut past Jim Wilson's racing yard and did not encounter too many hold-ups. The worst aspect was getting rid of the car since there never seems to be any room for trainers' cars in the Owners' and Trainers' car park during Festival week. Terry chatted to various car park attendants – they mostly knew him from previous years – and eventually we found a place but it was a struggle and we were not put in the proper car park. It annoyed me to think that we were bringing the Gold Cup favourite for everybody to see but we could not even park our car. It was not as if we had arrived late.

As we walked up from our new parking area, which was somewhere behind the racecourse stables, there was no escaping the crowds and we were recognised wherever we went. I suppose it was my blue suit, black furry hat and pearls that did it. The racegoers had remembered me from the previous year. I thought to myself, maybe next time I'll go in disguise – I could wear an overall and a rain hat and take my own hat in a carrier bag. We talked to all the people who stopped us and we signed endless autographs. There were so many well-wishers. I felt cheered by their support and the knowledge that so many people were willing Best Mate to win.

We attended the Tote lunch once again, in the Hatton's Grace suite, which seemed to be miles up in the new stand, but we only spent a short time at our table as we had Tusk to saddle in the first race. He looked good and we were hopeful of a big run but he raced too freely and faded in the closing stages. He had not been especially happy on the ground, which was reported as riding slightly dead, but both Terry and I concluded that he would never win a big race until he learnt to settle. We were disappointed, as he has a lot of ability and was well supported in the market before the race. In 4 minutes and 5.3 seconds the owners' dreams of a Festival winner were shattered but there would be another day.

The Gold Cup was the third race on the card and I made my way to the pre-parade ring in plenty of time. The omens looked bad since Baracouda had just been beaten in the Stayers' Hurdle – race two – which meant that two of the week's 'certainties' had gone down; Rooster Booster had been the first. Could Best Mate beat the hoodoo and get the punters out of trouble? In his walk up from the racecourse stables, he had been allocated five security men as well as three policemen. When he reached the pre-parade area, another policeman was there to meet him. Drew said that the guards were superb and that nobody was allowed near his charge bar Jackie Jenner, Dave

Reddy and himself. He reported that huge crowds were hanging over the plastic railings from the big entrance gates right down to the saddling boxes and he was thankful that an escort had been laid on. Everybody wanted to see the champion and there were mutterings in the crowds wherever he went. The fans were out in force; thousands of people thronged to the edge of the paddock and onto the stands overlooking the saddling boxes. It was a sea of faces and the atmosphere was electric.

Once again, I moved to our chosen saddling box for cover and felt a little more secure with three walls around me. I could hardly think straight and at times I again felt that I was living in a dream but it was not a dream, it was reality and Best Mate was there, at Cheltenham, attempting to make history. Could he do it? Could he beat the statistics? Could he equal Arkle's record? Terry was almost as shaky as myself – although he will deny this. Before the second race he'd taken me onto the course to inspect the ground on the Gold Cup track and to show me the unused strip of grass on the inner. This was where he wanted Matey to go and there would be very little margin for error. I had not been onto the course on Gold Cup day in 2002 or 2003 so I realised that Terry must be unusually anxious. If anything had gone wrong with his and Jim Culloty's plan, he wanted to make sure that I'd seen for myself the two different sorts of ground. In the middle of the fences the turf had been well used in December and January. There was less grass cover and if any more rain fell it could ride soft and tacky. I agreed with Terry's decision. There was no alternative – the better the ground, the better Best Mate would move and jump off it.

Terry and I saddled up our big-race favourite; he was alert and ready for action. Jim and Valerie Lewis, accompanied by a number of their supporters, had joined us outside the saddling box. We were all on tenterhooks. Jim had started the day badly by putting on the wrong overcoat when he'd set off from home for the racecourse. Being even more superstitious than myself – if that is possible – he'd telephoned a friend back home and described the coat to him and its whereabouts in a certain cupboard. Fortunately it arrived at Cheltenham just in time for the third race.

We followed our usual routine in the parade ring and I did not talk to Jim Culloty. All his instructions came through Terry and I did not want to confuse him nor break with tradition. I knew the tactics. I was almost paralysed with fear by this time and began to understand what a rabbit must feel like when it becomes frozen to the spot at the sight of a weasel, but Matey looked superb as he walked around the paddock and I was proud of him.

Once the jockeys were mounted and were walking their horses around the ring in preparation for the Gold Cup parade up the course, I made my retreat to that familiar little press tent behind the weighing room. I was pleased to find that it was smaller than in 2003 and its occupants were closely monitored. Last year it had been crammed with extras – with people who could in no way have been classed as members of the press. I was given a friendly welcome as I returned to my torture chamber and both Charles Egerton (Edgy) and Mick Easterby were allowed inside to sit with me in order to help calm my nerves. By this time however, there was little they could do – I was just really scared. I sat in my white plastic chair and my legs felt like jelly. It was an agonising race to watch. For the first circuit I could hardly bear to open my eyes at all; I kept my hands over my face and just allowed myself a few little peeps. I listened to the commentary and Mick added his own little quips. Then, as the race hotted up, I had some longer looks. Due to the ground and the tactical plan, Jim had gone the shortest way along the inside of the course. Matey had jumped brilliantly and had been travelling well. He was, according to Terry, always in the right place at the right time, but then the trouble began. As they turned for home and entered the final half-mile Jim tried to continue his run up the inner which meant keeping on the inside of First Gold. The French horse had made the running for the entire race until this point and Thierry Doumen, presumably sensing Best Mate's presence on his left-hand side, then moved across closer to the rails in order to close the gate in Matey's face. Simultaneously, Paul Carberry on Harbour Pilot and Andrew Thornton on Sir Rembrandt squeezed up our horse from the outer. Jim Culloty was now in a pocket and for three or four strides had nowhere to go. He was pushed back from second to fourth. I clung on to the arm of my chair with one hand and on to Mick Easterby with the other; whatever would happen next? 'I think you're in trouble, Hen,' said Mick, 'I think you're beat' – but Best Mate is a brave horse and a fighter; he would not give in. Jim switched him to the middle of the course and the champion caught sight of daylight. At the second-last fence he put in a tremendous leap and gained lengths in the air. All of a sudden he was in front and I'm told that the roar of the crowd had to be heard to be believed. He kept his head in front from then on and, following an economical but safe jump at the last, battled on gamely up the hill. Harbour Pilot kept going on the inside rail but Matey had gone a length and a half up. It seemed all over, but Sir Rembrandt was getting into his stride and making relentless ground up the stands' rail. Inch by inch he reeled in Best Mate but the post came in time. Our horse held on by half a length. I could hardly believe it – three Gold Cups.

'I wasn't particularly worried', said Terry afterwards, 'I was reading Jim's mind and knew he had to pull out. He made the right move at the right time and didn't wait until the last fence. He got his run and the horse galloped right to the line. Jim rode a brilliant race'. Jim Culloty was equally matter of fact: 'I got a grand run until it really mattered but Carberry was only doing his job keeping me in – it's the chance you take when you go down the inside. Best Mate has got all the class and ability but he has got bottle as well.'

It was an incredible result but the enormity of Best Mate's achievement did not immediately sink in. I remember a feeling of huge relief and a spontaneous desire to once again get to Terry and to the victor himself with his cool jockey. Everybody congratulated me in the press tent and showered me with kisses but now it was time for my own Gold Cup run and my own race down that well used pathway to the course. Once more, the cheers were ringing in my ears as I gradually built up speed on my way to the course gates. I was nearly two stone lighter in weight than in 2003 and my training sessions with Lee had helped my fitness. I knew that my action had been criticised in past years but this time I was determined to show the crowds that I too could quicken my steps like Best Mate. That run felt brilliant – it was pure magic. Everybody was shouting and waving and racecards were being tossed into the air. I could never again relive that experience; even describing it is hard. Suffice to say that it was probably the best feeling I have ever had in all my life. The whole racecourse, with its 69,000 spectators, seemed to have erupted and gone mad. There was bedlam. To think that 50 years ago I had been content to stay at home to ride my Shetland and Connemara ponies but now I was at Cheltenham, the Mecca of steeplechasing, and had trained the horse who had just made history, emulating Arkle by winning three Gold Cups in a row. Yet I could not have done it alone, it was one big team effort based on trust and belief in this special horse.

By now it was raining steadily but I barely noticed the change in the weather – it could have poured and poured for all I cared and that wonderful join-up with Terry was better than ever. I could have hugged him for hours but there was no time to delay and once again we set off up that hallowed walkway in front of the stands. By now I was in a total daze, Terry was crying, and, as in previous years, hundreds of arms were outstretched to us across the barriers. The cheers were indescribable. I wanted to stop and talk to everybody and to thank the racegoers for their brilliant support and their kind words. Cheltenham would never be Cheltenham without their enthusiasm. It is an amazing place and we had just witnessed a new chapter in its history.

The walk back to the winner's enclosure was much the same as it had been in the two previous years except that Terry was moving better and kept up with Best Mate all the way. The police were stricter than they had been before and formed cordons to keep back the crowds. Everybody wanted to touch Matey and get through the railings to be with him but the men with yellow fluorescent jackets did their job and kept them at bay – so much so that even Drew was pushed back and could not go through the entrance in his usual position to the right of Best Mate's head. A jubilant Jim Lewis met his hero as he touched the parade ring grass. He threw his hands into the air and signalled three Gold Cups by holding up three fingers. He said afterwards that 'Secretly this was the one I wanted to win more than anything else in the world – not for myself particularly but for all those followers who had always believed that at Cheltenham Best Mate was invincible'. He went on to say that in a previous television interview after the Ericsson Chase at Leopardstown that he had told the viewers: 'We have not yet seen all the attributes of Best Mate, there is another face yet to be seen', and he maintained that this was shown on Gold Cup day 2004 – 'Best Mate the street fighter'.

As Best Mate entered that hallowed enclosure, the cheering was deafening. The crowds were almost hysterical. His reception was unbelievable – the clapping, the shouting, the screaming and the waving. It was an occasion not to be missed and the whole unsaddling area was buzzing; it was hard to know which way to look or where to put oneself, yet the thought of Jim Lewis singing his Best Mate song on the podium appalled me, it would have been completely out of place. When Alastair Down told me that Jim was preparing his words, I let my true thoughts take over: 'That f***ing song', and it came out live on Channel 4. Oh dear! What would the racing public think of their Gold Cup trainer now?

Following a moving and joyous press debriefing – in my favourite little tent – it was time to saddle up Impek for the Cathcart Chase. Earlier in the day, I had thought he had a good chance but now that it had rained I was not so sure. I needed to go down to the start with the starter as Impek is sometimes temperamental in the preliminaries but on this day he behaved perfectly. It was strange to get away from the crowds and to walk around beside the starting gate, without any pressure. I leant on the railings and looked back across the course to those huge grandstands and the tented village. The enclosures were still packed with people. I could still hardly believe that 90 minutes earlier they had been cheering home Best Mate for his third Gold Cup. It was the first time that I'd ever been on my own that week at Cheltenham racecourse and it was a wonderful feeling. I was free at last and the pressure had been lifted. I hoped that Impek would run well but I would not be able to see the race from across the course. After the start, I jumped into the waiting Land Rover and hitched a lift back to the weighing room. Impek did not win but ran well and finished third. He had tired up the final hill; maybe he'd have done better over a shorter trip. It was five furlongs further than the Arkle Chase in which he finished second in 2003 but he had won over three miles at Sandown in between.

After the Cathcart it was back to the unsaddling enclosure for the second time that day and a chance to say goodbye to Jim Lewis and all his friends. There were several more interviews and two television appearances for news programmes. I was also presented with another Guinness Award – this time for the leading trainer on the final day of the Festival. At last, Terry and I could think about making our way home. As we made for the exit gate behind the paddock, we were again stopped by numerous fans who wanted us to sign their racecards and congratulate us on Best Mate's win. It was difficult to make much progress and the crowds were still elated but we eventually reached the horsewalk and made for the car park area via the racecourse stables. I put my arm through Terry's and we walked slowly down the hill. It was beginning to get dark and it was still raining but above us, in the sky, a little aeroplane was flying round and pulling a streamer behind it with the words 'Well Done Best Mate'. This was too much for Terry and he was reduced to tears yet again. It was certainly a touching sight and a wonderful tribute to our champion. He deserved the reception he received that day. He is a brave horse and worthy of Triple Gold. We would remember his performance for the rest of our lives. No wonder the crowds were happy – they were singing loudly – but it was time to leave them and say goodbye to our favourite racecourse. For once, I was almost reluctant to go home but we wanted to see everybody at West Lockinge and be there to greet our hero when he returned. There was a mighty reception back at the farm. Everybody knew it had been another magical day.

CHAPTER
TWENTY SEVEN

REFLECTIONS

Best Mate returned home to a hero's reception. As in 2003, the balloons and streamers were everywhere. There were even more banners and flags than I had remembered in the two previous years. This was no ordinary return from a day's racing; it was the welcome home for a superstar. Not only had all the staff in the yard waited to see the champion but a number of extra fans had turned up as well. These supporters lined the roadside as the horsebox entered the driveway. Christine had received numerous telephone calls from these special well-wishers. They all wanted to know when Best Mate was expected home. It was a cold, wet night but they waited patiently under their umbrellas until the headlights from the LRT vehicle shone round the corner of the road. Camera crews and newspaper reporters further made up the numbers and our greatest ally, Andrew Longmore, was hovering in the wings.

It was a touching occasion and everybody seemed to be on a high. Matey, himself, walked proudly back to his stable – the hero of the day and a proper pro. Jackie took off his travelling rug and boots and he looked superb; he glanced at his surroundings as if to say: 'Well, what's all this fuss about? I've done all this before'. His fans beamed as they gloated over their idol. They adored him and did not want to miss a moment of this unforgettable evening.

Once we had hugged and thanked our special horse, Terry and I made tracks to the house where, yet again, the fax machine and telephone were going mad. We fought our way through huge bunches of balloons and decorative plaques but there was no time for delay; we needed to plan the party for the following morning. Due to the deterioration in the weather, it was obvious that we would not be able to hold it in the garden. The forecast for Friday was not good – besides the rain there was also a mention of gales. No tents would be able to be pitched on the lawn. Fortunately, we had some space in one of the hay barns and we quickly arranged with Simon Florey, the marquee supplier, to build up a tented area within the barn. He is an expert when it comes to dealing with emergencies. Our regular caterers were also summoned and we put out the word to as many people as possible that Best Mate would be on show at 11am. I am told that Gill Draycott, who always prepares the scrumptious party food for West Lockinge Farm functions, had half expected a telephone call once she knew that Best Mate had won his third Gold Cup.

We spoke to numerous people on the telephone that Thursday night and, as in previous years, watched several replays of the race including Channel 4's coverage. I glanced at Ceefax and we watched the 10 o'clock news. I did not want to miss out on anything. Fortunately, we did not have to send for a Chinese takeaway as there was a big lasagne waiting to go in the oven. Andrew stayed for a while and we mulled over that amazing day – we were all extremely tired but it was difficult to unwind. My head was reeling. The staff, who, following evening stables, had celebrated Best Mate's win with glasses of champagne, unearthed by Christine from our cellar, later disappeared, for the second year running, to Luke Harvey's pub, the Blowing Stone. I am told it was some party. It went on until the early hours and there were certainly some sore heads the next morning.

As expected, Friday was wet and windy. How lucky that the barn was empty and would be able to save the day. Simon and his helpers did a marvellous job and their tent looked superb. Gill provided plenty of delicious eats and the champagne flowed for several hours. A whole host of supporters turned up to see the horse who had just made racing history and cameras were clicking everywhere from the moment Best Mate left his stable to stroll in the little paddock beside the barn, until the moment he once again disappeared from view. Everybody had an excellent opportunity to see and stroke the champion. I wonder what it was like in Ireland when Arkle returned home after his third Gold Cup victory.

Best Mate wore his special Gold Cup rug during the celebrations. He enjoyed all the extra attention from his adoring fans and behaved immaculately – like a true champion. Television camera crews and various members of the racing press merely added to the already huge numbers. For a spur of the moment, impromptu party it was a memorable occasion. The weather was dreadful but nobody seemed to care. There were so many happy, smiling faces.

Over the next weeks, sackfuls of congratulatory letters and cards were delivered to the farm. The postmen were superb. Some of the envelopes were barely addressed at all – 'Best Mate, Oxfordshire' or 'Best Mate, England'. I was overwhelmed by so many touching messages and I have kept a large envelope of 'special letters', ones that I will read over and over again when the fairytale has ended. A lot of them reduced me to tears. As in previous years I ordered a number of Cheltenham photographs depicting Best Mate on his glorious day of Triple Gold. In the weeks that followed, and once more helped by Clare Richmond-Watson, I managed to acknowledge almost all of this fan mail, although I confess to having missed out on some of the faxes and emails. I still cannot work the computer!

Best Mate's win at Cheltenham in 2004 did a lot for racing and many said that it gave the sport a big lift at a time when there had been several slurs on its public image. In the months preceding Cheltenham, it had received a lot of bad press and desperately needed a boost. It seemed as if Best Mate had been sent as its saviour.

In the *Sunday Telegraph*, Brough Scott wrote: 'For three weeks racing and my former jockey profession has been heaped with ridicule and shame. For three days the Cheltenham Festival has thrilled us and now Best Mate has given his answer. He has washed the old game clean'.

Apart from taking racing out of the doldrums, it has to be said that winning three Gold Cups is a huge achievement for any horse. It had been done previously by only three horses – Cottage Rake, Arkle and Golden Miller. The latter amazingly won the blue riband five times but the last treble was in 1966 and racing enthusiasts were longing for a new star to arrive on the scene and change the course of history. In 2002, I had been delighted for our stable to win one Gold Cup but at that time, if anybody had told me that the same horse would win the next two as well, I would have said that they were merely dreaming. I could not imagine that this would ever happen but I do enjoy dreams. With Best Mate in our midst, Terry and I have been given a huge responsibility and he has undoubtedly changed our lives and lifestyle. Yet we are so lucky to train a horse that is such a pleasure to have around. His charisma and charm continue to shine through. He is always willing to please and enjoys his work. Indeed, he gets bored if his holidays are too long.

Best Mate has been called the people's horse and the country's property. Jim Lewis, his owner, has said that he is happy to share his treasured possession with the nation. Best Mate is good for racing and so is Jim but he is well aware that his horse is already a valuable commercial commodity. He knows that certain people could be quick to jump on the bandwagon in order to make profits from his star.

There is a fine dividing line between allowing genuine fans access to the horse and protecting his commercial potential. The same applies to human athletes. Like Olympic champions, Best Mate should not be open to exploitation by anyone, so Jim Lewis has registered the Best Mate trademark in order to prevent sharp-eyed entrepreneurs from making unreasonable profits without his knowledge. Under the new trademark, royalties will be paid to a central trust fund set up by Jim's legal advisors. The chief beneficiaries of the fund will be Jim's chosen charities. He calls it 'Having the wherewithal to give money to those less fortunate than ourselves' and I know he will take particular satisfaction in sharing his own good fortune so directly with others. There are four registered signatories – the two Jims, Terry and myself – and any Best Mate promotions will have to be sanctioned by Jim Lewis before they can be allowed.

Following the March excitements, Best Mate was gradually let down in fitness and given time to unwind. It was requested that he do a number of parades but he only made one public appearance. This was at Newbury racecourse on 27 March. He received a great reception and a sum of money was given to last year's Open Day charities. If we were to accept all the invitations for Best Mate to appear and parade during the summer months, he would never have any holiday. He could easily become blasé about visiting racecourses. It is important for him to remember that he is still a racehorse, even if he is a celebrity as well. Parade rings are there to be taken seriously and to be associated with races to follow. They are not, as yet, for holiday walkabouts. Hopefully, there will be time to honour charity invitations when Matey's racing days are over.

The 2003/04 National Hunt season ended at Sandown on 24 April and, by virtue of the votes of Channel 4 viewers, Best Mate won the Horse of the Year Award. Jim Lewis was presented with a fine bronze head depicting Queen Elizabeth, The Queen Mother's Special Cargo, that great old Sandown favourite. In May 2004 The British Horseracing Board held a lunch in London for their own end-of-season Jump Racing Awards. Jim Lewis collected two more trophies for Best Mate, one for the BHB Steeplechaser of the Year and then the Horse of the Year Award. Matey is currently at the very top of the steeplechasing tree. How much longer he can stay there remains to be seen but at the time of writing he is in great heart and already preparing for his fourth Cheltenham Gold Cup in March 2005. He has summered particularly well and looks stronger than ever. We have Golden Miller's record well in our sights and will do our best to get the champion back to his favourite racecourse in prime condition next spring. Meanwhile plans are well under way for our Annual Charity Open Day in September and Best Mate is sure to have plenty of visitors. We are still dreaming. We are not yet ready for that dream to come to an end.

APPENDICES

BEST MATE'S RACING RECORD

CHELTENHAM (L-H) (GOOD)
Sunday 14 November 1999 WEATHER: overcast

NSPCC RACING TO HELP CHILDREN BUMPER STANDARD OPEN NATIONAL HUNT FLAT RACE CLASS B (4-6yo)
4:00   2m 110y (OldNHF) £7198 (£2180; £1065; £508)

Best Mate (IRE)	(Miss H C Knight) 4 11-00 J Culloty rangy: hid up in tch: hdwy over 3f out: rdn to ld wl ins fnl f		**1**	10/1
Hard To Start (IRE)	(P J Hobbs) 410-11 R Widger (3) w'like: leggy: lw: hid up: hdwy over 2f out: styd on u.p ins fnl f	¾	**2**	14/1
Southern Star (IRE)	(M Pitman) 4 10-13 L Corcoran (5) a.p:1ed over 3f out tl wl ins fnil	1¼	**3**	5/1(3)
Captain Zinzan (NZ)	(J L Dunlop) 4 11-00 A Thomton lt-f: hid up & bhd: sme hdwy fnl 2f: n.d	22	**4**	9/2(2)
Lord Scroop (IRE)	(D Nicholson) 5 10-11 O McPhail (3) bkwd: set stdy pce 5f: hrd rdn over 3f out: sn btr	2½	**5**	16/1
Pippin's Ford (IRE)	(P F Nicholls) 4 11-04 J Tizzard lw: hld up in rr: drvn along 4f out: no imp	1	**6**	6/1
Phal	(T G Mills) 5 11-07 L Cummins prom: led 11f out tl over 3f out: sn rdn & wknd: t.c	8	**7**	14/1
Inthemeantime (IRE)	(M Pitman) 6 11-00 N Williamson wl grwn: bkwd: hld up: drvn along 4f out: sn outpcd	2	**8**	11/2
Big Trouble	(N A Twiston-Davies) 4 10-11 J Goldstein (3) lw: str: bkwd:chsd ldrs over 12f:sn wknd t.o	15	**9**	16/1
Halexy (FR)	(Miss Venetia Williams) 4 11-04 A P McCoy hid up: hdwy ½-way: rdn & outpcd over 3f out	11	**10**	11/4(F)

SANDOWN (R-H) (Chase - GOOD: Hurdles – GOOD TO SOFT)
Friday 3 December 1999 WEATHER: cold & windy

EWELL 'NATIONAL HUNT' NOVICES' HURDLE CLASS D (4yo+)
3:40　　　　　　　　2m 110y (8 hdl) £3680 (£1115; £545; £260)

Best Mate (IRE)	(Miss H C Knight) 4 11-00 J Culloty a gng wl: hld up: led on bit 2 out: v.easily		**1**	5/4(F)
Rosco	(J T Gifford) 5 11-00 P Hide chsd ldr: led 4th to 2 out: unable qckn	10	**2**	100/30
Behamore (IRE)	(R Rowe) 6 11-08 T J Murphy lw: pild hrd: a.p: rdn appr 2 out: wknd appr las	7	**3**	13/2(3)
Light The Fuse (IRE)	(D G Bridgwater)7 11-00 N Williamson rdn & hdwy appr 2 out: wknd appr last	1	**4**	12/1
Running Water (IRE)	(P R Hedger) 6 11-00 L Aspell bhd to 3 out: stdy hdwy appr 2 out: shkn up appr last: fnd nil	10	**5**	12/1
Macaw-Bay (IRE)	(A W Carroll) 5 10-13 R Johnson chsd ldrs tl appr 2 out: sn wknd	5	**6**	10/1
Mister Graham	(P R Webber) 4 11-00 R Garritty lw: led to 4th: ev ch 3 out: wknd appr 2 out	1¾	**7**	16/1
Express Crusader (IRE)	(J S Moore) 6 11-00 S Durack bhd fr 4th: t.o		**8**	40/1

SANDOWN (R-H) (SOFT (Good to soft in places on chase course))
Saturday 8 January 2000 WEATHER: sunny

SUN 'KING OF THE PUNTERS' TOLWORTH HURDLE CLASS A GRADE 1 (4yo+)
2:35　　　　　　　　2m 110y (8 hdl) £16500 (£6325; £3163; £1513)

Monsignor (IRE)	(M Pitman) 6 11-07 N Williamson lw: chsd ldr: led 3rd: rdn appr 2 out: r.o w		**1**	11/8(F)
Best Mate (IRE)	(Miss H C Knight) 5 11-07 J Culloty hid up: chsd wnr fr 3 out: rdn appr last: unable qckn flat	2½	**2**	4/1(3)
Doctor Goddard	(P J Hobbs) 5 11-07 R Johnson lw:chsd ldrs: rdn appr 2 out:sn wknd	10	**3**	12/1
Snow Drop (FR)	(F Doumen) 41 0-04 T Doumen hdwy 3 out: 3rd whn hit 2 out: sn wknd	hd	**4**	100/30
Ballinclay King (IRE)	(Ferdy Murphy) 6 11-07 A Maguire lw: bhd whn mstke 1 st: hdwy 3 out: wind appr 2 out	17	**5**	13/2
Grief (IRE)	(D R C Elsworlh) 7 11-07b P Holley lw: led: mstke 2nd: hdd 3rd: 6th & wkng whn fell 3		**F**	33/1

CHELTENHAM (L-H) (GOOD)
Tuesday 14 March 2000 WEATHER: cloudy

CAPEL CURE SHARP SUPREME NOVICES' HURDLE CLASS A GRADE 1 (4yo+)
2:00   2m 110y (OldH) £46400 (£17600; £8800; £4000; £2000; £1200)

Sausalito Bay	(Noel Meade) 6 11-08 P Carberry led to 3 out: rdn to ld last: all out		1	14/1
Best Mate (IRE)	(Miss H C Knight) 5 11-08 J Culloty lw: hld up: hdwy appr 3 out: swtchd rt appr next: fin wl	¾	2	6/1(2)
Youlneverwalkalone (IRE)	(C Roche) 611-08 C O'Dwyer trckd ldrs: rdn appr last: styd on & edgd tf t flat	1¼	3	5/4(F)
Phardante Flyer (IRE)	(P J Hobbs) 611-08 P Flynn lw: a.p: led 3 out to last: one pce	¾	4	50/1
Rodock (FR)	(M C Pipe) 6 11-08 A P McCoy hid up: hdwy appr 3 out: ev ch whn hit last: one pce	shd	5	7/1(3)
Eastwell Hall	(T P McGovern) 5 11-08 P Hide l w: in tch: rdn & out pcd appr 2 out: subtr	5	6	150/1
Silence Reigns	(P F Nicholls) 6 11-08 J Tizzard lw: hid up in tch: blnd 1st: hdwy whn n.m. r appr 3 out: btn appr next	1¼	7	20/1
Ballet-K	(J Neville) 6 11-03 W Marston in rr: hit 4th: sn pushed along: n.d	6	8	33/1
Dusk Duel (USA)	(N J Henderson) 511-08 M A Fitzgerald chsd ldrs: hrd drvn & hit 3 out: sn btr	5	9	8/1
Evening World (FR)	(M C Pipe) 5 11-08 R Johnson plld hrd: prom tl mstke and wknd 5th	1¼	10	20/1
Dodjo (FR)	(E Leenders) 7 11-08tb J J Manceau hld up in rr: sme hdwy appr 4th: rdn & wknd appr 2 out	shd	11	150/1
Baclama (FR)	(M C Pipe) 4 10-09 R Greene chsd ldr to 5th: rdn & wknd appr next: t.c	14	12	100/1
Mr Lamb	(M C Pipe) 5 11-08 A Maguire hid up & bhd: hdwy appr 3 out: no ch whn fell last		F	16/1
Through The Rye	(M C Pipe) 4 11-00t B Fenton a in rr: fell 5th		F	40/1
Kaiserstolz (GER)	(Ian Williams) 7 11-08t A Dobbin lw: lost tch ½-way: p.u bef 3 out		P	66/1

AINTREE (L-H) (GOOD (Good to firm in places))
Friday 7 April 2000

MARTELL MERSEY NOVICES' HURDLE CLASS A GRADE 2 (4yo+)
2:00   2m 4f (11 hdl) £21000 (£8050; £4025; £1925)

Best Mate (IRE)	(Miss H C Knight) 5 11-01 J Culloty led to 5th, remained cl up, led again 8th, pushed out fr last		1	4/11(F)
Copeland	(M C Pipe) 5 11-06b A P McCoy trckd lders, wnt 2nd 2 out, rdn between last 2, kpt on, no imp on wnr	2½	2	9/2(2)
Harvis (FR)	(Miss Venetia Williams) 5 11-01 N Williamson cl up, led 5th until hded 8th, weakening whn hit 2 out	23	3	28/1
Barney Knows (IRE)	(M A Peill) 5 11-09 R Garritty hld up, pushed along and outpcd bef 3 out, sn lost tch	½	4	11/1(3)
Forest Ending (USA)	(J A B Old) 5 11-01 T J Murphy hld up, lost tch fr bef 3 out, t.o	28	5	25/1

EXETER (R-H)(GOOD)
Tuesday 17 October 2000 WEATHER: bright and sunny early, cloudy later

MANTECH NOVICES' CHASE CLASS D (5yo+)
4:10   2m 1f 110y (12) £3926 (£1208; £604; £302)

Best Mate (IRE)	(Miss H C Knight) 5 11-00 J Culloty lw: hld up in tch: led appr last: qcknd clr flat		1	1/2(F)
Bindaree (IRE)	(N A Twiston-Davies) 6 11-06 C Llewellyn lw: led 2nd to 7th: led appr 4 out to 3 out: disp ld 2 out: ev ch tl outpcd last	2½	2	3/1(2)
Shooting Light (IRE)	(P G Murphy) 7 11-00b L Aspell lw: a.p: led 7th tl after next: led 3 out: rdn & hdd appr last: wknd	5	3	7/1(3)
Prah Sands	(C Tizzard) 7 11-00 J Tizzard bit bkwd:led to 2nd: in tch tl wknd 8th: t.o	dist	4	14/1
Cold Encounter (IRE)	(S Mellor) 5 10-11 J Mogford (3) chsd ldrs tl lost tch 6th. t.a	22	5	100/1
Access Festivals	(R G Frost) 10 11-00 R Wakley chsd ldrs tl outpcd 5th: t.o when p.u bef 3 out		P	100/1
Mordros	(Mrs J Scrivens) 10 11-00 T Dascombe bit bkwd: blnd & uns rdr 3rd		U	200/1

CHELTENHAM (L-H) (GOOD TO SOFT)
Sunday 12 November 2000 WEATHER: unsettled

1985 INDEPENDENT NOVICES' CHASE CLASS A
(REGISTERED AS THE NOVEMBER NOVICES' STEEPLE CHASE) (GRADE 2) (5yo+)
2:15   2m (OldCh) £15000 (£5750;£2875;£1375)

Best Mate (IRE)	(Miss H C Knight) 5 11-04 J Culloty hld up: led 6th to 7th: hit 4 out: qcknd to ld 2 out: sn clr: easily		**1**	8/13(F)
Fatehalkhair (IRE)	(B Ellison) 8 11-00 R Johnson hld up: hdwy 5th: led 7th to 3 out: outpcd after 2 out	18	**2**	33/1
Dusk Duel (USA)	(N J Henderson) 5 11-00 N Williamson hld up: led 3 out: hdd whn slipped bdly 2 out: nt rcvr	11	**3**	100/30
Nordic Crest (IRE)	(P R Webber) 6 11 00 J A McCarthy w ldr: led 3rd to 6th: wknd 4 out	7	**4**	33/1
Prancing Blade	(N A Twiston-Davies) 7 11-07 C Llewellyn lw: led to 3rd: wknd 8th	12	**5**	7/1(3)
Khairabar (IRE)	(C Roche) 6 11-04 P Moloney hld up: nt fluent 8th: sn bhd: t.c	dist	**6**	20/1

SANDOWN (R-H) (HEAVY; *First hurdle on far side and pond fence omitted each circuit*)
Saturday 3 February 2001

WEATHERBYS SCILLY ISLES NOVICES' CHASE CLASS A GRADE 1 (5yo+)
3:05   2m 4f 110y (16) £24000 (£9200; £4600; £2200)

Best Mate (IRE)	(Miss H C Knight) 6 11-06 J Culloty j.w: trckd ldrs: cruised into ld after 2 out: sn clr: impressive		**1**	5/4(F)
Crocadee	(Miss Venetia Williams) 8 11-06 N Williamson trckd ldr: mstke 7th: led bef 2 out: rdn and hdd after 2 out: no ch w wnr	13	**2**	5/1(3)
Hannigan's Lodger (IRE)	(N A Twiston-Davies) 7 11-01 C Llewellyn led at gd pce: rdn and hdd on long nun to 2 out: wknd and fin tired	22	**3**	20/1
Logician (NZ)	(A W Noonan)10 11-06t B Fenton blnd bdly 1st: last and detached: wl bhd 6th: mstke next: running on but stl plenty to do whn blnd 12th: no prog after	13	**4**	12/1
Silver Streak (IRE)	(J T Gifford) 7 11-06 P Hide nt jump wl: a rr: lost tch 6th: t.o 3 out	dist	**5**	25/1
Redemption	(P R Webber) 6 11-06 A Thornton rr whn blnd 3rd: prog 6th: chsd ldrs next: blnd 12th: wknd bef 2 out: tired and slow jump last: virtually p.u	dist	**6**	8/1
Hurdante (IRE)	(E J Alston) 11 11-06 B Harding in tch to 6th: sn bhd: t.o whn p.u bef 1 0th		**P**	33/1
Exit To Wave (FR)	(P F Nicholls) 5 10-12 M A Fitzgerald chsd ldrs: mstke 6th: wknd 11th: wl bhd whn p.u		**P**	4/1(2)

AINTREE (L-H) (HEAVY)
Saturday 7 April 2001 WEATHER: Raining

MARTELL AINTREE HURDLE CLASS A GRADE 1 (4yo+)
2:55   2m 4f (11 hdl) £71400 (£26400; £13200; £6000; £3000)

Horse	Details		Pos	Odds
Barton	(T D Easterby) 8 11-07 A Dobbin trckd ldrs: styd on to ld between last two: drvn clr run-in: eased towards finish		1	9/1
Best Mate (IRE)	(Miss H C Knight) 6 11-07 J Culloty patiently rdn: effrt appr 3 out: outpcd next: styd on after last to take 2nd nr line	14	2	3/1 (F)
Mr Cool	(M C Pipe)7 11-07 A P McCoy wldr: led 7th tl between last two: wknd towards finish	1¼	3	16/1
Bounce Back (USA)	(F Doumen) 5 11-07 T Doumen trckd ldrs: effrt 3 out: sn wknd	18	4	9/2(3)
Teaatral	(C R Egerton) 711-07 N Williamson w ldrs: rdn and wknd 3 out	dist	5	6/1
Landing Light (IRE)	(N J Henderson) 611-07 R Johnson pushed along 5th: lost tch 8th: p.u bef 2 out		P	7/1
Mister Banjo (FR)	(P F Nicholls) 5 11-07 A Maguire led: reminders 6th: hdd next: lost pl bef 3 out: p.u bef 2 out		P	4/1(2)
First Ballot (IRE)	(D R C Elsworth) 511-07 T J Murphy lost pl and mstke 7th: sn bhd: t.o wUn p.u bef 2 out		P	20/1

EXETER (R-H) (GOOD TO FIRM (Good in places)
Tuesday 6 November 2001 WEATHER: Raining

WILLIAMHILL.CO.UK HALDON GOLD CUP CHASE (LIMITED HANDICAP) CLASS A GRADE 2 (5yo+)
2:30   2m 1f 110y (12) (£21000 (£8050; £4025; £1925)

Horse	Details		Pos	Odds
Best Mate (IRE)	(Miss H C Knight) 6 10-12 J Culloty j.w: chsd ldr: led 8th: clr appr 4 out: easily		1	8/13(F)
Desert Mountain (IRE)	(P F Nicholls) 810-13 J Tizzard hld up: hdwy 8th: wnt 2nd appr 4 out: no ch wwn	20	2	14/1
Fadalko (FR)	(P F Nicholls) 8 11-10 M A Fitzgerald hld up: rdn 7th: hdwy 8th: wnt 2nd briefly appr 4 out: sn wknd	35	3	7/2(2)
Cenkos (FR)	(P F Nicholls) 710-12b. TJ Murphy led: sn clr: hdd 8th: sn rdn and wknd qckly: t.o	dist	4	9/2(3)

ASCOT (R-H) (GOOD (Good to firm in places on Chase course)
Saturday 24 November 2001

FIRST NATIONAL GOLD CUP (LIMITED INTERMEDIATE CHASE)
SHOWCASE HANDICAP CLASS A GRADE 2 (5yo+)
2:30   2m 3f 110y (16) £30000 (£11500; £5750; £2750)

Wahiba Sands	(M C Pipe) 810-04 A P McCoy t.k.h: hid up in rr: nt fluent 9th: hit 12th: rdn and hdwy 3 out: ev ch next: drvn to ld last: rdn out		1	4/1(2)
Best Mate (IRE)	(Miss H C Knight) 611-10 J Culloty trckd ldr: nt fluent 12th: drvn to take narrow ld 2 out: hdd last: rallied gamely u.p: nt qckn cl home	½	2	8/13(F)
Dusk Duel (USA)	(N J Henderson) 6 10-04 M A Fitzgerald chsd : ldrs disp 2nd 7th to 9th: c wd bnd appr 2)out: edgd rt appr last: styd on wl but nt pce to chal	2	3	9/2(3
Logician (NZ)	(I A Balding) 10 10-01t F Keniry (3) led tl hdd 2 out: styd pressing ldrs tl outpcd run-in	¾	4	10/1

KEMPTON (R-H) (GOOD)
Wednesday 26 December 2001 WEATHER: fine & cold WIND: slt

PERTEMPS KING GEORGE VI CHASE CLASS A SHOWCASE RACE GRADE 1 (5yo+)
2:20   3m (19 fncs) £87000 (£33000; £16500; £7500; £3750; £2250)

Florida Pearl (IRE)	(W P Mullins) 9 11-10 A Maguire lw: prom: led 10th: mde rest: hrd pressed fr 3 out: r.o gamely flat		1	8/1
Best Mate (IRE)	(Miss H C Knight) 6 11-10 A P McCoy lw: settled in tch: trckd ldrs gng easily after 4 out: rdn 2 out: pressed wnr last: r.o but a hld	¾	2	5/2(2)
Bacchanal (IRE)	(N J Henderson) 7 11-10 M A Fitzgerald lw: led to 5th: led 9th to 10th: styd cl up: mstke 14th: pressed wnr after 4 out: ev ch u.p 2 out: one pce bef last	6	3	4/1(3)
First Gold (FR)	(F Doumen) 8 11-10 T Doumen racd wd: prom: led 5th to 9th: chsd wnr 10th to after 4 out: wknd next	26	4	6/4(F)
Legal Right (USA)	(Jonjo O'Neill) 8 11-10t J R Kavanagh hld up last pair: effrt 13th: pushed along and no imp on ldrs 4 out: wknd bef next	9	5	12/1
Fadalko (FR)	(P F Nicholls) 8 11-10 T J Murphy trckd ldrs: mstke 8th: pushed along whn nt fluent 15th: wknd 4 out	7	6	25/1
Go Ballistic	(Miss H C Knight) 12 11-10 D Gallagher lw: a in rr: pushed along 9th: lost tch fr 12th: bhd fr next: t.o whn j.lft last	8	7	33/1
Bellator	(Miss Venetia Williams) 8 11-10 B J Crowley ref to r		RR	66/1

CHELTENHAM (L-H) (GOOD (Good to soft in places))
Thursday 14 March 2002 WEATHER: overcast, str wind, drizzle from race 6

TOTE CHELTENHAM GOLD CUP CHASE SHOWCASE RACE CLASS A GRADE 1 (5yo+)

3:15   3m 2f 110y (Ne £174000 (£66000; £33000; £15000; £7500; £4500)

Best Mate (IRE)	(Miss H C Knight) 7 12-00 J Culloty lw: hld up in rr stdy hdwy 17th: trckd ldrs gng wl fr 4 out: qcknd to ld appr last: r.o wl		1	7/1(3)
Commanche Court (IRE)	(T M Walsh) 9 12-00 R Walsh bhd: stdy hdwy 15th: chsd ldrs 4 out: drvn to ld and hit 2 out: hdd appr last: rallied u.p: no imp cl home	1¼	2	25/1
See More Business (IRE)	(P F Nicholls) 12 12-00b J Tizzard trckd ldr: led 11th: hdd next: styd in 2nd: chal fr 18th: led 3 out: hdd and hit 2 out: outpcd run-in	8	3	40/1
Marlborough (IRE)	(N J Henderson) 10 12-00 D Gallagher hld up in rr: hit 16th: hdwy 17th: hit 4 out and next: no ch w ldrs whn j.slowly last: kpt on run-in	6	4	12/1
What's Up Boys (IRE)	(P J Hobbs) 8 12-00b7 P Flynn bhd: hit 8th and 12th: hrd drvn fr 18th: styd on fr 2 out: nl a danger	5	5	33/1
Alexander Banquet (IRE)	(W P Mullins) 9 12-00 B J Geraghty lw: bhd: hit 13th: sme hdwy and rdn 18th: blnd and wknd 3 out	½	6	12/1
Moscow Express (IRE)	(Miss F M Crowley) 10 12-00t J R Barry bhd: hdwy 13th: rdn 17th: sme hdwy again u.p fr 2 out: nvr a danger	¾	7	66/1
Cyfor Malta (FR)	(M C Pipe) 9 12-00 R Greene hit 7th: a bhd	12	8	25/1
Foxchapel King (IRE)	(M F Morris) 9 12-00 D J Casey chsd ldrs 8th: chsd ldrs 13th to next: blnd 18th: sn rcvrd: wknd after 3 out	3	9	12/1
Lord Noelie (IRE)	(Miss H C Knight) 9 12-00 Richard Guest lw: chsd ldrs to 18th: wknd 4 out	7	10	16/1
Florida Pearl (IRE)	(W P Mullins) 10 12-00 C O'Dwyer lw: trckd ldrs to 4 out: sn rdn and wknd	¾	11	10/1
Bacchanal (IRE)	(N J Henderson) 8 12-00 M A Fitzgerald in tch whn j.rt 5th to 6th: styd in tch: hit 12th: reminders 15th: wknd 18th	6	12	6/1(2)
Looks Like Trouble (IRE)	(Noel T Chance) 10 12-00 R Johnson lw: led: hit 10th: hdd next: led 12th: hit 13th: nt fluent 18th: hdd 3 out: sn wkkd: t.o: dismntd	dist	13	9/2(F)
Sackville (IRE)	(Miss F M Crowley) 9 12-00 J L Cullen chsd ldrs: bhd fr 12th: no ch whn fell last		F	33/1
Shotgun Willy (IRE)	(P F Nicholls) 8 12-00 T J Murphy chsd ldrs: reminders 10th: hit 13th: sn wknd: t.o whnp.u bef 4 out		P	25/1
Go Ballistic	(Miss H C Knight) 13 12-00 C Llewellyn bhd fr 13th: t.o whn p.u bef 2 out		P	66/1
Behrajan (IRE)	(H D Daly) 7 12-00 N Williamson in tch: blnd 9th: hdwy 13th: blnd 15th: hit 17th: sn wknd: t.o whn p.u bef 3 out		P	11/1
Shooting Light (IRE)	(M C Pipe) 9 12-00v A P McCoy a bhd: t.o whn p.u after 12th		P	10/1

255

HUNTINGDON (R-H) (GOOD TO SOFT (Soft in places)
Saturday 23 November 2002

MCCALLUM CORPORATE CONSULTING PETERBOROUGH CHASE CLASS A GRADE 2 (5yo+)

3:10 2m 4f 110y (16) £32725 (£12100; £6050; £2750; £1375)

Best Mate (IRE)	(Miss H C Knight) 7 11-10 J Culloty mde all: mstke 2 out: r.o wl		**1**	8/15(F)
Douze Douze (FR)	(G Macaire) 6 11-00 Jacques Ricou a.p: mstkes 7th: 9th and next: chsd wnr 2 out: mstke and j.rt last: wknd flat	8	**2**	7/2(2)
Geos (FR)	(N J Henderson) 7 11-00 M A Fitzgerald chsd wnr to 2 out:sn outpcc	2½	**3**	8/1(3)
Tresor De Mai (FR)	(M C Pipe) 8 11-10 A P McCoy hld up: hit 1 st: blnd 8th: wknd after next	dist	**4**	14/1
Castle Prince (IRE)	(R J Hodges) 8 11 00 Mr L Tibbatts prom: lost pl and dropped rr 5th: t.o fr 10th	dist	**5**	150/1

KEMPTON (R-H) (SOFT)
Thursday 26 December 2002 WEATHER: overcast with showers

PERTEMPS KING GEORGE VI CHASE CLASS A SHOWCASE RACE GRADE 1 (5yo+)

2:20 3m (19 fncs) (£87000 (£33000; £16500; £7500; £3750; £2250)

Best Mate (IRE)	(Miss H C Knight) 711-10 A P McCoy lw: cl up: trckd ldr 11th: led 15th: shkn up after 3 out: jnd after 2 out: hrd rdn flat: kpt on gamely nr fin: all out		**1**	11/8(F)
Marlborough (IRE)	(N J Henderson) 10 11-10 T J Murphy prom: rdn and sitly outpcd 4 out: rallied to go 2nd 2 out: sn jnd wnr: ev ch tl jst hid last 75y: fin tired	1½	**~2**	14/1
Bacchanal (IRE)	(N J Henderson) 8 11-10 M A Fitzgerald lw: led to 7th: chsd ldr to 11th: n.m. r bnd after next: rdn 14th: effrt u.p and cl up 2 out: one pce bef last	4	**3**	100/30
Florida Pearl (IRE)	(W P Mullins) 10 11-10 R Walsh chsd ldr tl j. slowly 4th: styd prom: chsd wnr after 15th tl wknd 2 out	12	**4**	8/1
Native Upmanship (IRE)	(A L T Moore) 9 11-10 C O'Dwyer hld up midfield: prog to trek ldrs gng easily 15th: rdn after 4 out: wknd bef next	13	**5**	7/1(3)
Wahiba Sands	(M C Pipe) 9 11-10 T Scudamore hid up last trio: nt fluent 9th: lost tch ldng gp fr 12th: sn wl bhd	18	**6**	66/1
Shooting Light (IRE)	(M C Pipe) 9 11 -10v R Greene lw: mstkes and nvrgng wl in last trio: lost tch 12th: t.o whn p.u bef 15th		**P**	25/1
Flagship Uberalles (IRE)	(P J Hobbs) 811-10 R Johnson lw: hid up midfield: lost tch ldng g pafter 12th: sn wknd:t.o whn p.u bef 3 out		**P**	10/1
Douze Douze (FR)	(G Macaire) 6 11-10 C Gombeau str: hid up tl plld way into Id 7th: hdd & wknd 15th: wl bhd whn p.u bef 2 out		**P**	12/1
Lord Noelie (IRE)	(Miss H C Knight) 911-10 J P McNamara lw: a last trio: lost tch fr 12th: t.o whn p.u bef 3 out		**P**	40/1

CHELTENHAM (L-H) (GOOD (Good to soft in places)
Thursday 13 March 2003 WEATHER: fine & sunny but chilly

TOTE CHELTENHAM GOLD CUP CHASE SHOWCASE RACE CLASS A GRADE 1 (5yo+)

3:15   3m 2f 110y (Ne) £203000 (£77000; £38500; £17500; £8750; £5250)

Horse	Details			
Best Mate (IRE)	(Miss H C Knight) 8 12-00 J Culloty lw: hld up in rr stdy hdwy fr 16th:trckd ldrs 4 out:chal 3 out: sn ld: c cir appr next: easily		1	13/8(F)
Truckers Tavern (IRE)	(Ferdy Murphy) 8 12-00t D N Russell lw bhd: hdwy 17th: styd on u.p appr 2 out: tk 2nd run-in but no ch w wnr	10	2	33/1
Harbour Pilot (IRE)	(Noel Meade) 8 12-00b P Carberry swtg: bhd: hit 7th and 12th: stl plenty to do u.p 3 out: kpt on fr next and r.o wl to take 3rd run-in	2½	3	40/1
Valley Henry (IRE)	(P F Nicholls) 8 12-00 B J Geraghty lw: in tch: chsd ldrs fr 10th: hit 4 out: sn revrd and drvn to chal 3 out: sn outpcd by wnr: no ex and lost 2nd run-in	1	4	14/1
Behrajan (IRE)	(H D Daly) 8 12-00 R Johnson w ldr tl led 5th: hit 11th and hdd: led next: hdd l7th: sn outpcd: rallied and kpt on again fr 2 out	1½	5	14/1
Commanche Court (IRE)	(T M Walsh) 10 12-00 R Walsh lw:bhd hdwy 18th: one pce after 4 out: nt fluent 2out and styd on again run-in	1½	6	8/1(3)
Chives (IRE)	(Miss H C Knight) 8 12-00 Richard Guest chsd ldrs: chsd ldr fr 13th tl led 17th: kpt narrow advantage tl hdd after 3 out:sn one pce:wknd appr last	4	7	25/1
See More Business (IRE)	(P F Nicholls) 13 12-00b J Tizzard lw: prom: chsd ldr 9th tl led after 11th: hdd next:wknd 17th	17	8	16/1
You're Agoodun	(M C Pipe) 11 12-00v A P McCoy hit 1st: j. slowly 1st: a in rr	¾	9	50/1
Colonel Braxton (IRE)	(D T Hughes) 8 12-00 K A Kelly chsd ldrs tl wknd 16th	12	10	33/1
Marlborough (IRE)	(N J Henderson) 11 12-00 M A Fitzgerald hit 16th: a in rr	10	11	20/1
Modulor (FR)	(M C Pipe)11 12-00v. R Greene w'like: slt advantage to 5th: wknd 12th	10	12	200/1
Beef Or Salmon (IRE)	(Michael Hourigan) 7 12-00 T J Murphy neat: hld up in rr: fell 3rd		F	5/1 (2)
Hussard Collonges (FR)	(P Beaumont) 8 12-00 R Garritty in tch: chsd ldrs 13th: wknd 17th: t.o whn p.u after 3 out		P	8/1 (3)
First Gold (FR)	(F Doumen) 10 12-00 T Doumen hit 1st and 13th: a bhd: t.o whn p.u bef 3 out		P	33/1

HUNTINGDON (R-H) (HEAVY)
Saturday 22 November 2003

TOTE PETERBOROUGH CHASE CLASS A GRADE 2 (5yo+)
2:55   2m 4½f (16fncs) £29000 (£11000; £5500; £2500; £1250; £750)

Jair Du Cochet (FR)	(G Macaire) 6 11-5 Jacques Ricou: led 1st to 5th: led again 9th: wnt lft and hit last: r.o wl run-in		**1**	100/30(2)
Best Mate (IRE)	(Miss HC Knight) 8 11-10 J Culloty: tkh early: a in tch: led 5th to 9th: mstke 4 out: shkn up appr 2 out: one pce run-in	8	**2**	8/13(F)
Valley Henry (IRE)	(PF Nicholls) 8 11-10 J Tizzard: trckd ldrs: mstke 3 out: rdn appr 2 out: no ex appr last	1¼	**3**	7/1(3)
La Landiere (FR)	(RT Phillips) 8 11-3 W Marston: led to 1st: in cl tch tl rdn and wknd 3 out: blnd next: t.o	dist	**4**	9/1
Strong Magic (IRE)	(JR Cornwall) 11 11-0 R Hobson: a bhd: lost tch after 9th: t.o	12	**5**	200/1
Venn Ottery	(OJ Carter) 8 11-0 PHide: mstke 4th: in tch to 9th: t.o	dist	**6**	500/1

LEOPARDSTOWN (L-H) (GOOD TO SOFT)
Wednesday 28 December 2003

ERICSSON CHASE GRADE 1 (5yo+)
2:40   3m (17fncs) £63311.69 (£18506.49; 8766.23; £2922.08)

Best Mate (IRE)	(Miss HC Knight) 8 11-12 J Culloty: trckd ldrs in 3rd: impr into 2nd 7 out: sent into ld on inner after 2 out: qcknd clr bef last: impressive		**1**	8/11(F)
Le Coudray (FR)	(C Roche) 9 11-12 BJ Geraghty: hld up in 5th: prog 6 out: 3rd 4 out: 2nd bef last: kpt on wout troubling wnr	9	**2**	14/1
Beef or Salmon (IRE)	(Michael Hourigan) 7 11-12 TJ Murphy: trckd ldrs in 4th: nt fluent and reminders 10th: 3rd 5 out: slt mstke 4 out: kpt on one pce fr 2 out	4	**3**	2/1(2)
Colonel Braxton (IRE)	(DT Hughes) 8 11-12 AP McCoy: 2nd and disp ld: led 10th: rdn and strly pressed bef 3 out: hddafter 2 out: 4th and no ex whn mstke last	14	**4**	16/1
Alcapone (IRE)	(MF Morris) 9 11-12 G Cotter: hld up: mod 5th 4 out: no imp whn slt mstke next	13	**5**	100/1
Alexander Banquet (IRE)	(WP Mullins) 10 11-12 DJ Casey: a bhd: trailing fr 6 out: kpt on fr last	20	**6**	40/1
Rince Ri (IRE)	(TM Walsh) 10 11-12 R Walsh: trckd ldrs tl fell 8th		**F**	11/1(3)
Batman Senora (FR)	(Ian Williams) 7 11-12b P Moloney: led and disp: mstke 3rd: bad mstke 5th: hdd 10th: sn rdn: wknd 6 out: t.o: whn fell last		**F**	20/1

CHELTENHAM (L-H) (GOOD)
Thursday 18 March 2004

TOTESPORT CHELTENHAM GOLD CUP CHASE CLASS A GRADE 1 (5yo+)
3:15   3m 2f 110y (22fncs) £203000 (£77000; £38500; £17500; £8750; £5250)

Best Mate (IRE)	(Miss HC Knight) 9 11-10 J Culloty: lw: trckd ldrs: hdwy 3 out: nt clr run and swtchd rt bnd appr 2 out: qcknd to chal and sn slt ld: drvn out		**1**	8/11(F)
Sir Rembrandt (IRE)	(RH Alner) 8 11-10 A Thornton: lw: j. slowly 4th: bhd: hdwy 16th: blnd 18th: pressed ldrs fr 3 out: hit 2 out: outpcd: rallied run-in: fin wl: tk 2nd nr fin	½	**2**	33/1
Harbour Pilot (IRE)	(Noel Meade) 9 11-10b P Carberry: swtg: led tl after 1st: hit next: trckd ldr: edgd lft bnd appr 2 out and slt ld: sn hdd: one pce run-in: ct form 2nd nr fin	1¼	**3**	20/1
Beef or Salmon (IRE)	(Michael Hourigan) 8 11-10 TJ Murphy: lw: hld up in rr: pushed along 16th: stl plenty to do 3 out: rdn and styd on sn after: kpt on wl run-in: nt pce to rch ldrs	1¼	**4**	10/1(3)
First Gold (FR)	(F Doumen) 11 11-10b T Doumen: w ldr: led 2nd nt fluent 4 out: rdn next: narrowly hdd appr 2 out: wknd bef last	10	**5**	12/1
Keen Leader (IRE)	(Jonjo O'Neil) 8 11-10 BJ Geraghty: lw: in tch: pushed along 16th: blnd 18th: no ch whn mstke 4 out: t.o	dist	**6**	10/1(3)
Therealbandit (IRE)	(MC Pipe) 7 11-10 AP McCoy: lw: hld up in rr: nt fluent 9th: hit 13th: effrt 18th but nvr rchd ldrs: wknd qckly 4 out: t.o	4	**7**	15/2(2)
Alexander Banquet (IRE)	(WP Mullins) 11 11-10 R Walsh: t.o fr 8th	3	**8**	80/1
Irish Hussar (IRE)	(NJ Henderson) 8 11-10 MA Fitzgerald: chsd ldrs: hit 7th and lost pl: sn rcvrd to chse ldrs: hit 13th and wknd: p.u bef 15th		**P**	16/1
Truckers Tavern (IRE)	(Ferdy Murphy) 9 11-10t A Dobbin: mstke 3rd: nt fluent 13th: a bhd: t.o whn p.u bef 4 out		**P**	22/1

BEST MATE'S FIRST POINT-TO-POINT

SECOND RACE : 1.30 p.m.

MAIDEN RACE FOR 4-Y-O MARES & GELDINGS

(Sponsored by LISMORE HOTEL & DECIE FUEL)

The Maiden Race of £400 and Maxwell Perpetual Challenge Cup , of which the second will receive £80 and the third £40. For Certified Hunters, aged 4 years old mares and geldings only, maidens at starting, the property of subscribers to any Hunt in Ireland. Weights : 11st 7lb. About 3 miles. Entry Fee : £10.00   The Stewards of the I.N.H.S. Committee have suspended Regulation 8 (v) for the purposes of this race.

Best Turned Out Horse in this race sponsored by
M. CONDON, FARRIER

1	BRUTHUINNE		Doneraile	11-7
	ch g 4 Vaquillo (USA) – Portane Miss	J J GORDON		Maroon, blue cap
	Half brother to Churchtown Port – won two chases & placed in two points + Aghawadda Gold, won point, three hurdles & three chases.			
2	GAMBIT MANNA		Scarteen	11-7
	ch m 4 Heavenly Manna – Lucy's Gambit	M N O'RIORDAN		Red, red & white slvs
	Dam (by Lucifer) is own sister to Mister Donut & won bumper and placed in hurdle & chase.			
3	RANDOM ORCHESTRA			11-7
	ch g 4 Orchestra – Another Bless	M N O'RIORDAN		Yellow, brown chevron; red cap
	Dam (by Random Shot) own sister to Another Shot. Full brother to Roundwood – won bumper, two hurdles and chases. Half brother to Furry Baby, winner of four hurdles.			
4	ALANNA SUPREME		Ward Union	11-7
	b m 4 Supreme Leader – Winter Dancer	EITHNE SLEVIN		White, red chevron; qtrd cap
5	FESTIVE ISLE			11-7
	ch m 4 Erin's Isle – Fiesta Femme	O J HIGGINS		Royal blue & red qtrd
	Dam (by Condorcet) placed once at 3. Half sister to Tessa – won once on flat & placed in hurdle; Kulikove, won bumper & placed two hurdles + Festival Project, placed three times flat.			
6	THE GREY EXECUTIVE		United	11-7
	gr g 4 Executive Perk – Tara's Lady	J BARRY		Lemon, black hoop; black cap, lemon hoop
	Half brother to Irene's Call – won two points & placed eight times + Boreen Lass – placed in two points. Dam by General Ironside.			
7	BALTIC DUST			11-7
	b g 4 Freddie's Star – Gentle Gill	C O'LEARY		Red & white
	Half brother to Keepoff-The-Grass – won hurdle & placed once.			
8	FIGHTALLTHEWAYHOME			11-7
	b m 4 Mister Lord (USA) – Sedate	M GALVIN		Blue, red X belts; red cap
	Half sister to point winners, Tranquil Lord & General Anasthetic + Winnipeg Duke, placed in three points.			
9	GAIHA LASS			11-7
	ch m 4 Commanche Run – Ragtime Lady	J WALSH		Purple & amber; same cap
	Dam (by Ragapan) placed in point & two hurdles.			
10	ROSIE STROUD			11-7
	br m 4 Mandalus – Galway Grey	T CONDON		Red & white
	Full sister to Dreamin George – placed in chase.			
11	SERIOUSLY NOW		Macroom	11-7

5

260

4/1 /13/

	b g 4 Fresh Breeze (USA) – Croziers Glimmer	G P KELLEHER	Blue, red stars
	Half sister to David's Way – placed in three hurdles + Pike's Glory, winner of two points.		
12	**NO MESSING**		**11-7**
	b g 4 Alphabatim (USA) – The Best I Can D BARROW	Blue & gold qtrd; gold cap, blue hoop	
	Dam by Derring Rose.		
13	**MOVE YOUR BODY**	Killeady	**11-7**
	b g 4 Mac's Imp (USA) – Like A Dove MISS Y HANLEY	Blue & white	
	Dam (by Ahonoora) placed nine times on flat. Half brother to Pigeon Hill Buck – placed in two points.		
14	**PROMETTEUSE** 1st	T DAVERN	**11-7**
	ch m 4 Bob Back (USA) – Astral Fields (FR)	Purple & brown	
	Dam (by Northfields) won at 4. Half sister to Be My Sir, two wins in Spain + Zorobabel – won five in Spain.		
15	**NATIVE CAPTION**	Island	**11-7**
	b g 4 Be My Native (USA) – Hard Lady I CONROY	Yellow & red	
	Half brother to Kiama Lady – placed in four points.		
16	**NATIVE PERFORMANCE**		**11-7**
	b g 4 Be My Native (USA) – Noon Performance D O'CONNOR	Yellow; black cap	
	Dam (by Strong Gale) own sister to Festival Dreams + Executive Options.		
17	**BROWN MINSTREL**		**11-7**
	b g 4 Black Minstrel – Royal Toombeola D O'CONNOR	Yellow, black cap	
	Dam by Royal Fountain.		
18	**BE MY MANAGER**	Co. Galway	**11-7**
	b g 4 Be My Native (FR) – Fahy Quay T COSTELLO	Yellow & blue	
	Dam placed in bumper. Half brother to Ballyvaughan, placed in hurdle.		
19	**RUGGED RIVER**	Co. Galway	**11-7**
	b g 4 Over The River (FR) – Early Dalus T COSTELLO	Yellow & blue	
	Dam by Mandalus.		
20	**BEST MATE**	Co. Galway	**11-7**
	b g 4 Un Desperado (FR) – Katday (FR) T S COSTELLO	Yellow & blue	
	Dam (by Miller's Mate) – won three on flat in France & placed in two hurdles.		
21	**MUSICAL MAESTRO**		**11-7**
	b g 4 Orchestra – Rovral Flo D McSWEENEY	Purple & amber	
	Full brother to Raggiepuss – won two bumpers, two hurdles + point winner, Rainbow Fantasia.		
22	**WELL THEN NOW THEN**	Limerick	**11-7**
	b m 4 Supreme Leader – Northern Dandy M HOURIGAN	Blue, brown diamond	
	Half sister to Sound Orchestra – placed in bumper & two hurdles.		
23	**TELLYOUONETHING** (GB)	Limerick	**11-7**
	ch m 4 Broadsword (USA) – Another Rumour M WADE	Blue, brown diamond	

7

BEST MATE'S PEDIGREE

BEST MATE IRE Bay Gelding	**Un Desperado**	Top Ville	High Top	Derring-Do
				Darius II
				Sipsey Bridge
			Camenae	Vimy
				Madrilene
		Sega Ville	Charlottesville	Prince Chevalier
				Noorani
			La Sega	Tantieme
				La Danse
	White Lightning	Baldric	Round Table	Princequillo
				Knight's Daughter
			Two Cities	Johnstown
				Vienna
		Rough Sea	Herbager	Vandale
				Flagette
			Sea Nymph	Free Man
				Sea Spray
Katday	Miller's Mate	Mill Reef	Never Bend	Nasrullah
				Lalun
			Milan Mill	Princequillo
				Virginia Water
		Primatie	Vaguely Noble	Vienna
				Noble Lassie
			Pistol Packer	Gun Bow
				George's Girl II
	Kanara	Hauban	Sicambre	Prince Bio
				Sif
			Hygie	Sunny Boy
				Hymenee
		Alika	Auriban	Pharis II
				Arriba
			Pretty Lady	Umidwar
				La Moqueuse

262

INDEX

The index is arranged alphabetically
except for subheadings, which
appear in approximate chronological
order.